Charles W. Woodworth:

The Remarkable Life of U.C.'s First Entomologist

By Brian Holden

Published in the United States by Brian Holden Publishing.

ISBN 978-0-9864105-0-5 (MOBI edition)
ISBN 978-0-9864105-1-2 (EPUB edition)
ISBN 978-0-9864105-2-9 (PDF edition)
ISBN 978-0-9864105-3-6 (Print edition)

Cover photo: Charles W. Woodworth at his microscope, owned by author.

Table of Contents

Table of Figures

Table of Tables

Introduction

There can be little doubt that my great-grandfather, Charles W. Woodworth, was a polymath. A polymath is someone who excels in many different sciences, and they are few and far between. His supple and comprehensive mind produced significant accomplishments in seven diverse fields: entomology (insects), plant pathology, public policy, optical physics, optical engineering, machine calculation, and distillate chemistry. Within entomology, he published in anatomy, classification, systematics, theoretical economic entomology and applied economic entomology.

He founded the Entomology departments at what are now the University of California, Berkeley and the University of California, Davis. He served as the Chief Entomologist at the California Spray Chemical Company, the enterprise that created the Ortho™ brand of pesticides.

He was happily married and had four children who all lived full and successful lives. He designed his family home, which became a Berkeley architectural landmark. A colleague referred to him in a speech as "a very modest and tolerant man."

His most famous Entomological accomplishment came early in his career and took the form of a suggestion. He was the first to cultivate in a laboratory the famous model species *Drosophila melanogaster* and suggested to W. E. Castle that it could be useful for genetic research. Thomas H. Morgan's official Nobel Prize biography credits him with this suggestion. Drosophila has gone on to become the central model species for biology and for many forms of genetic research. In the year 2000, the Drosophila was the first eukaryote species to have its genome sequenced.

He was the central figure in helping California agriculture, then California's leading industry, respond to many insect threats in the first three decades of the 20th century. He directed the world's first successful city-scale salt-marsh mosquito control effort, in San Rafael, California. He helped the region around Nanking (now Nanjing) control mosquitoes for the first time. He was an important early figure in what is now known as Integrated Pest Management. He also published papers in insect embryology, anatomy and classification.

His public policy accomplishments include writing California's First Insecticide Law in 1906, getting it passed in 1911, and administering that law until 1923. He also advocated for the development of better universities in China after his two periods there.

He defined the requirements for what is now Wellman Hall on the Cal campus, which was added to the National Register of Historic Places in 1982.

His optics achievements include early contributions to the science of multi-element telescopes, the technique that is used today in the world's largest telescopes. He attempted to build the world's largest telescope in his back yard. He published a new formula allowing a more convenient calculation of focal length. He contributed to the ability to analyze distortion, curvature, axial aberration, coma and astigmatism. He also created forms of optical calculations for lens design specifically tailored for machine calculation. In 1936, he taught classes in optical triangulation at Bausch & Lomb, the leading maker of optical weapon sights for the U.S. Navy in WWII.

In the field of chemistry, he developed and patented a low-temperature, short-path, thin-film distillation process that has echoes in the modern techniques used in the processing of certain food and pharmaceutical products.

The University of California named him Emeritus Professor upon his retirement. Four species of insects were named after him. Of these four, a planthopper, *Cixidia woodworthi,* now named *Epiptera woodworthi,* retains "woodworthi" in its modern name. The Pacific Branch of the Entomology Society of America has given out their C.W. Woodworth Award for achievement in entomology in the Pacific slope region over the last ten years since 1969.

His obituary was printed in *Science* and in the *New York Times.*

This book is intended to be the definitive biography of Charles W. Woodworth.

Timeline

1814-1859

- 11/27/1814 - C.W.'s uncle and later stepfather Stephen Woodworth is born near Seneca Falls, NY.
- 1/18/1819 - C.W.'s father Alvin Oakley Woodworth is born in near Seneca Falls, NY.
- 4/5/1842 - C.W.'s mother Mary Celina Carpenter is born near Syracuse, NY.
- 7/20/1848 - Stephen Elias Woodworth signs the Declaration of Sentiments, the founding document of the American Feminist Movement.

1860-69

- 11/6/1861 - C.W.'s parents are married in Buffalo, NY.
- 7/2/1862 - The Morrill Act passes, establishing land-grant colleges
- 4/9/1865 - Robert E. Lee surrenders, ending the Civil War.
- 4/15/1865 - Abraham Lincoln is assassinated.
- 4/28/1865 - C.W. is born in Champaign, Illinois.
- 3/2/1868 - The University of Illinois opens.
- 3/23/1868 - The Organic Act is passed, founding the University of California.
- 4/2/1869 - C.W.'s father Alvin dies of tuberculosis.
- 5/10/1869 - The Transcontinental Railroad is completed.

1870-79

- 1/22/1872 - Arkansas Industrial University opens.
- 9/4/1876 - C.W.'s mother Mary marries her late husband's brother Stephen Elias Woodworth.

1880-89

- 9/1882 - 6/1885 - C.W. attends the University of Illinois and graduates with a B.S.
- 3/31/1884 - His stepfather wins an insurance case that went to the U.S. Supreme Court.

- 1885 - Stephen Alfred Forbes arrives at the University of Illinois
- 9/1885 - 6/1886 – C.W. attends the University of Illinois and graduates with a M.S.
- 9/1886 - 6/1888 – C.W. attends Harvard University in a Doctor of Science program in the Zoology Department.
- 3/2/1887 - The Hatch Act is enacted funding the establishment Agricultural Experiments Stations.
- 9/1888 - accepts a job as Professor at Agricultural Experiment Station of Arkansas Industrial University (now the U. of Arkansas) as their first trained agricultural research scientist.
- 9/4/1889 - marries Leonora Stern in Rolla, Missouri.
- 1888 – 1891 - gets malaria.
- 1889 – becomes a charter member of the Association of Economic Entomologists, the older of the two roots of the Entomological Society of America.

1890-99

- 1890 – His oldest son Lawrence is born in Fayetteville.
- 11/1890 – Travels to his hometown to attend the second meeting of the AAEE in Champaign, IL.
- 9/1891 - accepts a job at the University of California as their first Professor of Entomology.
- 1891-189? – runs a one-person entomology program at Cal, teaches all classes.
- 1894 – middle son Harold is born in Berkeley.
- 1895 - thrown out of the Berkeley First Baptist Church for believing in evolution.
- 1895 – youngest son Charles is born in Berkeley.
- 11/1898 – elected chair of the Entomology Section of the Association of American Ag. Colleges and Experiment Stations.

1900s

- 9/1900 – takes a one year leave of absence from U.C.
- 9/1900 - 6/1901 - returns to Harvard University and completes dissertation.

- 1900 – makes the suggestion to W.E. Castle that Drosophila would be useful for genetic research.
- 12/1900 – works for a few weeks on the white fly at Florida Agricultural College (now U. of Florida).
- 2/1901 – fourth and last child, Elizabeth is born in Cambridge.
- 6/1901 - travels to visit entomology departments in Europe.
- 8/1901 - returns to the University of California.
- 9/1901 – identifies that what is now known as the grape whitefly, *Trialeurodes vittatas,* has two broods per year on different hosts.
- 1900-1905 – his wife comes down with Arthritis Deformans (Rheumatoid Arthritis)
- 1902 – C.W.'s dissertation for a Doctor of Science degree is rejected.
- 1902-3 – designs and has built their home at 2043 Lincoln St. in Berkeley
- 1903-1904 – directed the first successful city-scale salt marsh mosquito control effort, clearing the salt marshes in San Rafael, California. (John B. Smith had previously succeeded in clearing limited areas in New Jersey.)
- 1904 – defined the "superficial plans" for Agriculture Hall" (now called Wellman Hall) on the Cal campus, now on the National Register of Historic Places.
- 1904-1905 – is involved with Henry Qualye's successful salt marsh mosquito control effort in Burlingame, California.
- 1904 – promoted to Associate Professor.
- 1904 - *Caliothrips woodworthi,* now a synonym for *Caliothrips fasciatus,* named after C.W. by S.M. Daniel.
- 1905 – Bill establishing the University Farm at Davis (later U.C. Davis) passes.
- 6/30/1905 – got building permit for his home at 2237 Carleton.
- 4/18/1906 – The San Francisco Earthquake happens.
- 9/1906 – His rejected doctoral dissertation, *The Wing Veins of Insects,* is published UC with Contributions from the Zoological Laboratory of the Museum of Comparative Zoology at Harvard College".

- 1906 – proposed California's first pesticide law.
- 1906 – Two of his students discover that the lead arsenate form of arsenic minimizes foliage damage in the foggy weather of the Pajaro Valley.
- 1907 – These two students start the California Spray Chemical Corporation (their brand name is "Ortho").
- 1908 – publishes "The Theory of Parasitic Control of Insect Pests", one of the early works in today's theory of Integrated Pest Management.
- 1908-1915 Thomas Hunt Morgan and others use Drosophila to help define the role of chromosomes in inheritance.
- 1/1909 – The University Farm at Davis (later U.C. Davis) opens.
- 5/12/1909 – C.W.'s mother, Mary dies.

1910-19

- 1911 – secured the passage of California's first pesticide law.
- 1913 – completes the textbook *Guide to California Insects.*
- 1913 – promoted to Full Professor.
- 1914 - *Gypona woodworthi,* now the name of a variety of *Ponana pectoralis,* named after C.W. by Edward Van Duzee.
- 1916 - *Elidiptera woodworthi,* now *Cixidia woodworthi,* named after C.W. by Dr. Edward Van Duzee
- 1917 - *Myzocallis woodworthi,* now a deprecated name, named after C.W. by George O. Shinji
- 1917 – His son Lawrence serves in WWI as an Army Engineer.
- 1918 - takes sabbatical to China.
- 1918 – effects practical control of mosquitoes for the first time in Nanking.
- 1919 – Son Charles enters U.S. Army, but WWI ends before he is deployed.
- 1919 – C.W. steps down from being head of the Entomology Division. William B. Herms is chosen to head the division of Entomology and Plant Parisitology.

1920-29

- 1921 – 1924 - works for three years in Nanking China.

- 1924 – published "Microscope Theory" in Shanghai
- 9/7/1924 - C.W.'s wife Leonora dies from Rheumatoid Arthritis complicated by a kidney infection after gall bladder surgery.
- 1926 – visits Barro Colorado Island research station with his son Charles
- 4/4/1926 - marries Bernice Christopher.
- 6/20/1926 – Son Charles marries, and the reception is in C.W.'s home.
- Circa 1927 - starts work on building the world's largest telescope in his back yard, with a 3.4m segmented-mirror reflector.

1930-39

- 1/28/1930 – takes final 3-month sabbatical from U.C.
- 4/28/1930 – retires from U.C. at age 65 and is named Emeritus Professor.
- 5/6/1930 - C.W.'s second wife Bernice dies.
- 1930 - accepts the position of Chief Entomologist at the California Spray Chemical Company (CSCC)
- 1930 – 1932 - makes a journey for CSCC to Mexico and South America.
- 1933 – Thomas Hunt Morgan wins the Nobel Prize for his Drosophila-based work.
- 1935 - teaches a class on optical triangulation at Bausch & Lomb, the leading maker of WWII weapon sights for the U.S. Navy, and teaches at the Baptist Temple, both in Rochester, NY.
- 1935 – 1936 - takes a trip around the world.
- 8/16/1937 – applies for patent entitled "Low Temperature Oil-Refining Process".
- September 1937 – visits Barro Colorado Island again.
- 7/18/1939 – granted an oil refining patent.
- 12/1939 – invited to celebrate the 50th anniversary of the AAEE.

1940-49

- Circa 1940 – elected an honorary fellow of the Entomological Society of America
- 11/19/1940 – dies of prostate cancer.
- 11/1940 and 12/1940 – his obituary is published in the *New York Times* and *Science*.
- 1942-1945 – His son Charles E. Woodworth serves as Major in the U.S. Army's Sanitary Corps working to control mosquitoes in the Pacific theater and injures his lungs.
- 1948 – The 5.08m Hale telescope is completed using segmented mirrors.
- 1949 – His oldest child, Lawrence dies.

1950-59

- 1950's – U.C. Entomologists articulate the principles of Integrated Pest Management, greatly extending the concepts found in C.W.'s 1908 paper.

1960-69

- 1966 – His third child, Charles E. dies.
- 1969 – The C.W. Woodworth Award is established by the Pacific Branch of the Entomology Society of America. Maurice T. James is the first recipient.

1970-79

- 1971 – His second child, Harold, dies.

1980-89

- 1985 – His youngest child, Elizabeth, dies - the last of his children.

1990-99

- 1993 – His home becomes a Berkeley Architectural Landmark.
- 1993 – The Keck 1 ten-meter telescope is built on top of Mauna Kea in Hawaii using segmented mirrors.
- 1999 – His only biological grandchild, Elizabeth Woodworth Holden (my mother) dies.

2000-09

- 2000 – *Drosophila melanogaster* becomes the first eukaryotic species to have its genome sequenced.

2010-19

- 2011 – The 43rd C.W. Woodworth Award is presented to Dr. Frank Zalom of the University of California, Davis.
- 2015 – His biography is published by his great-grandson.

Author's Notes

What got me started on the project of writing this book was meeting the wonderful entomologists at the annual meetings of the Pacific Branch of the Entomological Society of America. They have been so welcoming to me in my annual trips to their conference to present the C.W. Woodworth award, now in its 46th year.

My family had lost the thread of all that C.W. had accomplished. My mother knew that he was an amazing person, and that he had done big things, but she was not scientific (and didn't like bugs) and so could not tell me what he really had done. In order to write this book, I read everything that he wrote and then three or four times as much other material to allow me to see his work in context.

I was continually amazed by what he accomplished in his life. I probably had a hundred "wow" moments in the course of this project. I hope you have at least a few along the way as you read this book

Organization of the book

When organizing this book, I was faced with the challenge of how to present the intensely multidisciplinary nature of C.W.'s work. A simple chronological narrative of his life that I started with was inadequate to capture the many threads of his research. Each general subject of his research needed a coherent, in-context presentation on its own. Conversely, a pure listing topic by topic did not capture the progression of his life.

What I settled on was a topic-by-topic organization with the topics arrayed generally chronologically. Within each topic, I endeavored to present the material in chronological order.

The general organization of the book is sections on his:

- Family of origin.
- Education.
- Entomology career by topic with the topics generally arrayed in the order that he did his most important work in that topic:
    - Teaching
    - Drosophila
    - General Entomology and Plant Pathology work
    - Species-specific work
    - IPM precursors
    - Mosquito control
    - China
    - Public policy
    - The Codling Moth and CSCC
- Optics and chemistry work.
- Wife and children along with discussion of his avocations.
- Landmarked home along with Agricultural hall.
- The C.W. Woodworth Award.
- Conclusions.

The appendices contain five organized lists of C.W's publications, divided by general topic. I have also included a list of selected references, a list of publications by his son, a list of research dead-ends, and some genealogy links.

Breadth of the material

Because C.W. really was a polymath, I struggled with how to make the material compelling to a broad range of readers. If you are an Entomologist, the material about lens calculation might make your eyes glaze over. Similarly, if you are an optics person, the section on scale insects might not catch your interest. However, this is his definitive biography, and this telling of the story of his life would be lacking if I had left out one subject area or another.

In the end, I decided to cover every area of his work. I tried to follow his lead in determining the depth of my coverage of each topic. I went where the story of his life led instead of trying to impose an artificial narrative onto his life. I endeavored to add introductory material to many sections to make that material more accessible. I also tried to tie each topic into the modern version of the same topic.

I apologize in advance if your eyes glaze over occasionally while reading some minutia about his research in this book, mine certainly did at times while reading the source material. My experience with the volume and breadth of his writing was that his remarkable mind would come shining through his writing time and time again and surprise me with another "wow" moment. To help capture that experience, I have included numerous passages of his writing to connect you directly with his mind.

Writing style

I tried to write this book in the full academic biography style. Since his life is so fascinating on its own, and he published so much, there was absolutely no need to embellish it with anything like reconstructed dialog or other such techniques that biographers sometimes use to bring historic figures to life.

The book is written in a third person omniscient point of view. I have made a conscious effort to give the source for each important statement in the book. Some items of introductory or general context are presented without sources for convenience. I have attempted to use the Chicago Manual of Style's endnote formatting.

Where I have added contextual items to quotes, I denoted each with a bracket, for example: "the insect [the Peach-Tree Borer] caused great injury." I have also added some asides written from my point of view on various topics denoted as [Author's note: …].

Final notes

I apologize in advance for any errors of omission or commission that are in this book. I worked diligently to make it perfect, but I know that there must be at least one and likely a number of errors contained in it somewhere - hopefully they are small.

I worked for five years on this book. I hope that you find C.W.'s life to be as fascinating and inspirational as I did.

Chapter 1 - Childhood and Family

On April 28, 1865, nineteen days after Robert E. Lee's surrender to Ulysses S. Grant at the Appomattox Courthouse, Charles William "C.W." Woodworth was born in Champaign, Illinois. Abraham Lincoln was assassinated thirteen days before he was born; Cornell University was founded the day before. His father was Alvin Oakley Woodworth, and his mother was Mary Celina (Carpenter) Woodworth. His father was a merchant who died when Charles was three. His mother was a homemaker and seamstress.

Alvin Oakley Woodworth

C.W.'s father, Alvin Oakley Woodworth, was born on Jan 18, 1819 in Seneca County, NY, probably in Tyre where his family lived. Tyre is in the Finger Lakes region northeast of Seneca Falls, north of Cayuga Lake. There is no known picture of Alvin.

The 1850 U.S. Census has him living in a boarding house in Seneca Falls and working as a merchant. In 1851 he married Cynthia Ward and in 1856 they had one child who died. Cynthia died in 1857. That same year he married Sarah Mandeville, who was also from the Seneca Falls area. They are recorded in the 1860 census as living in Champaign, IL, with real estate holdings of $4,000 and a personal estate of $500. They had one child, Alvin Orton Woodworth. Sarah died of typhoid fever shortly thereafter. Sarah's family raised Alvin Orton.

On November 6, 1861, Alvin married Mary Celina Carpenter in Buffalo, New York. They had five children including C.W., only two of which lived past the age of two.

Alvin died on February 4, 1869 of consumption (tuberculosis) after having it for twelve years and is buried in the Mount Hope Cemetery in Champaign, IL. C.W. was three years and nine months old when he died.

Mary Celina Carpenter

C.W.'s mother, Mary Celina Carpenter Woodworth, was born on April 5, 1842 in Manlius, New York, just southeast of Syracuse. Her father, Thomas Carpenter, is recorded as living in Kingsbury, NY in 1840, two years before her birth. Kingsbury is near Hudson Falls, 50 miles north of Albany, NY. He was born in 1812 in Sandy Hill, NY, which is a part of the modern Hudson Falls, NY.

Figure 1 C.W.'s mother, Mary Celina Carpenter Woodworth, circa 1863, age circa twenty-one[1]

Mary Celina Carpenter is said to have pronounced her middle name with its Anglicized pronunciation "Sa-line-na" and not the Spanish pronunciation "Sa-lee-na". [2] One of her great-grand-daughters, who is alive today, is named Celina and also pronounces it that way.

On 9/16/1850, the U.S. census records her family as farming in Pompey, Onondaga County, New York, which is southeast of Syracuse on the Eastern edge of the Finger Lakes region.[3] Ten years later, on 9/27/1860, the U.S. census records her father working as a merchant living in Champaign, Illinois, where Mary would live the rest of her life, but Mary is not found in the census record. Just over a year later on November 6, 1861, Mary wed Alvin Oakley Woodworth in Buffalo, New York. One possibility is that, since both the Carpenter and Woodworth families were from the Upstate New York region, they chose Buffalo, in far Western New York, as the site of their wedding as a central meeting point for the families between central New York and Champaign, Illinois. Another possibility is that one or both of them had moved to Buffalo for employment. They were married for seven years until his death in 1869, when C.W. was just three.

Figure 2 C.W.'s parent's marriage certificate[4]

Mary's parents were named Mary Barney and Thomas Carpenter. The photo below is the only known to exist. The Barney family had been in Taunton, Massachusetts, which is about 20 miles northeast of Providence, Rhode Island, for four generations.

Figure 3 C.W.'s maternal grandfather, Thomas Carpenter[5]

C.W.'s niece, Mary Young Detrich, reported that her mother, Minnie Woodworth (C.W.'s half-sister) had said that their mother Mary refused to clean C.W.'s room after a certain point because "there were creepy crawlies in there".[6]

Mary was recorded as being a tailor in 1877. She designed early athletic uniforms for some University of Illinois women's sports teams in the "bloomer" style.[7]

Figure 4 Mary Celina Carpenter Woodworth, June 1904[8]

C.W. travelled to Champaign to see his mother numerous times. A voucher for reimbursement of some portion of a business trip from Berkeley to Champaign is found in a Report of the Illinois State Entomologist.[9] Mary died on May 12, 1909 at age 67.[10]

C.W.'s childhood home

C.W. lived at 610 East Clark Street in Champaign, IL. This is the only known photograph of that house.

Woodworth House
610 E. Clark St. Champaign, IL

Figure 5 C.W.'s childhood home in Champaign[11]

Unfortunately, the house has not survived. An apartment building now occupies this site, which is a half block from the University of Illinois campus, towards the northwest corner. The close proximity of the house to the U. of I. campus likely played a positive role in the graduation of all four of her surviving children from the University of Illinois.

Stephen Elias Woodworth

C.W.'s Stepfather and Uncle Stephen Elias Woodworth was born on Nov 27, 1814 in Tyre, Seneca County, New York and grew up on the Woodworth farm there. Tyre is five miles north of Seneca Falls, New York in New York's Finger Lakes region. The 1820 and 1830 U.S. Census records show a likely entry for him in Tyre (those early census records only list the name of the head of household plus the number of people living in the household, divided by age group and gender). In 1850, the U.S. Census shows him in nearby Seneca Falls. The 1860 and 1870 U.S. Census records show Stephen in Montezuma, NY, which is nine miles northeast of Seneca Falls, on the other side of the Montezuma Swamp, a wetlands area at the north end of Cayuga Lake, where the lake gradually flows into the Seneca River. Part of these wetlands form the modern Montezuma National Wildlife Refuge.

In July of 1848, Stephen signed the Declaration of Sentiments, the founding document of the American Feminist Movement.
(See the section entitled Declaration of Sentiments later in this chapter.)

Stephen had a dry goods store in Seneca Falls in 1848. In Judith Wellman's 2004 book, "The Road to Seneca Falls" there is an imaged re-creation of Elizabeth Cady Stanton's walk to the Seneca Falls Convention (see later in this book) on the morning of July 19, 1848. That re-creation contains the following mention of S.E.'s store derived from mentions and advertisements found in the *Seneca Falls Courier*:

> At the very end of the bridge, she could see the Seneca House and the brick stores built by Ansel Bascom. Woodworth's general store was there. So was Miss Gilbert's millinery shop. Miss Gilbert, it was rumored, would soon be married to S.E. Woodworth, in spite of his bankruptcy last winter. Woodworth and his brother, "the People's Agent," were the young merchants of the village. They sold everything: ready-made clothing (sewn on the premises by William R. Goetchius with thirty assistants), dry goods, groceries, carpets, boots and shoes, hats, crocks, "candies, toys, and Yankee notions," even books. ... They advertised as the "cheapest bookstore in the United States," with the most competitive prices in town. "Farmers, Mechanics, Laborers, Men, Women and Children, young and old draw near with pockets full of rocks, and you will not be permitted to go without purchasing, if you are satisfied to buy goods cheap," they claimed.[12]

Later in the book she mentions, "S.E. Woodworth, despite his reputation for honesty, failed three more times in business during the 1850s." (Perhaps people took him up on the rocks-for-books offer.) "His niece Grace Woodworth became a photographer in Seneca Falls."[13]

Around the time of the convention, Stephen E. Woodworth was a widower with one child, Thomas Bell Woodworth. S.E. married Ann Gilbert in 1847 or 1848. They had two children, Mary E. Woodworth born circa 1848 and Ann E. Woodworth, born circa 1858. Ann Gilbert Woodworth died in 1875.

Figure 6 C.W.'s Stepfather and Uncle, Stephen Elias Woodworth[14]

On September 5, 1876, Mary Celina Carpenter Woodworth married her late husband Alvin's older brother Stephen Elias "S.E." Woodworth in Champaign, Illinois. S.E. thus became Charles' stepfather along with the Uncle that he already was. Mary was a widow, and Stephen had already become a widower twice. There was a twenty-seven year age difference between them. They were married for eleven years until his death in 1887.

Both Mary and Stephen were tailors. He is reported as sometimes being gone as he stayed with the families that he was making clothes for.[15]

Stephen is unique in having been:

1) both the Stepfather & the Uncle of a famous scientist.
2) the plaintiff in a case that went before the U.S. Supreme Court (as we will see in the next chapter).
3) a signatory of the founding document of the American feminist movement (as we will see later in this chapter).

[Author's note: It is probable that there has never been another person that has met even two of the above conditions.]

C.W.'s Siblings

C.W.'s family was stalked by death. His extended family had twelve children, born from seven different adults. Five of those seven adults died while their children were still small. Between four and six of the twelve children died as children. The families lived in upstate New York in the 1840's and 1850's. Some of them moved westward to Champaign, Illinois. Many of the deaths occurred in the years surrounding the U.S. Civil War. It is easy to imagine that the primitive health care of that mid-nineteenth century was delivered in a less than optimal way in the small communities that they lived in, a situation only made worse by the thankfully distant Civil War.

The drawing of C.W.'s extended family that follows is interpreted as follows:

1. The seven parents are shown in bold type
2. The twelve children are shown in a normal typeface.
3. A timeline is presented vertically with the oldest event shown at the top of the page (1841) and the most recent event shown at the bottom (1905).
4. The adults are placed on the chart at the time of their marriage to one of the three central adults, Alvin Oakley Woodworth (C.W's father), Mary Celina Carpenter (C.W.'s mother), and Stephen Elias Woodworth (C.W's uncle and stepfather).
5. The children are placed on the chart at the time of their birth.
6. C.W. himself is near the center of the drawing.
7. The birth and death dates, as far as they are known, are below each of the names.

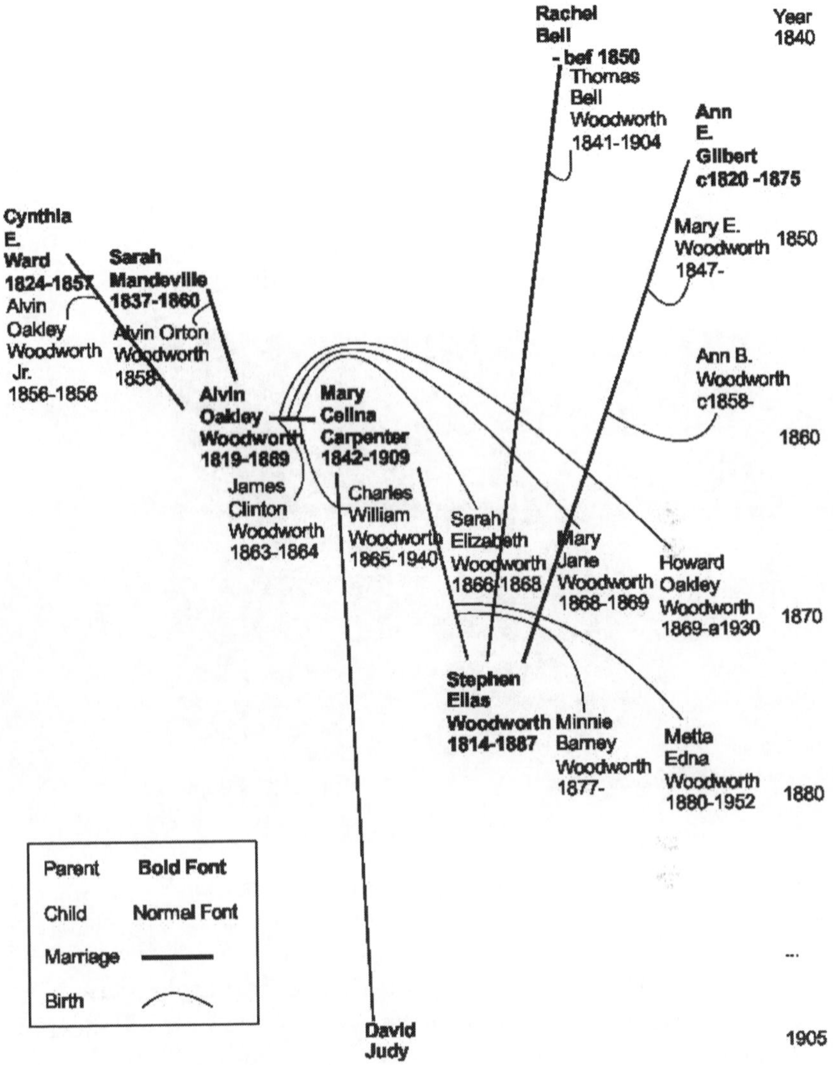

Figure 7 C.W.'s extended family

C.W.'s immediate family in the main portion of his childhood was his mother and brother Howard. His three other full siblings died before they were three.

As previously mentioned, when C.W. was ten, his mother remarried his father's older brother Stephen "S.E" Woodworth. Fifteen months later, his half-sister Minnie was born and three years after that, his other half-sister Metta was born. The following picture was taken in 1935 of the four youngest living siblings, Minnie, Howard, Metta, and Charles as well as Metta's daughter-in-law June, who was married to Metta's son Donald. The four siblings are all graduates of the University of Illinois.

Minnie W. Young Metta Burkhart June Burkhart
Howard Woodworth Charles W. Woodworth
June 10, 1935

Figure 8 C.W., his three youngest living siblings, and a nephew's wife[16]

Mary Young Detrich, the daughter of Minnie Barney Woodworth, C.W.'s half-sister, told me that at least some of the constellation of half-siblings would call each other "Cousin" to ease the burden of explaining their complex relationship.

Figure 9 C.W. visiting Minnie's family in Kansas City in 1924-5 with Jack, Mary [the same Mary who spoke in 2007 and 2008 to the PBESA] & Celina Young[17]

Howard Oakley Woodworth

C.W.'s younger brother Howard Oakley Woodworth graduated from the University of Illinois with a Bachelor's Degree in 1893. He then got a Masters from Cornell University in 1895. In July 1895 C.W. recommended him for a job at the University of Illinois Agricultural Experiment Station.[18] He worked as a Field Assistant Entomologist for the University of California from 1897 to 1898. He took an exam for assistant entomologist for Illinois in December 1898.[19] He worked for Stephen A. Forbes in 1899 and 1900 when Forbes was the Illinois State Entomologist.[20][21]

Howard worked in the poultry industry and published articles in poultry journals. He also worked as a bookkeeper. He married Elsie Victoria Weeks and had seven children, 4 of whom lived. [Author's note: I have visited his grave in the Pinewood Cemetery near Phelps, NY, north of the Finger Lakes.]

Metta Woodworth

C.W.'s half-sister Metta graduated from the University of Illinois with a degree in Domestic Sciences in 1902. She married Henry Burkhart, had four children, two of whom lived.

Metta Woodworth is recorded in a 1904 Oakland Tribune article as being the only woman in the United States to serve as a lecturer in Agriculture in a University Extension. She was a lecturer in domestic sciences. She also spoke at farmer's institutes on the subjects of "House Building and Home Making", "The Preservation of Foods", and "Food Economy".[22]

In 1918, she is listed as an Assistant in Agricultural Extension.[23] In 1920, she is listed in a directory as Specialist in the Agricultural Extension Farm Bureau in Riverside, California.[24] In both of these listings, she uses her maiden name as her professional name, listed as "Mrs. M.H. Woodworth."

Minnie Woodworth

C.W.'s half-sister Minnie Woodworth also graduated from the University of Illinois and became a music teacher. She married a fellow U of I graduate, John Hayes Young, and had four children, three of whom lived. Minnie's middle name was Barney, which was her maternal grandmother's maiden name.

[Author's note: Minnie is the mother of Mary Detrich, whom I used as a source numerous times in this book. Mary spoke to the PBESA annual meeting in both 2007 in Portland and 2008 in Napa.]

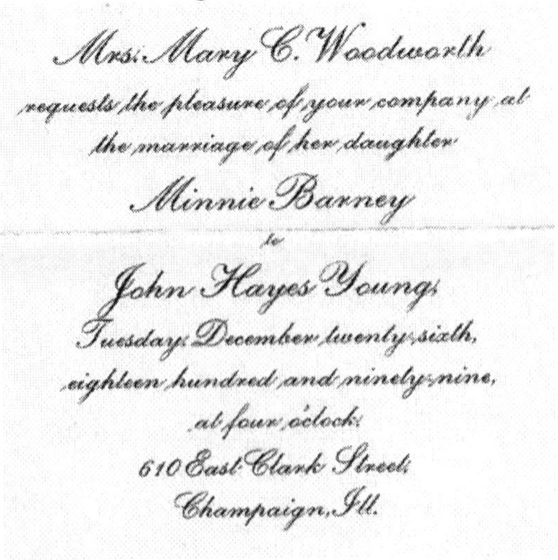
Mrs. Mary C. Woodworth
requests the pleasure of your company at
the marriage of her daughter
Minnie Barney
to
John Hayes Young,
Tuesday, December twenty-sixth,
eighteen hundred and ninety-nine,
at four o'clock.
610 East Clark Street,
Champaign, Ill.

Figure 10 Wedding announcement for C.W.'s sister's 12/26/1899 marriage at C.W.'s childhood home in Champaign[25]

Alvin Orton Woodworth

C.W.'s half-brother, Alvin Orton Woodworth, is shown in the 1870 census at age 12 living with his late mother's family, Saul and Mary Mandeville, also in Champaign. In 1926, a Santa Cruz, CA directory shows him as a locksmith at 33 Soquel Avenue in downtown Santa Cruz, where the Gap store is now.[26] C.W. worked extensively with the California Spray Chemical Company, which was headquartered down the road from Santa Cruz in Watsonville, so it is not unlikely that they stayed in contact. Alvin Orton Woodworth died in San Mateo, CA, which is on the San Francisco peninsula across the water and south of Berkeley, in 1941.[27]

Household in the 1870 Census record

The transcript of the 1870 U.S. census record of his family living in Champaign, IL illustrates the nature of C.W.'s childhood.

- His father is dead.
- They have a good-sized house.
- Their wealth of $1300 in real estate and $200 in personal estate is way down from the $4,000 plus $500 that was recorded in the 1860 census.
- They have a female boarder who works as a music teacher.
- His mother's invalid 31-year-old brother lives with them (perhaps made an invalid in the Civil War).
- His late father's brother's widow & her daughter live with them.
- Nobody aside from the boarder is recorded as working, although his mother Mary was recorded in 1877 as a tailor, so she may well have done sewing work of some sort in 1870.

Illinois, Champaign County, Champaign, Roll M593_193, page 24, image 48, Dwelling 55, Family 55

Relation-ship to C.W	Name	Age in 1870	Sex	Occupation	Real/ Personal Estate	Birth State
Mother	Woodworth, Mary	29	F	Keeping House	$1,300 $200	NY
Self	Woodworth, Charles	5	M	At House		IL
C.W's Brother	Woodworth, Howard	1	M	At House		
C.W's Uncle	Carpenter, J.W.	31	M	Invalid		NY
(presume-ably boarder)	Illegible, but not Carpenter or Woodworth	20	F	Music Teacher		KY
C.W.'s	Woodworth,	49	F	Keeping	$0	NY

late father's brother's widow	Mary			House	$200	
Cousin	Woodworth, Mary	10	F	At House		NY

Table 1 Woodworth Household in the 1870 U.S. Census

Household in the 1880 Census record

The situation as recorded in June 6, 1880 looks much better economically than that of 1870.

- C.W.'s mother has married her late husband's brother.
- C.W.'s stepfather (and uncle) is working as a tailor,
- A younger sister Minnie has arrived,
- They have three boarders to help pay the bills.

The 1880 census did not collect the real estate or personal estate values, so we do not have any more specific economic information.

Illinois, Champaign County, Champaign, District 3, Roll T9_179 Film 1254179, page 24B, image 0050.
East Clark St., Dwelling 53, Family 57.

Relation-ship to C.W	Name	Age in 1880	Sex	Occu-pation	Birth State	Birth State of Fa-Ther	Birth State of Mo-ther
Stepfather and Uncle	Woodworth, S. E.	63	M	Tailor	NY		
Mother	Woodworth, Mary	38	F	Keeping House	NY	NY	NY
Self	Woodworth, Charles	15	M		IL	NY	NY
Brother	Woodworth,	11	M		IL	NY	NY

	Howard						
Half-Sister	Woodworth, Minnie	3	F		IL	NY	NY
3 boarders							

Table 2 Woodworth Household in the 1880 U.S. Census

Declaration of Sentiments

On July 19th and 20th, 1848 in Seneca Falls, New York a convention was held "to discuss the condition and rights of women". The convention drew members of the community, both male and female, as well as some early leaders of the American feminist movement.

The "Declaration of Sentiments" was signed in 1848 by 68 women and 32 men in what is now known as the 1848 Women's Rights Convention. The principal author of the Declaration of Rights and Sentiments was Elizabeth Cady Stanton. The document followed the form of the United States Declaration of Independence. It was quickly published by Frederick Douglass, whose attendance at the convention and support of the Declaration helped it pass. The document was the "grand basis for attaining the civil, social, political, and religious rights of women."[28] It is often called the founding document of the American Feminist Movement.

The United States National Park Service established the Women's Rights National Historic Park at the site of the convention in downtown Seneca Falls, New York.[29] Because the significance of the Declaration of Sentiments grew as the years passed, the site of the convention was not well preserved and went through many uses including as a laundry. The overall history of the convention had to be carefully reconstructed by historians.

[Author's note: In my case, the memory of S.E. Woodworth being a signatory of the Declaration of Sentiments had been lost to my family's memory. I stumbled upon this fact while doing genealogy research into Woodworth's living in Seneca County, NY. I then carefully researched this connection.

The historian of the National Historic Park had independently done similar research and had come to the same conclusion, that Stephen Elias Woodworth was the "S.E. Woodworth" who signed the document. The only thing that she did not know about was S.E.'s connection to C.W. The results of that genealogy research follow.]

C.W.'s uncle & stepfather Stephen Elias "S. E." Woodworth has been accepted by the National Park Service historian as a signatory of the 1848 Seneca Falls Declaration of Sentiments. The evidence for this is the following:

1. There is a signatory of the document named "S.E. Woodworth".
2. The Seneca Falls Convention is known to have drawn attendees from the area
3. S. E. Woodworth had lived within 10 miles of Seneca Falls his entire life to that point.
4. The October 19, 1850 U.S. census records both Stephen E. Woodworth, age 30, working as a merchant and his daughter Mary, age 2 as living in Seneca Falls. Both ages are perfect.
5. There are no other Woodworth's whose first name starts with S. in Seneca County in the 1850 census
6. He used his initials S.E. in other records including the Supreme Court case (see the Education section later in this book).
7. The fact that both of his daughters, Minnie and Metta, graduated from the University of Illinois is evidence that he was likely supportive of women's rights.
8. The fact that his third wife had designed athletic uniforms for University of Illinois women's sports teams in the bloomer style is evidence that he was likely supportive of women's rights. (Amelia Bloomer was involved with the

women's rights movement, and bloomers were a symbol of the movement.)

9. The fact that his sister-in-law, Mary Gilbert, also signed the Declaration of Sentiments.
10. The historian of the National Park Service's Women's Rights National Historical Park in Seneca Falls, Anne DeRousie, said in an email to me in June of 2008: "We do believe that Stephen Elias Woodworth was a Signer and are aware of all of the information that you cite, except for the information concerning Charles W. Woodworth."
11. Judith Wellman, in her 2004 book "The Road to Seneca Falls", mentions Stephen and the Gilbert sisters.

Figure 11 Preserved site of the 1848 Seneca Falls Convention[30]

Figure 12 S. E. Woodworth's name on the wall of signatories at the National Historic Park (middle right)[31]

Judith Wellman's 2004, "The Road to Seneca Falls"[32] talks about S.E. in several places. This book is a well-written scholarly picture of the confluence of historical events that led to the Seneca Falls Convention. It presents what is known about the signatories. She found numerous advertisements in the "Seneca Falls Courier" for S.E.'s Dry Goods and tailor businesses as well as the millenary business of Mary, Ann, and Ruth Gilbert. The book mentions that S.E. was the fiancée of Mary Gilbert, who also signed the Declaration, but it is actually likely that he was either the fiancée or new groom of Mary's sister Ann at the time. A family bible lists S.E. and Ann's wedding as in 1847. S.E. and Ann can be found together in the 1850, 1860, and 1870 census records first in Seneca Falls and then in Montezuma, N.Y., about 15 miles northeast of Seneca Falls in the two later records.

After Elizabeth Cady Stanton read the proposed declaration in the Convention, Lucretia Mott added a response. S.E. is recorded as then, among others, as "having added his comments".[33]

The book also mentions, as part of an analysis of the religions of the signers, that "Only one Baptist endorsed it, and his motive may have been as much personal as political. S.E. Woodworth was engaged to marry Mary [probably sic, should be Ann] Gilbert, a local milliner. With her sisters Ann and Ruth, Mary Gilbert made most of the ladies' hats in town. Woodworth and Gilbert attended the woman's rights convention together, and both signed the Declaration of Sentiments."[34] The book's suggestion that social reasons may have underlain S.E.'s decision to sign the Declaration would seem to hold true, whether it was his fiancée, his fiancée's sister, or his new bride's sister who also signed.

[Author's note: My assumption is that the advertisement for the convention drew the attention of one of the Gilbert sisters and/or S. E. Woodworth, who all lived in Seneca Falls. S.E. and his sister-in-law Mary Gilbert attended together. Either the Declaration of Sentiments or the leadership of the movement must have impressed them, and they both signed the document. 300 people attended the convention, but only 100 signed the Declaration. S.E.'s signing is evidence of his positive thinking towards the place of women. Further evidence of S.E.'s thinking is: 1) that both of his daughters, Minnie and Metta, graduated from the University of Illinois and 2) that his wife designed athletic uniforms for University of Illinois women's sports teams in the bloomer style.]

C.W. had another connection to the Declaration of Sentiments. Late in life, when he was 61, C.W. married 45-year-old Bernice Christopher, who was the great-niece of Mary Gilbert, who also signed the Declaration of Sentiments. Bernice was both his first cousin once removed and his much-older and raised-in-a-different-household stepsister's daughter.

[Author's Note: I have two more connections to the Declaration of Sentiments aside from the connections on my mother's side to S.E. Woodworth and Mary Gilbert. On my father's side, I am related to the Nantucket Folger family. This is the Folger's Coffee family, although my connection to the coffee part of the tree is very distant. Through a closer part of the Folger family, I am related to the sisters Lucretia Mott and Martha Coffin Wright. They are both my fourth cousin four times removed as well as my third cousin seven times removed. (Given that Nantucket was a small and isolated island, seven other more distant cousin relationships to them also exist.)

The historic genealogy of Nantucket is amazingly well documented. There was a genealogist who, in the 19th century documented the family trees of nearly everyone who had ever lived on the island. The early female astronomer Maria Mitchell was also from this extended family and is a second cousin four times removed.]

Caleb and Elizabeth Woodworth

Alvin & Stephen Woodworth's parents were named Caleb Woodworth and Elizabeth Crane Woodworth. Caleb was born in 1786 in Mayfield, Fulton County, New York. Mayfield is at the southern end of the Adirondacks, northwest of Albany. Elizabeth was born in 1787 in Montclair, Essex County, New Jersey, which is six miles Northwest of Newark, NJ. In 1895, long after her death, Elizabeth's half great-great nephew, Stephen Crane, would write *The Red Badge of Courage*. She was also the great great granddaughter of the governor of Connecticut and co-founder of Newark, NJ, Robert Treat.

C.W.'s grandfather. Caleb, grew up in Tyre, NY, just northeast of Seneca Falls. Caleb's (born 1786) father Caleb (born 1763) purchased their land in Tyre, Seneca County, New York from Colonel James Livingston, who in turn had been granted the property in the Central New York Military Tract in return for his service in the Revolutionary War. The Military Tract was two million acres of land in New York's finger lake region that the state of New York used as compensation for its soldiers in lieu of cash. The counties and some cities in the tract are named for Greek and Roman persons and locations. This naming has been attributed to a clerk in the office of New York's Surveyor General's office who had an interest in antiquities. Tyre was an ancient Phoenician town in what is now southern Lebanon. Colonel Livingston had been involved with the defense of the St. Lawrence and Hudson rivers and played a role in the discovery of Benedict Arnold's treason.

The History of Seneca Co., 1786-1876 says:

> "CALEB WOODWORTH [born 1763] had bought Lot No. 36 of COLONEL LIVINGSTONE some time prior to 1802 ... [Caleb Woodworth then sold off a portion of that land.] Woodworth moved upon his lands in 1805, and there sojourned till the occurrence of his death five years later. ... [He had sold another portion before he died.] The four hundred acres of Woodworth were divided among heirs, and in time passed to other hands."[35]

Caleb and Elizabeth are buried on the outskirts of Tyre, NY in a small cemetery just west of the corner of Gravel Road and Durling Road, just south of the New York State Thruway (I-90). His tombstone is tipping over, but is otherwise in good shape. Hers is in worse shape. [I trimmed the grass away from both tombstones to allow better photos. A broken portion of his second wife's stone is nearby.]

Figure 13 C.W.'s paternal grandfather Caleb Woodworth's tombstone[36]

Figure 14 C.W.'s paternal grandmother Elizabeth Crane Woodworth's tombstone[37]

Caleb Woodworth's brother Hiram's original homestead house is still standing nearby at the end of E. Tyre Rd., just south of the New York Thruway. C.W.'s second cousin twice removed, Edward Lawrence, owns it. It was built of cobblestones by laborers who had previously worked on the Erie Canal.[38]

Figure 15 C.W.'s Uncle Hiram Woodworth's homestead house. C.W.'s second cousin twice removed, Edward Lawrence in front[39]

Extended Family

C.W was the 4th great grandson on his father's mother's side of Robert Treat, who was an American colonial leader. He served as governor of Connecticut and was the co-founder of Newark, New Jersey. Treat was involved in the Charter Oak Incident where the charter of the colony of Connecticut was hidden from a new British governor-general in an oak tree.

University of Connecticut

Figure 16 The oak leaf in the logo of the University of Connecticut represents the spirit of Connecticut as exemplified by the Charter Oak Incident[40]

C.W. is thought, although there is lack of firm evidence, to be a direct descendant on his mother's mother's side of Colonel Adrian Scrope, who was a member of parliament and a signatory of the death warrant for King Charles II during the English Civil War.

C.W. was a half second cousin once removed on his father's mother's side of Stephen Crane, the author of *The Red Badge of Courage*.

Figure 17 Stephen Crane[41]

C.W. was a second cousin three times removed on his father's mother's side of Robert Treat Paine, who signed the Declaration of Independence.

Figure 18 Robert Treat Paine's signature on the Declaration of Independence[42]

He was a fourth cousin once removed on his father's mother's side of inventor Thomas Edison.[43]

Figure 19 Matthew Brady image of Thomas Edison[44]

C.W. was also fourth cousin once removed on his mother's maternal side of General Douglas MacArthur.

Figure 20 General Douglas MacArthur[45]

Chapter 2 - Education

C.W. had a wonderful education for his era. He attended public high school in Champaign, Illinois before graduating from the University of Illinois with first a bachelor's and then a master's degree. He then entered Harvard where he spent two years in a Doctor of Science program before leaving to start a job at the newly organized Arkansas Agricultural Experiment Station. Twelve years later, he returned to Harvard in an ultimately unsuccessful attempt to finish his doctorate.

Primary and Secondary Education

Nothing is known about C.W.'s primary education aside from the fact that his family lived on East Clark Street in Champaign, Illinois.

For his secondary schooling, he went to Champaign High School.[46]

University of Illinois

Charles graduated with a Bachelor of Science in 1885 and with a Master of Science degree in 1886 from the University of Illinois at Urbana-Champaign.

The University was opened in 1868 as Illinois Industrial University. In 1877, authority to confer degrees was given. In 1885, the year of his bachelor's degree, the modern name, the University of Illinois, was adopted,[47] so his was the first class to have their diplomas say the University of Illinois. His was one of only four master's degrees granted by the entire University in June of 1886 (only 29 bachelor's degrees were granted then as well).[48]

> A 1897 college guide reports: "[The University of Illinois] embraces colleges of literature and the arts, of engineering, of science and agriculture, a graduate school, and that of pharmacy, each of which offers special courses. Admission is by examination, and on the certificates of 134 accredited schools. All of the first year's work and part of the second is prescribed. That of the two remaining years is large elective. Military drill is compulsory for all able-bodied men through six university teams. Attendance at chapel is voluntary. The degrees are A.B. and B.S. in architecture; civil, electrical, and mechanical engineering, agriculture; chemistry; and pharmacy. The master's degrees, conferred after graduate study correspond to these. The doctor's degree is conferred after three years, one of which must be resident."[49]

The university was also reported in the same 1897 guide as having 114 instructors, 855 students, 17 buildings, 36,000 books, and an income of $140,000. It was a co-educational, non-sectarian school. While there was no tuition, there was $157 in expenses for the year.

He became a member of Sigma Xi, the Scientific Research Society, either while he was at Illinois, or shortly thereafter.[50]

A happy occurrence for C.W. and one that was central for his entire career was that during the period of 1885-1886 at the University of Illinois, he was an assistant to the prominent economic entomologist and ecologist Stephen Alfred Forbes.[51]

C.W.'s Advisor Stephen Alfred Forbes

Figure 21 Stephen Alfred Forbes[52]

Stephen Alfred Forbes was born in 1844 and was a Civil War veteran. His first published works appeared in *American Entomologist and Botanist* in 1870, and a new plant species, which he was the first researcher to describe, was named *Saxifraga forbesei* in his honor.

Forbes was named director of the new State Laboratory of Natural History in 1877, and in 1882 he became both the Director of the State Laboratory of Natural History and the State Entomologist of Illinois. Forbes moved from Normal, IL to Urbana, IL in 1885 to accept a position with the Illinois Industrial University, which renamed itself to the current University of Illinois that same year. He also gained approval from the state legislature to transfer the State Laboratory of Natural History along with its staff, library, and research collections from Normal to Urbana.[53] This post was renamed the Illinois Natural History Survey in 1917, at which time he became the first director. He stayed in this post until his death in 1930.

Forbes was a noted economic entomologist, the field that C.W. spent much of his career in. Economic entomologists are sometimes colloquially called "bug killers". They study the impact of insects on crops & humans and often work to develop methods of chemical and biological control of those insects when they become pests.

Forbes was also a central figure in the development of American ecology and helped lay the groundwork for the concept of ecosystems.

His biographer, L.O. Howard, wrote in 1931 "All of his writings on entomological topics stand out conspicuously from the mass of publications on this subject. Here for the first time in the history of economic entomology a man not only of striking originality but of very broad biological sympathies and experiences found himself engaged in the multifarious problems of insect damage to human interests. None of his predecessors or contemporaries in this field had his broad experience in biology or his broad outlook on nature."[54]

His biography also has a beautiful extended account of a 14-year-old Stephen Forbes witnessing one of the Lincoln-Douglas debates. There was an extended sequence of slights by Douglas against Lincoln's supporters and responses by those supporters. This was followed by Douglas' rebuff of those responses. At the end of the rebuff, Stephen called out "Lincoln didn't use any such talk". After being "sharply reproved by those around him", the young Stephen Forbes was gratified when Lincoln echoed his outburst and defended the behavior of Douglas' supporters. The account continues: "With this elaboration of my own sentiments I need not say that I was relieved and delighted or that I joined in the hearty laughter and applause with which ... his rejoinder was received."[55]

Professor Forbes published papers in 1886 and 1887 on a pair of topics that would be important in C.W.'s later career. It is fair to assume that C.W. was involved in these experiments as an assistant. In 1886, Forbes published "Experiments on the codling moth and circulious".[56] In 1887, Forbes published "Arsenical poisons for the codling moth - record and discussion of experiments for 1885 and 1886."[57]
(See *Chapter 11 - The Codling Moth and the California Spray Chemical Company* - "Ortho"for a detailed discussion.)

C.W.'s Professor Thomas J. Burrill

In C.W.'s paper, "The Wing Veins of Insects", he says: "The author desires to acknowledge the inspiration and encouragement of Professors Burrill and Forbes of the University of Illinois, with whom his first work on this subject was begun, ..."[58]

Figure 22 Plant Pathologist Thomas J. Burrill[59]

Thomas J. Burrill, 1839-1916, was a botanist. He was a pioneering scientist who first discovered the bacterial basis for certain diseases. One of his biographers, Dean A Glawe said, "Perhaps no other American plant pathologist is so deserving of the title 'Pioneer of Plant Pathology' as Thomas J. Burrill."

He was born in Massachusetts, but was raised in Illinois. He received a Bachelor's degree from Illinois Normal University (he received a number of honorary degrees later). Burrill joined John Wesley Powell on an expedition to Colorado in 1867. In 1868 he joined Illinois Industrial University (later the University of Illinois)

He served the University in many ways including as Vice-President and Acting President/Regent (four times). He taught courses in general horticulture, pomology, forestry, floriculture, vegetable physiology, cryptogamic botany, microscopy, and bacteriology. Glawe says: "His connection with the University was long-lived and deep." He was a hard worker and served the University in many different ways. Glawe quotes Burrill's friend:

> "He taught most of the days, was horticulturist to the experiment station, planted with his own hands or saw to the planting of most of the trees on campus, after he had laid it out for treatment, wrote reports, lectured here and there, served on innumerable committees, collected specimens up and down the state, and, lest some remnant of his time should be unoccupied, was charged by the Board with the sale of mules, whose labors on the south farm showed that they were not so able to stand the strenuous life as he was. His professorship began at sun-up and lasted indefinitely, and included everything that needed doing."

His plant pathology research is particularly known for the determination that fire blight is due to a bacterial infection and not a fungal infection.[60]

It is a reasonable assumption that C.W.'s expertise in plant pathology as well as his lifelong interest and expertise in optics started with Professor Burrill. If we had a copy of C.W.'s transcript, it would likely show that he took both plant pathology and microscopy classes from Professor Burrill. C.W. may have modeled some of his hard and multi-disciplinary work habits after Burrill's.

Silkworm experiments at Illinois

His niece, Mary Young Detrich reported that her mother Minnie told her that she and Metta had picked many baskets of mulberry leaves for C.W. to help feed his silkworm experiments.[61]

C.W. continued his investigations on silkworms for much of his career. This early work with silkworms may have also been an important link in the chain of events that led him to spend four years in China later in his career.

His first publication – Jassidae of Illinois

On September 10, 1887, over a year after C.W. had graduated from Illinois with his master's degree and during his first period at Harvard, what is presumably his master's thesis is published by the *Bulletin of the Illinois State Laboratory of Natural History*. The 37 page paper was entitled "Jassidae of Illinois" and was C.W.'s first professional publication.

Article II.—Jassidae of Illinois. Part I.

By Charles W. Woodworth, M. S.

Figure 23 Section of cover of his first professional publication, "Jassidae of Illinois. Part 1"

There is a note about the "Part I" designation on the first page; it says that "The present article includes only the subfamily Tettigoninae. I hope soon to complete the remaining part." There is no evidence that a "Part II" of this paper was ever published, although that is not too surprising given that he was enrolled in a doctorate program at Harvard, which itself was interrupted by his employment at the Arkansas Agriculture Experiment Station at Arkansas Industrial University.

The family Jassidae is now known by the name Cicadellidae and have the common names of hoppers or leafhoppers. This family of insects includes a number of economically important species including the glassy-winged sharpshooter, which has recently emerged as a threat to California's vineyards. Leafhoppers have piercing and sucking mouthparts and commonly live off of sap from plants. Some of the damage caused by these insects is through the transmission of plant viruses enabled by their piercing of the plants.

Of course, this sort of species description and organization document from 125 years ago does not match what has been produced by modern science. Today's versions of such a document have the taxonomic descriptions paired with clade diagrams that have been sourced by DNA analysis and derived computationally. Many of the species names in C.W.'s paper have been changed beyond recognition, although some are still the same.

A modern non-DNA version of C.W.'s 1887 paper is the 2005 paper in the *Florida Entomologist* by C.H. Dietrich, also of the Center for Biodiversity, Illinois Natural History Survey entitled "Keys to the Families of Cicadomorpha and Subfamilies and Tribes of Cicadellidae (Hemiptera: Auchenorrhyncha)".[62] The Illinois Natural History Survey is the modern name of the Illinois State Laboratory of Natural History. They even have a quote from C.W.'s advisor Steven A. Forbes on their website:

> "The first indispensable requisite is a thorough knowledge of the natural order - an intelligently conducted natural history survey. Without the general knowledge which such a survey would give us, all our measures must be empirical, temporary, uncertain, and often dangerous."[63]

One of the species named after C.W., now known as *Elidiptera woodworthi* is in this "Jassidae" (Cicadellidae) insect family.
(See the Chapter 6 section entitled *Species named after C.W.*).

C.W.'s paper was an important input into Edward P. Van Duzee's 1890 "A Catalogue of the Described Jassoidea of North America", published in the Transactions of the American Entomological Society. The interaction between the authors of the two papers is likely to have been the start of their lifelong affiliation. Van Duzee eventually became a member of the Cal faculty many years later.

New England Mutual Life Ins. Co. v Woodworth

A significant aspect of C.W.'s education is how it was likely funded.

On September 21, 1869, Ann E. Gilbert Woodworth, S.E. Woodworth's second wife, took out a life insurance policy on herself with the New England Mutual Life Insurance Company in Michigan. Her husband Stephen E. Woodworth was the beneficiary. She then died in New York, and her husband moved from New York to Illinois. She died intestate (without a will), so an Illinois court passed judgment on the disposition of her estate. The company did not pay the policy claim because they did not recognize the authority of the Illinois court. An Illinois court then passed judgment against the insurance company. The insurance company appealed, saying that the judgment was invalid since the suit should not have been filed in Illinois.

The appeal of the case reached all of the way to the United States Supreme Court. It was argued on March 18, 1884 and was decided on March 31, 1884. It is known as New England Mutual Life Ins. Co. v Woodworth. The Court reaffirmed the general rule that simple contract debts, such as a policy of insurance not under seal, are, for the purpose of founding administration, assets where the debtor resides, without regard to the place where the policy is found.[64] In plain English, the court reaffirmed the general rule that in simple financial disputes, the person who did not get paid can sue in the state where he or she lives.

Since C.W. graduated in 1884, he was likely in his junior year of college when the funds arrived. The funds received from the payout of the insurance policy following the judgment in this case are likely to have helped pay for C.W's and his sibling's education. Charles and all three of his immediate siblings, Howard, Minnie & Metta received degrees from the University of Illinois. The combination of these funds and living a couple of blocks from campus likely helped ensure that C.W. received a high quality education. Having educated siblings also has a way of pushing the intellectual development of a young person along.

The New England Mutual Life Insurance Company merged with the Metropolitan Life Insurance Company or "MetLife" in 1996. It demutualized in 2000 and trades on the NYSE under the symbol "MET".

MetLife®

Figure 24 Logo of the Metropolitan Life Insurance Company[65]

Illinois alumnus

A photo exists of recently widowed C.W. at a University of Illinois alumni event in 1925 with his mother's blind brother.

Alumni Parade 1925
Charles W. Woodwoorth and Harvey Carpenter
(Mary Celina's blind brother)

Figure 25 C.W. (dark suit & hat) in a University of Illinois alumni parade along with his Uncle Harvey Carpenter (cane) in 1925[66]

Harvard University 1886-88

From 1886 to 1888, C.W. studied in a Doctor of Science program at Harvard University under Dr. H.A. Hagen, who, at the time, was the leading entomologist of the United States. He arrived at the age of twenty-one.

The Doctor of Science (Sc.D.) degree that C.W. was trying to get was an academic research doctoral degree awarded by research universities. In the U.S., research doctorates, be they either Sc.D. or Ph.D. degrees, are largely a 20th century phenomenon. Harvard University granted its first Ph.D. degree in 1873, only 15 years before C.W.'s first time there.[67] Similar degrees to the Sc.D. exist today in degrees such as Doctor of Engineering and Doctor of Education.

C.W.'s Advisor Herman August Hagen

Figure 26 Hermann August Hagen[68]

H.A. Hagen was born in 1817 in Königsberg, East, in the country of Prussia. Königsberg is now known as Kaliningrad and is the capital of Russia's Kaliningrad Oblast, which is that small, disconnected part of Russia on the Baltic Sea coast between Poland and Lithuania. He received his M.D. degree from the University of Königsberg in 1840. At the time of his death it was written about him: "For the last 250 years, some ancestor [of his] has been connected to the University of Königsberg." [69]

He practiced medicine in Königsberg until 1867 while publishing in entomology. He received an honorary degree of Ph.D. from the University of Königsberg in 1863 and was received into membership of many scientific societies.

He was invited to come to Harvard University by Louis Agassiz and arrived in 1867. He became the Head of Entomology at the Museum of Comparative Zoology there starting in 1867 and a Professor of Entomology from 1870 until his death in 1893. He specialized in Neuroptera. He was the first Professor of Entomology at an American university.

His publications include more than 400 articles. His most important publication is the "Bibliotheca Entomologica". His New York Times obituary called him "one of the greatest scientists in the world".[70]

In the 1906 published version of C.W.'s failed doctoral dissertation, he calls out "the invaluable assistance and advice of that honored and lamented prince of entomologists, Dr. Hagen, whose invariable kindness during the two years' work in his laboratory can never be forgotten…".[71]

Psyche

When C.W. arrived at Harvard, he joined the Cambridge Entomological Club and helped restart the publication of journal, *Psyche.* He published in Psyche in 1888 and again in 1889.
(See the Chapter 3 section entitled Cambridge Entomological Club)

The Hatch Act and C.W.'s departure

C.W.'s first departure from Harvard is directly related to the passage of the Hatch Act of 1887, which officially established the concept of the Agricultural Experiment Station. It gave $15,000 to states for the purpose of establishing Agricultural Experiment Stations that would be formed in association with universities that had been formed by the 1862 Morrill Act. Those universities are commonly known as land-grant State colleges and universities.

An article on the Oklahoma Agricultural Experiment Station at Oklahoma State University about the Hatch Act says:

> The Hatch Act attacked general ignorance of growing conditions, helping to make American agricultural producers more productive. Research findings from experiment station systems across the country revised farming methods to fit the diverse geography of America and improved farm animals to meet public needs. Hatch Act funding has resulted in a federal-state research partnership that has largely removed the specter of hunger and the drudgery of subsistence agriculture production.[72]

An article on the website of the Virginia Tech Agricultural Experiment Station reads:

> With the organization of the additional stations in 1888, the demand for trained entomologists far exceeded the supply, and many men were appointed who for one reason or another seemed qualified for the work. The appointments resulted in the development of many who became prominent as economic entomologists.[73]
>
> They eventually organized, establishing the American Association of Economic Entomologists. That group was the precursor of the current day Entomological Society of America.[74]

An article on the website of the University of Florida's Institute of Food and Agricultural Sciences says:" ... the land-grant tripartite mission rests originally on the Morrill Act of 1862 [land-grant colleges], the Hatch Act of 1887 [agricultural experiment stations] and the Smith-Lever Act of 1914 [cooperative extensions]."[75]

The provisions of the Hatch Act of 1887 were amended by the Adams Act of 1906, the Purnell Act of 1925, the Bankhead-Jones Act of 1935 as well as in 1946, 1955 and 2002; they are still in force. The grants are administered by the USDA's National Institute of Food and Agriculture (NIFA).[76]

C.W.'s first time at Harvard ended when he got a job that had been created by the grants from the Hatch Act at what is now the University of Arkansas as an entomologist and botanist. C.W. would not return to Harvard for another twelve years.

It is easy to imagine that this must have been a difficult choice for him to make - finish your doctorate at Harvard or take a solid job with the chance to make an immediate impact.

In C.W.'s outgoing address as President of the Cambridge Entomological Club in 1891, while he was at Arkansas, he said "Economic entomology is upon the verge of an era of great advancement. The establishment of the agricultural experiment stations have added to its ranks more young men of scientific training and ability perhaps than have ever engaged in this line of investigation."[77]

Harvard University 1900-01

In 1900, after a twelve-year gap, a thirty-five year old C.W. took a leave of absence from the University of California to attempt to complete his Doctor of Science degree. He studied from 1900 to 1901 in the laboratory of a thirty-three year old Dr. William E. Castle. Dr. Edward L. Mark, professor of Zoology was also involved with reviewing his dissertation. Dr. Hagen, C.W.'s advisor during his first stay, had died in 1893, long before C.W.'s return.

The undated and ink-stained, draft first page of a letter C.W. was writing to his Harvard advisor E.L. Mark is contained in the UCB correspondence collection. The letter would have been written in early 1900. It is unclear what the final letter C.W. actually sent to Dr. Mark said.

"I have now matured my plans for the coming year and feel very much like going to Europe but I have the idea that I can get hold all that is latest in methods etc. better in your laboratory than elsewhere.

Now it occurred to me that I might compromise the matter if it would be feasible as follows: Spend the first term at Harvard, complete my work towards the S.D. [Doctor of Science degree] and then on to Europe. I suppose it would be called Non-Resident. After studying your catalogue and letter I believe there would be no difficulty in the matter of requirement and I have the subject I proposed for thesis so well in hand that I will have no difficulty in having it ready by Christmas. I have already fulfilled the minimum residence requirement and Dr. ..."[78]

He actually stayed in residence at Harvard for the full year, travelling to Europe in the summer of 1901.

[Author's note: This letter shows that C.W. underestimated how difficult it would be to get a doctoral dissertation past a Harvard review committee.]

In September of 1900, he reported back to U.C. President Benjamin Wheeler at the end of a letter about the Cuban school that:

Since leaving Berkeley I have visited about a score of colleges and spoken at a majority of them. I have availed myself of every facility afforded me of acquainting myself with the work of the colleges and experiment stations and feel that the trip has been very profitable. I have already arranged to take a trip through the southern states this winter but the greater part of my time I will spend here in scientific work.

We are located very pleasantly in the midst of the historic part of old Cambridge and have renewed many memories of my former college days.

I am pleased to learn of the increased numbers at Berkeley and will not be sorry when my year is up and I again take up the work there."[79]

The following is C.W.'s February 1, 1901 bursar bill from Harvard University. The tuition for the "first and second thirds of 1900-1901" was $100 and the lab fees were $20. This is around $3000 in 2008 dollars according to an online inflation calculator (in real dollar terms and not in purchasing power parity terms).

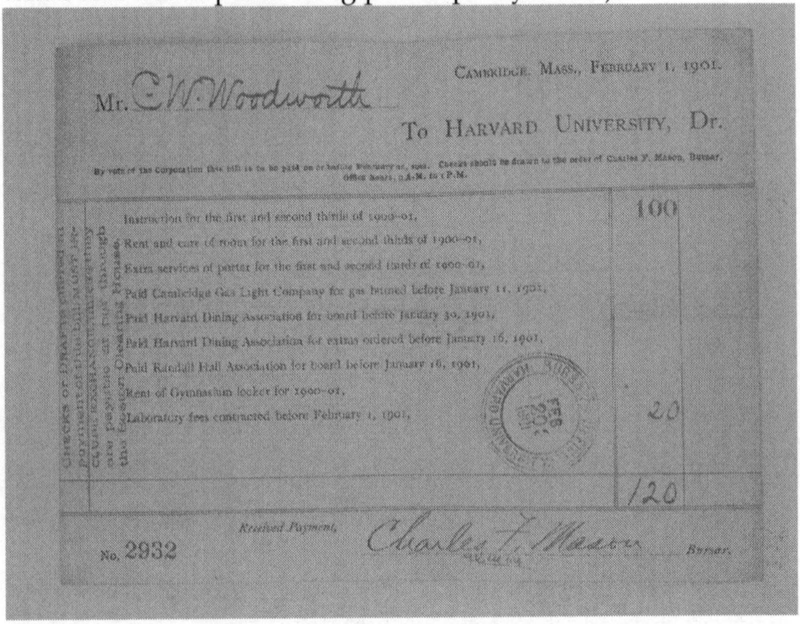

CAMBRIDGE, MASS., FEBRUARY 1, 1901.

Mr. C. W. Woodworth

To HARVARD UNIVERSITY, Dr.

Instruction for the first and second thirds of 1900-01,	100
Rent and care of room for the first and second thirds of 1900-01,	
Extra services of porter for the first and second thirds of 1900-01,	
Paid Cambridge Gas Light Company for gas burned before January 11, 1901,	
Paid Harvard Dining Association for board before January 30, 1901,	
Paid Harvard Dining Association for extras ordered before January 16, 1901,	
Paid Randall Hall Association for board before January 16, 1901,	
Rent of Gymnasium locker for 1900-01,	
Laboratory fees contracted before February 1, 1901,	20
	120

Received Payment, Charles F. Mason, Bursar.

No. 2932

Figure 27 C.W.'s 1901 Harvard Bursar Bill[80]

During his second visit, from 1900-1901, his fourth and last child, Elizabeth, arrived. A letter from E.W. Hilgard concludes with "I congratulate you upon the auspicious event in your family. I suspect the climatic conditions [of Cambridge] have helped the matter along, in accordance with the accepted ideas regarding the beneficial effects of a change of climate!"[81]

C.W.'s Doctoral Dissertation

C.W. completed most of his doctoral dissertation "The Wing Veins of Insects" while he was there and refined it over the next year while back in Berkeley. It is interesting that he chose a subject in insect morphology rather than in economic entomology where he had spent the bulk of his career to that point and had already published thirty-two papers. Four factors may have led to his choice of topic.

1. His first advisor, Dr. Hermann August Hagen, was a major figure in the study of insect wings.
2. Harvard had (and still has) the prominent Museum of Comparative Zoology, whose entomology collection had been started in 1859 by Samuel Scudder.[82]
3. Entomology at Harvard University at that time was likely more about studying insects instead of killing them.
4. He appears to have had a long-standing interest in insect wings. The study of insect wings is a classic subject of interest to amateur entomologists because they are easy to observe with only a magnifying glass.

Dr. Hermann August Hagen was a principal researcher in the study of insect wings. In the preface of his 1918 landmark book "The Wings of Insects", John Henry Comstock says "It is now more than thirty years since I began a special study of the homologies of the wing-veins of insects, a subject in which my interest had been awakened a decade before by my teacher, Dr. Hagen."[83] In the same book, he continues: "It seems probable that the short paper published by Dr. Hagen in 1870 entitled 'Ueber rationelle Benennung des Geäders in den Flügeln der Insekten' [About the rational naming of the veins in the wings of insects] was the beginning of the series of efforts to establish a system of terminology of the wing-veins of insects applicable to all orders of insects."[84]

His advisor E.L. Mark wrote C.W. on September 4, 1901:

> Yesterday I sent by registered mail a pkg. containing your thesis, bound in two parts, and the discovery outline which you made for my use in getting the lettering done. I have forgotten just what we were planning that you should do with the thesis - you probably remember better. In a general way I had the impression that we were to get it published and presented as a thesis next June in printed form. I have no doubt but that the acceptance of the thesis by the committee would be extended to the paper in printed form. If so, I am not sure that it is necessary to have another copy made. Perhaps I ought to have settled this point with you before forwarding it and thus have saved expense - was I to have gone thro' it again before your return? I was away till middle of July - a hot summer - and since my return have been so busy. I've not had a chance to look at it Please write to me at once your remembrance of what we planned to do."[85]

His advisor E.L. Mark wrote him on September 17, 1901:

> "Yours of 11th duly rec'd. I always think in June that I have an endless vacation in the summer in which to do all the things I want to do and cannot do during term time! So I did expect to through your ins. [paper] again before sending it to you; but was not able to. I think there is no question that you had better revise it with the utmost care, so that when I do go over it again there will be as little change as possible. The result will indicate whether is better to send to you or the printer final."[86]

The drafts of his dissertation do not survive, but the failed dissertation was published five years later by the University of California. He says in the introduction to that monograph:

> "The studies of the author have been under way since 1884 [when he was 19], and have included the study of microscopical preparations of the wings of about two thousand species representing all the principal groups, the examination of a much larger series of insects with spread wings, and the inspection of practically all the published figures of insects wings."

The paper is filled with his novel observations. For example, page 30 advances the theory that a function of the air sacs in certain insects is to help the recoil of the wing stroke. Page 39 describes the several features of the articulation of dragonfly and harvest fly wings. Pages 42-47 provide an articulate and ultimately correct falsification of the theory of "pretracheation" (see further discussion of this below).

His dissertation was ultimately rejected, and he did not receive a doctorate from Harvard.

[Author's note: Two obvious objections to the dissertation appear to be that it contained too few references and did not connect enough to other threads of research. If you look at a typical modern dissertation, endnotes are spread liberally through every page and point at 30 or 40 pages of references. When C.W.'s dissertation was ultimately published five years later, it had no endnotes and just six pages of general references.]

Oral exam

C.W.'s advisor, Professor E.L. Mark sent C.W. a letter on January 25, 1902.

"There are, so far as I know, no further 'formalities' to go through; but of course you will not fail to realize the searching character of an oral examination, which in your case - considering the outcome of the first one - will scarcely be made easier. I trust that you will not allow your many duties to prevent that thorough preparation of the examination that will ensure success.

Of course we shall to arrange beforehand the precise day for the exam. When you can foresee the date you prefer (let it be as near June 1st as convenient. Please let me know, and I will have the day set."[87]

This letter indicates that C.W. had gone through an earlier oral exam for his S.D. degree, presumably in the June, 1901 timeframe, at the end of his year there, and had failed. One way or the other, C.W. failed the second oral exam as well.

[Author's note: In today's scientific world, most papers have numerous co-authors, which are often a collection of collaborating professors and Ph.D. students. C.W.'s papers, throughout his career, were uniformly only credited to him, with acknowledgements often given in the course of the text. Collaboration was more difficult in his era given the lack of telephones during part of his career and email during all of it. C.W.'s position on the West Coast may have added to his difficulty in collaborating. In his era, much of the activity in academic entomology was happening at Cornell, Harvard and the USDA, all four-day train rides away from Berkeley.

C.W.'s work is rich with observation and reporting of the natural world; it is less full of the incremental advance of science that is the hallmark of today's world. Today's scientist cites twelve other papers and runs a finely tuned experiment to show why a certain aspect of a theory is subtly wrong. C.W. would have an idea, design an experiment to prove that idea, carry out that experiment, and write up a paper describing the results, along the way advancing three or four additional theories, one of which would be right on the mark and really important in the end.

It is easy to imagine C.W.'s oral exam committee members asking him about how the work of a list of other professors connected with his own. C.W. may not have had good, comprehensive answers these questions.]

Later publication of his dissertation

His 152-page dissertation was later published jointly in September, 1906 by the University of California with "Contributions From the Zoological Laboratory of the Museum of Comparative Zoology at Harvard College, Under the Direction of E.L. Mark". It was the first publication of the University of California Publications in Entomology, a monograph series that continues to this day.

A lengthy and highly critical review was published by James G. Needham of Lake Forest University (later at Cornell) in *Science* on February 8, 1907. James G. Needham was born in 1868 and studied at Cornell under Dr. Comstock. He was a professor at Lake Forest University from 1898 to 1907 and then at Cornell University from 1907 until his retirement in 1935. He succeeded Dr. Comstock as the head of the Department of Entomology at Cornell in 1914.[88]

Figure 28 Dr. James G. Needham (pointing) circa 1920[89]

Dr. Needham and Dr. Comstock together developed the "Comstock-Needham System" nomenclature for the veins of insect wings in 1898. Their naming system is the one that prevailed and has found its way into the textbooks. The theory underlying their system was partially based on Dr. Needham's "pretracheation theory". This theory asserted that the means of the development of the trachea of insect larva was the best guide to the development of veins in the wings of the adult. Pretracheation theory was finally discredited for good in the 1920's and 30's after some further counter examples were found.[90] However, the naming system of the various aspects of wing morphology did not have to change in response to this later change in the underlying theory.

Insects do not have lungs, hearts, and blood cells carrying oxygenated hemoglobin like vertebrates (including humans) do. Instead, insects have air pipes called "trachea" that reach into every part of their body that deliver ambient air directly, near to every cell of their body. The trachea connect to the outside world through vent structures called spiracles. They also connect to the smallest areas via small tracheas or tracheoles. This simple and efficient respiration system is part of the formula that has allowed insects to dominate our natural world. While a trachea system is ideal for small animals, it does not scale up sufficiently to deliver enough oxygen to the organs of large animals. This limitation is an important factor why there are not any insects as large as even medium-sized vertebrates.

In his review, Dr. Needham criticized many aspects of C.W.'s paper. His principal objections were:

1. That C.W. ignored some other published research.
2. That C.W. minimized the role of trachea in the morphology of the wing veins.
3. That C.W. overemphasized the role of mechanical requirements in the layout of the wing veins of insects.
4. That C.W. underemphasized the pliancy requirements of the trailing edges of wings to allow insects to scull in the air.

5. That C.W.'s proposed yet another nomenclature scheme for the elements of insect veins instead of using or modifying Redtenbacher's work or the "dozens" of other systems.
6. That C.W. inverted the order of development of independent veins that grow inward from the margin.
7. That C.W. misspelled some names.

[Author's note: Some of Dr. Needham's criticisms appear to be valid. Responses to these criticisms are:

1. Criticism #1 is somewhat unfair given that the paper was largely written five years before it was published. No intermediate versions of his dissertation survive to allow us to see how it might have changed between 1901 and 1906.
2. Numerous counter-examples to the Comstock-Needham theory of pretracheation that underlie Needham's criticisms #2 above were found in the 1930's, falsifying it as the central theory.
3. C.W. was ultimately proven correct, given the collapse of the pretracheation theory, the mechanical aspects of the wings the key aspect of wings that receive evolutionary pressure.
4. This may be a valid complaint.
5. The "dozens" of nomenclature systems are all arbitrary, but I do agree with Dr. Needham that it was not helpful to add yet another system of names. C.W. does justify the change by saying that Comstock's naming system overemphasizes the role of venation.
6. Possibly.
7. True.]

John Henry Comstock referenced C.W.'s paper in his landmark 1918 "The Wings of Insects", published twelve years later.

Dr. Needham's published response got unprofessional in a few places. He says on page 222 that "It is safe to say that no other venation theorist has ridden his hobby so far as this". Later on that same page near the end of the review Dr. Needham says: "There is a mysticism about the account of the genesis of the venation that is somewhat unusual in a scientific paper: page 79 is full of it; and the statement that the primary vein was developed to be the dominant vein (p. 144) reminds one of the statement of that other narrative of *Genesis* that the lights of the firmament of heaven were to be for signs."

[Author's note: This over-the-top wording is particularly in conflict with the fact that C.W. had been thrown out of a church eleven years earlier for believing in evolution. When I read pages 79 and 144 of the paper, I do not see any such mysticism. What I see is Dr. Needham railing against a criticism of his own concept, pretracheation - a concept that would be later disproven.]

One possibility is that the excessively critical nature of Dr. Needham's review is just the normal back and forth of passionate and dedicated scientists. Another possibility is that Dr. Needham made his review excessively critical as part of his attempt to get a better job. This paper was published just before Dr. Needham left Lake Forest University for Cornell University. Dr. Needham was 38 at the time, so it not fair to chalk this excess up to the excesses of youth.

There may also have been cultural issues at play. When C.W. hired William Herms away from a doctorate program at Harvard in 1908, Herms' advisors told him that the University of California was a "dead end academically and the population of California was uncultured."[91]

[Author's note: C.W.'s experience of coming so close, but ultimately failing to get his doctorate from Harvard could have been an important crucible in the molding of his character. Early failure is found so many times in the background of great persons to be a coincidence. I have had a long and wonderful career as a Silicon Valley electrical engineer and have seen first-hand the power of failure to produce the set of experiences that lead to later success. Silicon Valley engineers wear their failures like war wounds, and some say that the success of the valley is partially due to its social tolerance of failure. Many of C.W.'s greatest achievements happened after this failure.]

Through the course of his long and wonderful career, C.W. was always referred to as "Professor Woodworth" and not "Dr. Woodworth".

C.W.'s Advisor, Dr. Edward L. Mark

Edward L. Mark was a Professor of Zoology at Harvard. He was involved in reviewing C.W.'s dissertation.

Figure 29 Painting of Edward L. Mark by Leopold Seyffert[92]

Edward L. Mark was appointed a professor emeritus of Harvard University after serving there for 44 years in the Department of Zoology.

He was born on May 30, 1847 in Hamlet, Chautauqua County in western New York. He graduated from the University of Michigan in 1871. In 1873, he enrolled in the University of Leipzig under Professor Rudolf Leuckart, an authority on parasitic animals. Mark received his Ph.D. in 1876.

Dr. Mark was appointed an instructor of zoology at Harvard in 1877 and then assistant professor in 1880. He was involved in research into the eggs of the slug *Limax* and advanced knowledge about the polarization of eggs generally. Mark also had a particular aptitude for organizing the department and in teaching. The Zoological Laboratory under his direction produced 332 contributions.

"Dr. Mark is, doubtless, the zoologist of his generation who has trained the greatest number of biologists and through his own work and that of his pupils combined has had the greatest influence on science in America."[93]

Dr. William E. Castle

Figure 30 William Ernest Castle[94]

Dr. Castle was the professor who took C.W.'s suggestion that *Drosophila melanogaster* would make a good species on which to conduct genetic research on.

William E. Castle was born in 1867 on a farm in Ohio. He graduated in 1889 from Denison University and taught Latin at Ottawa University in Ottawa, Kansas. Botany was an avocation of his. He got a second bachelor's degree from Harvard in 1893, a master's in 1894, and a Ph.D. in 1895. He taught for one year at the University of Wisconsin and for one year at Knox College. He returned to Harvard in 1897.[95]

A retrospective on his life, published in 1993 in *Genetics* by George D. Snell and Sheldon Reed, says: "Castle's early work at Harvard was concerned with vertebrate embryology, but with the rediscovery of Mendel's laws in 1900, his interest soon shifted to mammalian genetics. Interestingly, Castle was the first to use drosophila for genetic experiments. With some colleagues, he did an extensive study of inbreeding and selection, which was published in 1906. It was through Castle's influence that drosophila became known to geneticists, most notably T. H. Morgan ..."[96]

Castle became the director of Harvard's Bussey Institution for Applied Biology in Jamaica Plains, MA. He "became the director because of his soft-spoken, kindly but firm, even-handed diplomacy." He published "242 papers, three books, and a genetics laboratory manual."

One of his books, published in 1921, was unfortunately entitled "Genetics and Eugenics: A Textbook for Students of Biology and a Reference Book for Animal and Plant Breeders". He was on the board of the Eugenics Record Office, an organization that was founded in 1910 (well after C.W.'s time with him in 1900-1901) that advocated for forced sterilization of the "feebleminded".

At age 70, after his retirement from Harvard, he joined the University of California as a research associate in mammalian genetics. C.W. would have been 72 at the time that Castle arrived in Berkeley. It seems reasonable that they must have spent some time together then. He died in 1962 at age 95.[97]

C.W.'s lucky start

C.W. received a spectacular education for his era, initially aided by some good luck. His luck came in three ways:

1. He grew up a half block from what would become the University of Illinois.
2. His family ended up with enough resources to send him and his siblings to college.
3. Stephen A. Forbes worked at the University of Illinois.

After this lucky start, the rest seems to be all his doing.

Chapter 3 – General Aspects of His Working Career

After the passage of the Hatch Act, in 1888, C.W. got a job at the newly formed Arkansas Experiment Station. After getting malaria there, he moved to Berkeley where he worked for the University of California.

The University of Arkansas

As a result of the Hatch Act, in 1888, C.W. was appointed entomologist and botanist at the Arkansas Industrial University's newly formed Agricultural Experiment Station in Fayetteville, now known as the University of Arkansas.

"Advantage was soon taken of the provisions of the Hatch bill and the experiment station was immediately organized, February 17, 1888. A brick building was erected at a cost of $4,000, and it was supplied with apparatus and material at an additional cost of $4,100, all of which was paid for out of federal funds, though the law said that not more than one-fifth of the first appropriation could be used for building purposes. ...

The first staff [at Fayetteville] was as follows:" [98]

Name	Position
A.E. Menke	Director
William Trelease	Consulting Botanist
S.S. Twombly	Chemist and Vice-Director
F.W. Simonds	Biologist
S.H. Crossman	Entomologist
S.H. Crossman, deceased	Vice-Entomologist
C.W. Woodworth	Entomologist
E.H. Richman	Horticulturist

R.R. Dinwiddle	Veterinarian
C.B. Covingwood	Chemist
G.A. Humphrey	Assistant Chemist

Table 3 First staff at Fayetteville

The first entomological bulletin published by any of the experiment stations was issued in April 1888, from the Arkansas station by Mr. S.H. Crossman, and was entitled "The Peach Tree Borer and the Codling Moth."[99] S.H. Crossman graduated from Cornell University in 1888.[100]

An 1897 college guide records the Arkansas Industrial University as having 73 instructors, 964 students, an income of $60,000, and 7,000 books.[101]

Figure 31 1908 postcard of the Agricultural Experiment Station (the entomology facility is the small red building on the left)[102]

Stephen F. Strausberg's book, "A Century of Research: Centennial history of the Arkansas Agricultural Experiment Station" states that C.W. was considered the first trained agricultural research scientist employed by the Arkansas Agricultural Experiment Station and includes a photo of him.

He writes: "Also, in an effort to directly assist the farmers, Charles W. Woodworth, the state entomologist, offered to identify any insect that was sent to the Experiment Station and forward suggestions as to control technology."[103]

Strausberg continued: "Charles W. Woodworth began a survey of plant pests and diseases in Arkansas. He had been trained under Professor Stephen A. Forbes at the University of Illinois. As a student he had imbibed his professor's philosophy on pest management, which has remained a hallmark of the Experiment Station till the present. Woodworth emphasized the importance of timely applications of poison, advising farmers to keep fields clean to prevent pests from taking control. Over application of insecticides, he said, had an adverse impact on crops. After becoming ill [from successive attacks of malaria], Woodworth later left to serve in the California Experiment Station where he perpetuated his views on pest control."[104]

While he was there, he published three papers, two of which were republished. Those papers were:

1. Entomological Notes: Life history, injuries, and remedies of the tarnished plant-bug, Bulletin No. 10, Arkansas Agricultural Experiment Station, June 1889, pp18

2. Entomologist's Report: Treatments of the grape leaf-folder, life history, natural enemies, and remedies, First Annual Report, Arkansas Agricultural Experiment Station, 1889, pp. 121-127

3. Entomology (Bulletin 13 of the Arkansas Industrial University, Agricultural Experiment Station, 1889)

C.W. got married and became a father during his time in Fayetteville.
(See the Chapter 14 section entitled Marriage to Leonora Stern.)

University of California (Berkeley)

He left Arkansas in 1891 to become an assistant professor in entomology at the University of California. Cal was then the only campus of the UC system and was then called simply the University of California. It is now known as "California", "Cal" and the University of California, Berkeley.

Cal is today one of the United State's preeminent public educational institutions. U.S. News and World Report ranked Cal's undergraduate program as the top public university in its 2012 list of "National Universities". As of the fall of 2011, it has 36,142 students and occupies a 1,232-acre campus. Its faculty, alumni, and researchers have been awarded 70 Nobel Prizes and counting.

When C.W. was hired, the situation was much different. The university was only 23 years old, had many times fewer students and was still suffering from growing pains, already being on its seventh university president. The first graduating class of 12 students had graduated in 1873, only 18 years before. An 1897 college guide records the University of California as having 234 instructors, 2400 students, an income of $285, 237, and 65,000 books.[105] The distinctive Beaux-Arts buildings of its core campus would not arrive for several decades.

Figure 32 1891 Birdseye real estate map of Berkeley[106]

Figure 33 (detail of previous figure) Westward looking 1891 real estate drawing of the main buildings of the Cal campus, South Hall on the upper left still stands, the newly built Agricultural Extension Building is not shown on either view, but would have been behind and to the right[107]

[Author's note] The author likes to think that his great-grandfather held up his part in helping Cal as an institution make that transformation from small outpost of learning in the West to world-class university.

The situation at Cal immediately before C.W. was hired

Before C.W. was hired, E.J. Wickson, who was an agronomist and not an entomologist, labored to teach the entomology classes that were offered.

Figure 34 Edward J. Wickson, later in his career[108]

The *College of Agriculture Report* for 1899 describes the situation:

> "The instruction in Elementary and Economic Entomology has been continued by Mr. Wickson as in former years. As has been noted in previous reports, this work is done by him as a volunteer instructor, and he is willing to continue it until so important a subject is better provided for on the University staff. Mr. Wickson makes no pretensions as a professional entomologist, but he has for a number of years followed the subject as an amateur, and has gained a fair acquaintance with California insect pests, their identification, life-history, and the means most successful in checking their increase. His work, therefore answers immediately needs fairly, but, as I have repeatedly urged in previous reports, there is imperative demand for a thoroughly trained entomologist, who shall act as a Professor of Entomology in the University and as a State Entomologist in the service of the public at large. The demand upon the University for this class of work becomes the more direct because the study of entomology is now prescribed in the public schools, and teachers are required to fit themselves for examination in this subject when applying for certificates. This consideration is perhaps more forcible in connection with University equipment than is the popular demand for advice and information concerning the myriad pests which are undermining our agricultural industries; but both branches of the work can fortunately be met by the same officer, and thus the suggestion becomes doubly strong.

> In the meantime Mr. Wickson has been conducting his growing classes in entomology to the best of his ability, and the correspondence with those who send insects for determination and ask for remedies, occupies much of his time. In the fitting-up of the lecture-room on the second floor of the Experiment Station building, a table has been extended along the north side of the room which receives the light from four large windows and gives the class the illumination most desirable for entomological and especially for microscopic work. This table is fitted with drawers for each student to keep his outfit of appliances, and with shelves above for the larger appliances and for bottled specimens. Two breeding cages, after the pattern of Professor Riley, United States Entomologist, have been secured, and three small compound microscopes have been purchased for use of students. The foregoing with the Ricksecker collection of Coleoptera which was donated several years ago, constitute the entomological outfit of the department. It is exceedingly meager, considering the character and popularity of the work, but it is made the best of in class instruction. Mr. Wickson's private microscopial outfit and collection of entomological books and reports are also in constant use."[109]

In the same report a year later, Dr. Hilgard reports that "the shoe has begun to pinch", referring to Dr. Wickson's workload.[110]

1891 - C.W.'s hiring

E.W. Hilgard was the Director of the Agricultural Experiment Station and hired C.W. E.W. Hilgard joined the faculty in 1875 and laid the foundations of the College of Agriculture. He was one of the "nation's great geologists and soil chemists"[111] and has been honored on campus with Hilgard Hall and Hilgard Way. U.C.'s journal of agricultural research is named *Hilgardia* in his honor. A peak in the Sierra is named Mt. Hilgard.

Figure 35 Eugene Woldemar Hilgard at Cal[112]

Hilgard wrote in the *Report of the Agricultural Experiment Station* for 1890 [113] a mention of C.W.'s hiring.

> "The station has been fortunate in securing the services of C.W. Woodworth, M.S., as assistant in entomology. Mr. Woodworth's training as an entomologist, and his work in both the scientific and economic branches of his profession, attest his fitness to extend the efficiency of the station in directions of the greatest importance to California agriculturists."

Hilgard made another mention of C.W. in the *College of Agriculture Report* for 1891:

> "In the preparation of the entomological portion of the report, Assistant C.W. Woodworth has made important contributions, and we look forward with confidence to a material development of the entomological work of the station under his hands, already well trained and proved in former fields."[114]

C.W. received a letter of congratulations dated from Clinton D. Smith of the University of Minnesota on May 28, 1891 saying "You are to be congratulated on your new appointment. Dr. Luggar says that you have a rare chance to do good work and having been there and looked the ground over carefully he ought to know. ... California is such a glorious State that you cannot help but be contented there."[115]

In the 1952 book California Agriculture, Ralph E. Smith wrote:

> "In 1891, after ten years of insistent agitation, the University was at last able to announce the appointment, as Assistant in Entomology, of C.W. Woodworth, a graduate of the University of Illinois, who had worked under the well-known Illinois entomologist, S.A. Forbes, and had later been Entomologist and Botanist at the Arkansas Experiment Station. He was the first college-trained entomologist connect with any institution in California, and the first (from a professional standpoint) qualified to teach the subject. Only a year later, both Stanford University and Pomona College began offering instruction in the same subject."[116]

An 1892 announcement lists a total 44 professors and instructors on the Berkeley campus.

His wife's journey west

C.W.'s wife Leonora sent him a telegram on June 5, 1891 from Burrton, Kansas saying "We [presumably her and their almost one year old son, Lawrence] leave here at eight this evening - we took your route."[117]

Burrton was a connecting point on the Atchison, Topeka & Santa Fe Railway where the line from Topeka met the line from St. Louis. She would have connected to a train on the St. Louis line earlier in the journey at Monett, Missouri after travelling north from Fayetteville, Arkansas.[118][119]

Facilities of the Agricultural Experiment Station

Cal had a 25-acre university farm on campus in that era. It was in the northwest corner of the campus, north and west of the North Fork of Strawberry Creek. The orchard where he did several insecticide studies was about where Giannini Hall is today.

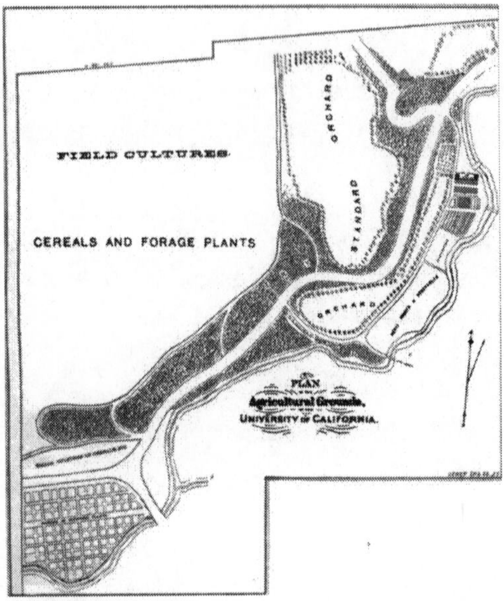

Figure 36 Diagram of the 25 acre University Farm in the northwest corner of the Cal campus, the Agricultural Extension Building is shown at a point that is now midway between the southern ends of Giannini and Haviland Halls just above the western bank of the North Fork of Strawberry Creek[120]

Figure 37 The Agricultural Experiment Station Building in an 1890 report[121]

In his memoirs, William Herms described the building in 1908 as "The small and rather creaky wooden building known as the Entomology Building".[122]

At Cal, C.W. founded and built up the Division of Entomology. He rose to become Associate Professor in 1904, Professor in 1913, and was named Emeritus Professor upon his retirement in 1930.

Figure 38 C.W. in front of the "Entomology Lab" (written on back), this is the eastern, back side of the Agricultural Experiment Station shown above, which was east of where Giannini Hall is today near the North Fork of Strawberry Creek[123]

A social invitation

Not long after he arrived he received the following invite: "Professor and Mrs. Kellogg [Cal Acting President Martin Kellogg] will be happy to see Mr. C.W. Woodworth on Friday evening June 19th to meet the graduation class of the University. Berkeley - June 16th 1891."[124]

Figure 39 Cal President Martin Kellogg (Acting President 1890-1893, President 1893-1894)[125]

Cal Teaching and Textbooks

1892-94 – Greatly expanded course offerings

C.W. wrote a report to Professor E.W. Hilgard that was published in the "Report of the Agricultural Experiment Station for 1892-93 and part of 1894" that "The work of instruction has in this department been greatly increased by the addition of advanced courses. The amount of additional work thus incurred can be seen from the fact that when I took up the work, two hours of class exercises with no laboratory was all that was offered in this subject, while now twenty credit hours, or actually forty hours, of work, including the laboratory is now taken. The number of students at first was larger than now, because of the fact that entomology was required to be taught in the public schools. Now that that artificial stimulus has been removed the present may be considered to represent more nearly the normal attendance."

Laboratory manual for the course in elementary and economic entomology at the University of California (1893)

One of C.W.'s first efforts at Berkeley was to produce a laboratory manual for the basic entomology class that he was teaching. An excerpt from the book is:

> "Eighth Week
>
> In this and the three succeeding weeks twelve species are to be determined as nearly as may be with the available literature. This twelve must include at least one each of the following orders: Hymenoptera, Lepidoptera, Diptera, Coleoptera, Hemiptera and Orthoptera. Make notes and drawings freely while making the determinations and note particularly the publications used and the results obtained.
>
> HYMENOPTERA. Cresson's Synopsis is the basis for determinations in this order. Consult also manuscript synopses of particular groups. For a reference to the described species compare Cresson's Catalog of the species of Hymenoptera. ..."

1896 – Eight classes

The "Report of the Agricultural Experiment Station" from 1896-1897 year has C.W. as a one-person entomology department. Of the twenty-four courses in Agriculture offered by the University of California, C.W. is teaching eight of them:

- 7(a) - Elementary and Economic Entomology - Lectures and laboratory work
- 7(b) - Elementary and Economic Entomology - Supplementary laboratory work
- 8(a) - Apiculture - Lectures, laboratory and apiary work
- 8(b) - Apiculture - Supplementary laboratory and apiary work

- 9(a) - Parasitic Plant Diseases
- 10 - Systematic Entomology
- 11 - Structural Entomology
- 12 - Entomological Laboratory[126] [127]

1897-99 – 7 and a half classes

The Report for both the 1897-1898 and 1898-1899 years have C.W. still as a one-person department down to teaching a slightly more reasonable 7 and a half classes.

C.W. helped lead a two day farmer's institute in Maennerchar Hall in San Luis Obibspo on September 24th and 25th where he taught sessions entitled: Spraying, Unpleasant Insects, How Plants Feed, and Scale Insects.[128]

1900 – A visit by J.H. Comstock and preparations for a return to Harvard

Professor Comstock was teaching for an interval at Stanford. C.W. received a note on February 7, 1900 from Professor Comstock saying:

> "My dear Professor Woodworth:
> Mrs. Comstock and I accept with much pleasure, your invitations for the 16th instant [of this month].
> With kindest regards, very sincerely yours, J.H. Comstock

Figure 40 John Henry Comstock[129]

Figure 41 Anna Botsford Comstock, entomological illustrator and instructor[130]

C.W. received a letter from Stanford's Entomology Professor Vernon Kellogg saying:

> "Professor Comstock tells me that you and he have decided on March 9 as the date for his lecture. With regard to my own date [to give a lecture at Cal] I can come either on February 16 or perhaps better at some time after Professor Comstock's lecture. On the whole I think we had better make it some time in March or April as best suits your convenience."[131]

Figure 42 Vernon Lyman Kellogg[132]

After teaching at Cal for nine years, C.W. applied for a leave of absence to return to Harvard for a year. He received a letter from the University President Benjamin Wheeler on April 27th about it:

> "The matter of leave of absence will be brought before the Regents on May eighth. I have no reason to doubt that the leave will be granted, but until the matter is officially settled I cannot officially commit myself to Mr. Carroll Fowler [C.W's stand-in]. He may, however, regard the matter as settled for I have no idea that there will be any opposition to the arrangement. I shall be glad to have you take your own time in regard to leaving Berkeley. All that we desire is that the date of your leaving be entered in the book kept by the Recorder, and that your address be left with us."[133]

C.W. received two letters from Carroll Fowler about preparing to fill in for him while C.W. was at Harvard.[134]

C.W. visited Lawrence Gillette at Colorado State, H.E. Summers at Iowa State and Lawrence Bruner at the University of Nebraska on his way east to Cambridge.[135][136][137] He also visited the University of Colorado, Boulder. He lobbied unsuccessfully to get U.C. to pay to send him to a meeting of the Association of Economic Entomologists in New York, although $39.30 did come later from the College's funds. E.J. Wickson complained to him in a letter that "Personally I am suffering grieveously from inability to push things off to you and Mr. Bioletti. It is just the season of the year for that sort of thing. I am counting considerably upon Mr. Fowler coming soon as school shall close at the south."[138]

1901 – A trip to Europe and return from Harvard

The introduction to the 1901 Bulletin #135 of the Agricultural Experiment Station, *The Potato Worm In California,* by Warren T. Clarke, shows that C.W. also supervised student research.

> "Note - The present paper has been prepared in accordance with the policy of permitting properly qualified students of the Agricultural Department to take part in the actual work of the Experiment Station. The insect treated is probably the most injurious species attacking truck crops in the State, but has hitherto received but little attention by entomologists. The study here reported constitutes a very material advance in our knowledge of the life history and habits of the insect and of the problem of its control."[139]

Warren Clarke is shown as being an assistant entomologist in a 1902 staff listing in an Agricultural Experiment Station bulletin.

Because C.W. was at Harvard, the interactions between C.W. and his boss, E.W. Hilgard were captured in writing. Several of them are interesting.

C.W. and E.W. Hilgard had a correspondence about whether General Zoology should be a prerequisite to C.W.'s introductory entomology course while C.W. was on leave at Harvard. The academic committee had made it so. C.W. argued that he taught enough introductory general biology to do without the prerequisite. Hilgard said in response:

> "But if you go so far as to systematically teach biology, you do precisely what in our present financial and overcrowded condition of the University the president is justly striving to do away with: the duplication of courses while calling for additional instructors. That is the fight I have still on hand with the Chemistry dept., and expect to win. The president [Benjamin Wheeler] is quite determined to put an end to the states-rights doctrine that has prevailed between the several 'colleges', so miscalled, and make the university more of a unit in practice as it is in theory."[140]

C.W. tried to get UC to pay for a professional trip to Europe at the end of his time at Harvard. On March 29th, he got a reply saying that it would not happen from E.W. Hilgard:

> "I have delayed some time my reply to yours of the 15'th in order to see how the land lies without risking a point-blank refusal on the part of the Pres't, which it is best to avoid. I now feel pretty certain that he would not be in favor of such a proposition, from the tenor of discussions we had in connection with other meetings to occur in Europe and for which men now there might be utilized. His ideas on the subject of University representation there are pretty high-strung, and I think it best not to submit the proposition to him. If you are financially able to go it would be an excellent thing for you, for if you can make a visit there it would be a high feather in your cap. As in any case no financial allowance would be made this year, it would be all the same whether you are officially accredited or not, if you can score a point, or several."[141]

C.W. did go on the journey to Europe. He received a letter from E.W. Hilgard dated July 22 that says:

> "I have yours of the 26'th, from Paris, and as you are by this time afloat on the broad Atlantic, I wrote to the remote corner of Maine which you gave me as your next address. Your letter must have gone by a belated cattle steamer.
>
> Now as to your home-coming: I think it very inadvisable for you to defer your coming until the regular opening of the Univ. You have been absent a long time and during the last session the entomological classes were almost nil. If you want to recover your full attendance you must be on hand to answer personally the numerous questions which are already coming to me regarding the manner in which your new arrangement will work."[142]

1904 - Promotion

C.W. was promoted to Associate Professor.[143]

1905 – Acting Director

C.W. served as the Acting Director of the College of Agriculture for ten days filling in for E.J. Wickson who was away testifying before Congress. E.J. Wickson was serving as Acting Director in the place of E.W. Hilgard at the time.[144] Hilgard was 72 at the time and would work five more years, until 1910.

Figure 43 E.W. Hilgard near the end of his career, published as the frontispiece of the 1913 report of the Expermient Station[145]

E.J. Wickson is honored with Wickson Way on the Cal campus. It is the road that loops in front of Wellman Hall.

Figure 44 Edward J. Wickson[146]

1906 - Overworked

At some point in 1906 C.W. appears to have become overworked and frustrated at Cal. There is a letter from the William A. Henry, Dean of the University of Wisconsin's College of Agriculture[147] saying that there was not any opening at the moment there. It reads:

"Yours of the 20th to hand. I am rejoiced to know that you have a good hold on California. Do not leave it. Put up with anything for the present. Our lines are such here that we cannot do anything in entomology for the present.

What are we to do under the tremendous pressure holding all the time? More work, more calls, more opportunities! Part of the time I cannot help being discouraged over the much pressing for attention, with my most limited powers for accomplishment—still it is glorious work."[148]

1907 - Davis Agricultural Experiment Station

C.W. also participated in the development of the Agricultural Experiment Station, now known as University of California, Davis, and is also considered the founder of the Entomology Department there.[149] Davis is one of California's two most important agricultural education institutions, along with the much younger U.C. Riverside.

On March 18, 1905 a bill was passed establishing the University Farm in Davis. It accepted 40 students in January 1909. It was established as the agricultural extension of the then only campus of the University at Berkeley. The location of Davis on the main railroad tracks from Berkeley to Sacramento may have had a role in its selection. Passenger rail service on this route continues to this day by Amtrak's Capitol Corridor service, which connects San Jose to Sacramento with stops in Berkeley and Davis. My father rides this same train down to our house when he visits us.

The location of Davis in the middle of California's central valley was likely also a key criterion. Even though Berkeley and Davis are only sixty miles apart, their climates are drastically different, particularly during the summer growing season. Berkeley has cool, foggy and windy summers; Davis has hot and dry summers with cool evenings. The core of California's agriculture is in the central valley. While the climate differs somewhat from one end of the valley to the other, particularly in the summer evenings, Davis is a reasonable representative of the valley as a whole. Its proximity to California's lawmakers in Sacramento may have also played a role, given the intense public policy issues surrounding agriculture such as access to water, amelioration of hunger, access to marketplaces, environmental pollution and pesticide regulation, which were all somewhat in play already when Davis was founded.

During "Ranchers Week" at Davis in 1909, C.W. gave a class on "Control of Grasshoppers" and "Insecticides".[150]

An official UC history document states:

> "The Department at UC Davis began as a subunit of the Department of Entomology and Parasitology at UC Berkeley and was closely entwined with the department at Berkeley for more than 50 years before it became autonomous. The first record of entomology being taught at Davis occurred when Professor C.W. Woodworth from UC Berkeley spoke to the State Farmers' Institute at the University Farm on October 30, 1907 on the "Whitefly Situation in California." This was a forerunner to the Farmers' Short Course (three to six weeks) that began in the fall of 1908. In 1913 a two-year nondegree program in entomology was established at Davis. Degree work in entomology was offered at Davis in 1923-24 when S.B. Freeborn was transferred from Berkeley to Davis to head the expanding program. At this time a course was also offered in veterinary parasitology."[151]

Davis is on the train line between the Bay Area and Sacramento. C.W. almost certainly rode the train there many times. His journey probably started on the Shattuck-Adeline Key System trolley line near his home in downtown Berkeley, riding it down to the Emeryville Southern Pacific station at the base of the Key System pier. From there he would have boarded the Southern Pacific train headed towards Sacramento. His journey would have taken him through Richmond and over the Carquinez Strait on the Benica-Martinez rail bridge. The train would then have sped through the Suisun marsh to Fairfield where the tracks turn and enter California's central valley. He would have passed through Dixon before stopping in downtown Davis. From there it is an easy walk to campus.

Figure 45 C.W.'s daughter Elizabeth's friend Mastick Gilbert's float at Davis Picnic Day, 1920, Picnic Day is still going strong at Davis[152]

[Author's note: I am an alumnus of U.C. Davis. While I was a student there, I did not know that my great-grandfather is considered the founder of a major department there. I remember seeing George Carlin at Freeborn Hall, the main concert venue at the time on campus in about 1980, never knowing that Stanley B. Freeborn had worked for C.W. in the Entomology Division long before becoming Davis' Dean of the College of Agriculture.]

1908 – A detailed look at a photograph of C.W. in his Cal office

Figure 46 C.W. at his desk in the Entomological Building, circa 1908[153]

This beautiful picture of C.W. at his desk is from his daughter's photo album. You can see her writing at the bottom. On the reverse of the photo's album page is a photo of his wife that is dated 1908. It is taken utilizing natural light, indoors on what appears to be an overcast day. It is a relatively long exposure, perhaps a second long, given the motion of a paper drooping out of a slot in the desk near his right hand and his relatively stiff pose.

He is about 43 years old in this photo. He holds a fountain pen in his right hand. He has a distant gaze, as if contemplating. This is one of the few photos of him where you can see his eyes clearly, and his irises are light. His suit coat is of relatively heavy material, although this does not indicate the season given Berkeley's somewhat foggy summer climate.

He is sitting in a wooden chair that has turned supports for the backrest. His desk is a roll-top. The photo on the wall above his head is of a man holding an object up with both hands outstretched as if to get a good look at it in the light.

A telephone mouthpiece mounted on a scissor gear is near his right elbow. This mount would have allowed him to have his right hand free as his left hand held the earpiece. Telephones were gaining adoption during this era, although the first coast-to-coast call would not happen until 1915.

There is a bare clear electric light bulb mounted on the wall sideways behind his left temple [hard to see] that would shine onto the area of the typewriter. A book is attached to the wall in front of the bulb, perhaps serving as an improvised shade for the light. The light bulb began to assume its modern form around 1880, and electricity distribution began to become widespread around 1890.

The typewriter appears to be an Underwood 1, the "first widely successful modern typewriter"[154], which was introduced in 1896. There is an empty metal chair in front of the typewriter, indicating that it may have been shared.

This photo shows that he was an adopter of the most important information technologies of his day, the telephone and the typewriter. The letters and notes that are from him that survive, those to E.P. Van Duzee[155], do not have any secretary's initials on them, so he may have typed them himself. If he did type the letters and notes, he was an accurate typist as the letters contain virtually no errors or even mis-struck keys.

1913 - Promotion

C.W. was promoted to Full Professor.[156]

Guide To California Insects (1913)

In August, 1913, C.W. finished a 360 page textbook entitled "Guide To California Insects. It was published by the Law Press, Berkeley. It is filled with 361 figures. This book was listed by E.O. Essig in C.W.'s *Science* obituary as one of his outstanding publications.

The book's preface starts:

> "Students in entomology need an outline of the species inhabiting the region in order that they may comprehend the relationship that the special forms under consideration in the various courses bears to the whole assemblage of insects. This is the more necessary since insects affect human interests in such a variety of ways, requiring that they be studied from diverse and narrowing view points."[157]

Two typical quotes from the book (page 4 and page 34) are:

"At a later period a similar ingrowth from the hind end of the ventral plate produces the intestines and just before the closing in of the back of the embryo a third portion of the digestive tract is formed as a single layer of cells which envelop the remains of the yolk and finally becomes the stomach." [158]

"The sphinx moths include two important pests; the tobacco or tomato worm Protoparce and Pholus that attacks the grape and Ampelopsis. Other species of little economic importance are: Sphinx on willow, Pachysphinx on willow and poplar. Hylolcus on wild cherry; ash and privet, and Celario on portulaca and other weeds."[159]

1914 – No respite

In 1914 he wrote:

"It was thought a year ago that the class work might be diminished as the result of the reorganization of the curriculum of the College of Agriculture. There has been no appreciable change, however, in this respect and the departure of Mr. Bridwell simply increased the work of the other members of the staff, as did also Professor Quayle's absence during the first half-year. I have personally shouldered much of the added work. This has involved no special hardship, but has interfered with research work."[160]

School of Fumigation (1915)

In 1915, a 184 page stenographic record of a course that C.W. gave was published. It was entitled "School of Fumigation". It was published by the Braun Corporation.

Figure 47 Cover of the textbook, "School of Fumigation"[161]

1919 – Correspondence Courses

The University Agriculture Experiment Station offered some free correspondence courses in 1919. C.W. taught one in bee-keeping. The listing starts with:

> "Course 15 Bee-Keeping
> C.W. Woodworth, Professor
> 14 Lessons
>
> Required of each student: (1) To have a swarm of bees with which to work; (2) to be in a position to study the bees during the daytime and carry on some experiments; also to study California honey plants. Those unable to meet these requirements should not apply for the course.
>
> The course consists of fourteen lessons, two preliminary ones, and one for each month of the year, thus requiring at least twelve months' time for completion."[162]

In 1919 C.W. also stepped down from being head of the Entomology Division. William Herms was chosen to head the newly formed Division of Entomology and Plant Parasitology.[163]

1921 – Optics courses

In the summer session of 1921, he taught two optics courses for the Agriculture Department:[164]

- 104 - The Theory of the Microscope
- 202 - Research in Geometric Optics

Figure 48 C.W. teaching, circa 1920[165]

1928-29 – Staff Listing

A listing of workers at the Agricultural Experiment Stations in California for the year 1928-1929 lists the following:

At Berkeley - W.B. Herms, E.O. Essig, F. Lamiman, H.H. P. Severin, Jocelyn Tyler, E.C. Van Dyke, C.W. Woodworth

At Davis – S.B. Freeborn, T.I Storer, H. Vansell, F.H. Wymore

At Riverside – A.J. Basinger, A.M. Boyce, Harold Compere, J. Quayle, H.S. Smith, R. H. Smith, P.H. Timberlake

At San Jose – L.M. Smith[166]

1930 - Retirement

C.W. retired from Cal on his 65th birthday and was promoted to Emeritus Professor.[167]

(See the Chapter 14 section entitled *Retirement*.)

1935 – An offer by C.W.

Five years after his retirement, C.W. offered to contribute his services to Cal, presumably in response to budget cuts induced by the Great Depression. A letter from Robert G. Sproul, the president of the University of California (and for whom Cal's central Sproul Plaza and Sproul Hall, and Davis' administration building, Sproul Hall are named) is in the UC archives. The letter is addressed to C.W. in Rochester, NY. It reads:

"Thank you for your generous letter of July 28, offering to contribute your services to the University during the present emergency, either in the Department of Entomology, where you served so long, or in some other department having to do with Mathematics or Optics. You may be sure that your offer will be called to the attention of the chairman of the departments concerned."[168]

Apparently there was not a need as there was another letter from Robert Sproul four months later that read:

I look for much good to come from your Adult Education venture and you are correct in your assumption that I might be interested in knowing about it. Study for the adult, as well as for the youth, not only brings pleasure but kindles enthusiasm.[169]

Photos of his staff

Figure 49 C.W.'s staff working[170]

Written on the rear of this photo is the caption:
"Prof Woodworth's staff of assistants sealing insects in gelatin capsules. Jars in foreground contain specimens. Each of the bags strung across room contains an experiment. Left to right - Gilbert, Baebec [hard to read], Van Devort, Wells, Lewis, Martin, Bartez [hard to read]"

Figure 50 Photo of his staff in 1914[171]

The caption of this photo reads: "Experiments with insecticides must be conducted in long series with many repetitions. Sixty thousand lots of scale insect eggs were used in the cyanide experiments this season."

University of California Salary

His salary for both the 1910-1911 and 1911-1912 school years was $2,700.[172] According to two different online inflation calculators, this is equivalent to about $60,000/yr in 2011 dollars.

In 1911-1912, the total budget for salaries for the Universities was $720,000. Agriculture had by far the largest budget at $107,000. The administration department was second with a $43,000 budget. The Lick Observatory was third with a budget of $32,000. U.C. President Benjamin Wheeler received $12,000, Director of the Agricultural Experiment Station E.J. Wickson received $4,000, Emeritus Professor E.W. Hilgard received $2,666, Associate Professor William Clarke received $2,400, and Assistant Professor William B. Herms received $1,800. Professor of Architecture John Galen Howard received $4,000.

The Temple Institute

In 1935 and 1936, during his retirement, he spent some time as the Director of the Temple Institute at the Baptist Temple in Rochester, NY.[173] There he ran an educational enterprise and taught some adult education classes. He also gave at least two classes in Optical Triangulation to employees of Bausch & Lomb also in Rochester.
(See the Chapter 12 section entitled Course in Optical Triangulation (1936).)

The Baptist Temple is a congregation that in 1893 built itself a fourteen-story office building that included a large sanctuary. Although the church moved out in 1965, the building still stands and is bounded by Franklin Street, Liberty Pole Way, and Achilles Street.[174]

Professional Societies

American Association of Economic Entomologists

C.W. was a founding member of the American Association of Economic Entomologists. The members of the founding group of this organization were those entomologists that were hired with the establishment of the State Agricultural Experiment Stations after the passage of the Hatch Act of 1887. This group was the precursor of the current day Entomological Society of America.[175] His advisor from Illinois, S.A. Forbes, was the first Vice President of the Association.

He attended the second annual meeting of the Association, which was held in his hometown of Champaign on November 11, 1890.[176] He is listed as a member of the Association of Economic Entomologists in the 1895 edition of *Insect Life*. [177] He is also listed as a member in 1909.[178]

In 1900, in the "Proceedings of the Twelfth Annual Meeting of the Association of Economic Entomologists", which records this meeting held in New York City June 22-23, 1900, he begins his paper "Notes From California": "This being, I believe, the first time a member from California has attended a meeting of this Association, it will be quite appropriate to give a general account of the entomological situation in the State rather the usual notes on the insects of the year."[179] C.W. studied at Harvard in the 1900-1901 year, and travelled east at the end of May in part to attend this conference. In this paper he gives a survey of all of the California agricultural zones, their crops and their insect pests.

In 1927, the AAEE had 892 total members. In 1937 it had 1,350 members.

On December 28, 1939, C.W. was invited to the 50th anniversary celebration of the AAEE. He was honored among the 23 founders of the AAEE in the program as the "Pioneers of Economic Entomology." His photo was included along with five of the seven then-living founders. The founders were: [180]

Then living (1939)	Name of founder	Original location
	Riley, C.V. (First President)	Washington, D.C.
*	Beckwith, M.L.	Delaware
	Bethune, C.J.S.	Canada
	Campbell, P.J.	Georgia
	Comstock, J.H.	Cornell University
	Cook, A.J.	Michigan
	Fletcher, J.	Canada
	Forbes, S.A.	Illinois
*	Garman, H.	Kentucky
*	Gillette, C.P.	Colorado
	Hargitt, C.W.	Syracuse University
	Harvey, F.L.	Maine
*	Howard, L.O.	Washington, D.C.
	Lintner, J.A.	New York
	Lugger, O.	Minnesota
*	Osborn, H.	Iowa
	Reed, E.B.	Canada
	Saunders, W.	Canada
	Smith, J.B.	New Jersey
	Webster, F.M.	Purdue
*	Weed, C.M.	Ohio
	Wickson, E.J.	California
*	Woodworth, C.W.	Arkansas

Table 4 Founding members of the AAEE

Pacific Slope Branch of the American Association of Economic Entomologists

C.W. was the founding President and a charter member of the Pacific Slope Branch of the American Association of Economic Entomologists (PSBAAEE), which was organized in 1909.[181]

The first meeting of this group was held on April 20-23, 1909 in Berkeley. Seven papers were presented and there were several exhibits and a visit to an Oakland formicary. A constitution was adopted and officers were selected. A vice president was selected to represent each of the 12 states and one province in attendance. The initial name that was chosen was the Pacific Slope Association of Economic Entomologists, but that was changed later to the PSBAAEE. The group was also associated with the American Association for the Advancement of Science (AAAS) and planned to hold a future meeting in conjunction with an AAAS meeting.[182]

This can be also considered as the first meeting of the Pacific Branch of the Entomological Society of America (PBESA) given the later merger of the AAEE and the ESA.

C.W. is shown as the president of the Association in the Proceedings of the Second Meeting, held in Berkeley in the Entomology Building on March 31 to April 1, 1911. C.W. presented three papers, "The Leakage Problem in Fumigation", "The Educator", and The Quantity of Spray Required".[183]

He is also shown as the president of the Association in the Proceedings of the Third Meeting, held at Stanford in room 432 of the Zoology Building on April 5-6, 1912. C.W. presented his paper "The Insecticide Industries in California."[184]

In 1916, the PSBAAEE was represented at a grand meeting of twelve scientific organizations that took place in San Diego concurrently with the 17th Annual meeting of the Cordilleran Section of the Geological Society of America (GSA). Ernest Hilgard, who hired C.W., is mentioned in the article as being a founding member of that section of the GSA.[185]

The fourth meeting of the PSBAAEE was held in Riverside, California in 1919. The Chairman was H.J. Qualye.[186]

The fifth meeting of the PSBAAEE was held at the University of Washington in 1920.

A meeting of the PSBAAEE was held on August 4-6, 1923 at Cal. C.W. arranged a field excursion for the following day.[187] C.W. was on a break from his second period to China during that summer.

U.C. Entomological Society

From January 2, 1895 to May 23, 1895, C.W. put out 118 issues of **The Entomologist's Daily Postcard: A California Journal of Entomology - Official Organ of the U.C. Entomological Society.[188]** The fee was $2.00 per year.[189]

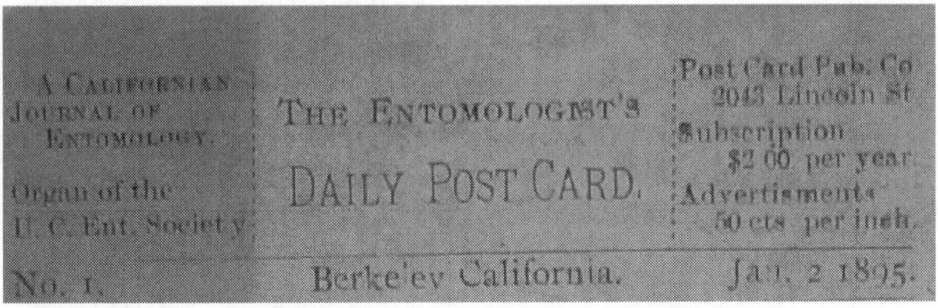

Figure 51 Title of the first issue of the Entomologist's Daily Post Card[190]

He gave a lecture entitled "The Theory and Use of the Microscope" before the Entomology Club on January 29, 1916.[191]

Entomological Society of America

He is listed as a member of the Entomological Society of America in the University of Illinois Alumni Directory.[192] He was elected Temporary Chairman in charge of the 1915 California summer meeting. He presented his paper "Quantitative Entomology" at that meeting.[193]

The Pacific Branch of the Entomological Society of America (PBESA) presents annually the C.W. Woodworth Award. The Entomological Society of America merged with the Association of Economic Entomologists in 1953. Shortly before he died, "he had recently been elected an Honorary Fellow of the Entomological Society of America".[194]
(See Chapter 17 - The C.W. Woodworth Award for an extensive discussion.)

Association of American Agricultural Colleges and Experiment Stations

He was elected chair of the entomology section of the Association of American Agricultural Colleges and Experiment Stations on November 15-17, 1898 meeting in Washington, D.C.[195] He corresponded with H. Garman about writing a paper for the November 1900 meeting in New Haven, Connecticut.[196]

Société Entomologique de France

He is listed as a member of the Société Entomologique de France in the University of Illinois Alumni Directory.[197]

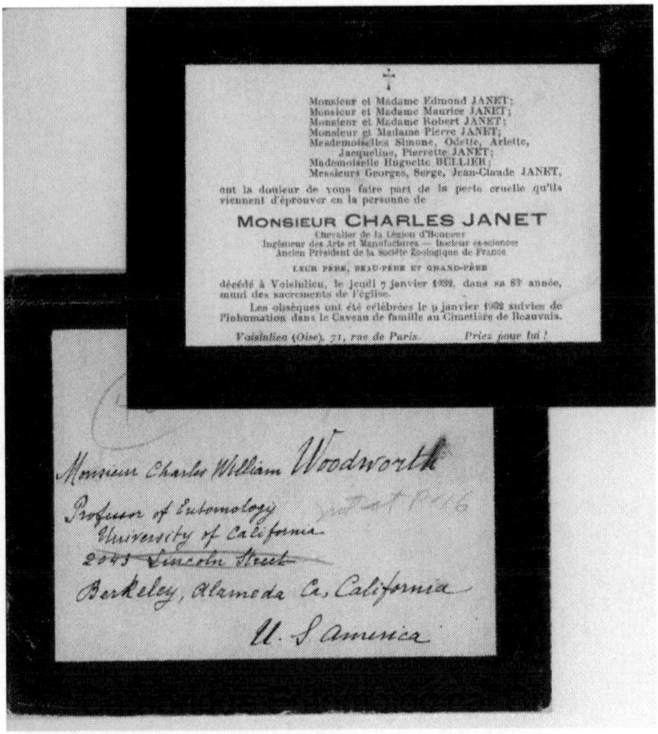

Figure 52 Death announcement for Charles Janet, the former president of the Société Entomologique de France[198]

Cambridge Entomological Club

C.W. jointed the Cambridge Entomological Club when he arrived at Harvard in 1888. The publication of their journal, Psyche, had slowed to a halt. In a letter to E.P. Van Duzee on November 11, 1887, he writes:

> "You know that our Entomological Club publish[es] a paper "Psyche" or at least used to. We are endeavoring to again set it on its feet. Can we look to you for support? What we want especially is short articles of general interest such as would make a live Entomological journal, such for instance as notes of habits, accounts of early states, interesting captures, notes on distribution, variation, and malformation, things which every observer now and then comes across - observations which for want of a ready channel for communication are oft to be lost."[199]

PSYCHE,

A JOURNAL OF ENTOMOLOGY.

[Established in 1874.]

Figure 53 Title of Psyche[200]

On December 10, 1887 he wrote to Van Duzee:

> "I am glad to inform you that "Psyche" will resume publication at once. The first number of the new volume will appear early in January. We will attempt to keep up the good points of previous volum[e]s and improve it by 1st issuing regularly about the first of each month 2nd by devoting more space and making a more prominent feature of the journal minor communications.
>
> To do this we require the hearty support of working entomologist[s], especially for the earlier numbers, and I write to you now partly to ask for some short communications for the January and February numbers."[201]

When Samuel Hubbard Scudder retired, C.W. became the President of the Cambridge Entomological Club from May of 1890 to January of 1891, while he was an entomologist and botanist at the Arkansas Industrial University's Agricultural Experiment Station. Two of C.W.'s advisors had also been president of the club, E.L. Mark in 1881 and S.A. Forbes in 1886. C.W.'s other advisor, H.A. Hagen was the founder of the club, having invited twelve to his home for the first meeting on January 7, 1874.[202]

On January 6, 1891 when C.W. was stepping down as President of the club, he gave an address entitled "On the Relation Between Scientific and Economic Entomology." In this address, he lays out this relationship:

> "I believe that the pure sciences are distinct from the economic sciences; that this is primary division of science. We seem to be prone in this utilitarian age to try to find excuse for the pursuit of pure science by holding up the possibility of applying our discoveries for economic ends. Let us recognize and not act as though we are ashamed of the fact that the sole aim of the student of pure science is the discovery of truth, catering to human wants being entirely out of his province."

Later he says:

> "Perhaps if we could see all the intimate relations sciences have to each other we should say that every fact belongs to every science; at any rate we could scarcely name a fact which when closely viewed has not more than one bearing. ... For economic purposes it is the facts which are appropriated, and in the same way that the biologist appropriates the facts discovered by the chemist. Economic sciences by using some of the same facts than biology becomes a department or application of chemistry."

At the end of the speech he recommends that their club focus on scientific entomology:

> "Finally, to recapitulate, scientific entomology is a department of biology, economic entomology of agriculture. They have all the difference between them that there is between a pure science and an economic science. Can we as a society [the Cambridge Entomological Club] include them both? I think we should not. On the other hand the economic entomologists are nearly all at the same time scientific entomologists. These we can and do welcome."[203]

International Zoological Congress (1901)

C.W. attended the International Zoological Congress in Berlin in the summer of 1901 at the conclusion of his second period at Harvard.[204] This was a few years before the formation of the International Congress of Entomology, which met for the first time in 1910.

American Academy for the Advancement of Science

A letter from C.W. to President James Fletcher is recorded in the minutes of the Entomological Club of the AAAS meeting at the University of Toronto on August 28, 1889.[205]

C.W. was elected to the American Academy for the Advancement of Science on February 8, 1901.[206] He published extensively in their journal, *Science* in both entomology and optics. His obituary was printed in the December 20, 1940 issue of *Science*.

Chapter 4 - *Drosophila melanogaster* (1900)

One of C.W.'s singular accomplishments took the form of a suggestion.

Thomas Hunt Morgan's Nobel Prize biography says:

> "It appears that *Drosophila* was first bred in quantity by C.W. Woodworth, who was working from 1900-1901, at Harvard University, and Woodworth there suggested to W. E. Castle that Drosophila might be used for genetical work. Castle and his associates used it for their work on the effects of inbreeding, and through them F. E. Lutz became interested in it and the latter introduced it to Morgan, who was looking for less expensive material that could be bred in the very limited space at his command. Shortly after he commenced work with this new material (1909), a number of striking mutants turned up. Morgan's subsequent studies on this phenomenon ultimately enabled the determination of the precise behaviour and exact localization of genes."[207]

Alfred Henry Sturtevant in the book "*History of Genetics*" says:

> "The first person to cultivate *Drosophila* in the laboratory seems to have been the entomologist, C. W. Woodworth. Through Woodworth, Castle learned of the advantages of the animal; and it was through Castle's work that it became known to other geneticists."[208]

Herbert C. Morse III in the book "The Mouse in Biomedical Research" says:

> "Remarkably, the underpinnings of Morgan's use of *Drosophila* can be traced back to the Bussey [The Bussey Institute for Research in Applied Biology at Harvard]. In the first years of the twentieth century, C.W. Woodworth at Harvard leaned how to breed *Drosophila* in large number. Being acquainted with Castle's efforts to study the effects of inbreeding, he made the suggestion that *Drosophila* might provide an important experimental tool. During the course of this work, Frank E. Lutz became impressed with their utility and, with Castle, introduced them to Morgan."[209]

Drosophila melanogaster, commonly known as the fruit fly, is an excellent species to use as a model organism for doing genetic research. Some of the reasons that fruit flies are useful are that they:

- Are small - they can fit in a laboratory
- Are inexpensive - they do not eat much
- Are safe - if they happen to escape, they are merely annoying and not dangerous
- Are quick breeding - they reproduce approximately every two weeks
- Have distinctive phenotypes - they have significant numbers of traits that are visible with a low-powered microscope or magnifying glass
- Have observable genotypes - they have a polytene (giant) chromosome in the cells of their salivary glands that can be stained and examined under a conventional microscope

C.W. would have been very aware of *Drosophila* because he was an economic entomologist. Then as now, numerous species in the genus *Drosophila* are significant agricultural pests. The 1895 edition alone of "Insect Life", one of the major journals in economic entomology that he would have read contains six mentions of the *Drosophila ampelophila,* the older name for *Drosophila melanogaster*.

Edward B. Lewis, in his article "Thomas Hunt Morgan and his Legacy", wrote:

> "During the Columbia period Morgan was clearly in his prime. His style of doing science must have been of paramount importance. He was not afraid to challenge existing dogma. He had become dissatisfied, even skeptical, of the formalistic treatment that genetics had taken in the period between the rediscovery of Mendelism in 1901 and 1909. He ridiculed explanations of breeding results that postulated more and more hereditary factors without any way of determining what those factors were. He wanted to know what the physical basis of such factors might be. At the time it was generally assumed that chromosomes could not be the carriers of the genetic information. He wanted a suitable animal and chose *Drosophila*, because of its short life cycle, ease of culturing and high fecundity. Also, large numbers of flies could be reared inexpensively - an important factor during this period when there were very few funds available to support basic research."[210]

To give an idea of the continuing importance of the use of *Drosophila* as a model organism to biology, Michael Ashburner and Casey Bergman of the University of Cambridge wrote in 2005:

"It is almost 100 years since William Castle introduced *Drosophila melanogaster* to the pleasures and rigors of biological research (Castle 1906). Four major phases of *Drosophila* research can, perhaps, be distinguished. The period 1910–1940, of classical genetic analysis was a period of rapid development in which most of the major principles of classical genetics were established: the chromosome theory of heredity, the nature of genetic linkage and genetic maps, the genetic behavior of chromosome aberrations, the induction of gene and chromosome mutations by radiation, the discovery of mitotic recombination, and so on. This was followed by a long period, 1940–1968, of growth but relative sterility, a period in which many of the best minds in genetics turned their attention to microbes and phage. The period from, roughly, 1968–2000 was a renaissance, witnessed by many molecular biologists moving into the field, creating an analytical, rather than descriptive, study of development and behavior. This metamorphosis was fueled by many major technical advances within the field, for example, the invention of *in situ* hybridization, of the *P*-element-based transformation technology, of powerful methods for clonal analysis, the discovery of potent chemical mutagens, and by the extraordinary external advances in molecular biology. New generations of researchers selected *Drosophila* as a model organism for the study of fundamental problems in biology. From 2000, fly research has matured into its fourth period: the genome era, for, on March 24, 2000 the first release of the "complete" genomic sequence of *Drosophila melanogaster* was published, timed to coincide with that year's annual fly meeting in Pittsburgh. Five years into the postgenomic era we can begin to ask: What have we learned and what may lie ahead?"[211]

Chapter 5 - General Entomology and Plant Pathology Research

This chapter presents much of the non-species specific work that C.W. did.
(See Chapter 6 - Species-Specific Entomology and Plant Pathology Research for his research specific families or species of plant pathogens or insects.)

Studies on the Embryological Development of *Euvanessa antiopa* (1889)

C.W. did the research for his one and only embryology paper during his first time at Harvard. It was published in 1889, shortly after his departure to Arkansas in "The Butterflies of the Eastern United States and Canada with Special Reference to New England, Vol. 1", by Samuel Hubbard Scudder.

Samuel Scudder was one of the nineteenth century's definitive observers of the natural world and a prolific writer. He trained under Mark Hopkins at Williams and Louis Agassiz at Harvard.

Figure 54 Samuel Hubbard Scudder[212]

C.W. provides a description of the ontogeny of the *Euvanessa antiopia,* a type of butterfly, also known as the Mourning-cloak butterfly. The caterpillar is known as the spiny elm caterpillar. Aside from providing the description, C.W.'s major points in this paper are:

The formation of the syncytium was not due to cell fusion [later proven to be correct - it is due to nuclear division without cytokinesis]

In one section, he ponders the function of the nucleus. This was long before the role of the chromosomes in inheritance was determined by Morgan and others.

> "The egg, as already remarked, is apparently without a nucleus and it suggestions the question: What is the function of the nucleus? Is it the motor power that impels the cell to the exercise of its functions?

[Author's note: We now know that the nucleus is the cell's information center and director. The mitochondria are the cell's chemical powerhouses. In a loose sense, the nucleus could be termed the cells information "motor power that impels the cell to the exercise of its functions." He was half way there. To be fair to C.W., the notion of general information computing engine was also a half-century away.]

Although he talks about different species, he also makes no mention of the themes of evolutionary development biology, which is the idea that evolution has tended to reuse mechanisms in the embryological development between species. Thus, it is possible to see commonalities between the embryos of species that share portions of an evolutionary path.

He has a long section about the development of the ovaries and how they appear to develop from different germinal layers. He provides examples from four species and concludes that this must be an illusion. He proposed in the paper's conclusion, he provides a new term for ovary development, ovarigenesis as opposed to organogeny, development of all other organs. [This division and the name ovarigenesis did not catch on - the development of the ovaries is treated as one of the many processes of embryo development].

A Synopsis of the Families of Insects, prepared for the use of the unscientific public (1893)

Not long after he arrived at Berkeley, C.W. produced this guide to help farmers to identify insects. He writes: "The synopsis is in simple English, all scientific terms being left out , unless really necessary, and these are fully explained by the figures and by the 'Explanation of terms' at the end."[213]

The guide has 266 steps for complete identification. The first 21 get you to the order of the insect. The most complex order in the guide is Coleoptera, which has 79 steps unto itself.

It is actually unclear whether the hardy farmer would actually get all the way to the end. For the farmer who is holding a *Carabidae,* it takes 20 steps just to get to the decision that you have an adult Coleoptera insect, then another 16 steps to get to step #155 which has the statement: " If the antennae are fastened to the front of the head, it is one of the *Cincindelidae*. If the antennae are fastened to the sides of the head it is one of the *Carabidae*."

That said, it does seem like a worthy project. It also might have been a bit of self-defense for C.W. who was overwhelmed with correspondence from farmers looking for insect determination. He wrote in 1892 "The correspondence has increased steadily, and become indeed, at times, quite burdensome, especially as it is, to so large an extent, a repetition of the same set of questions. The publication of special Bulletin A, giving the remedies most commonly in use, has proven a great help, and indicates that further publications of this type will be most useful."[214]

Remedies for Plant Diseases (1894)

C.W. published a two page summary paper in 1894 that delivers a short list of the best practices for handling six different situations:

- powdery mildews – use sulphur dust
- fungi – use Bordeaux mixture
- fungi and scale insects together - use lime, salt and sulphur in the winter
- scale insects, insects – use a resin soap with different mixtures for summer and winter
- insects in general – use an emulsion
- fruit or leaf-eating insects – use Paris green (arsenite)

This list shows how small the toolbox was for economic entomologists in 1894.[215]

A Laboratory of Plant Diseases (1894)

Plant pathology, the study of plant diseases caused by agents such as virus, viroids, fungi, bacteria, parasitic plants and other non-insect sources, had not yet been fully divided from entomology in C.W.'s era, particularly in economic entomology, C.W.'s specialty. As such C.W. taught and did some research and taught courses in what is now known as plant pathology. "The subject of plant diseases is now and will continue to be associated with that of entomology, so that the same equipment, to a considerable extent, serves for the two subjects."

Because of this, C.W. set up a laboratory specifically for the purpose of both teaching and doing research into plant diseases as well as other insect work. He published a two-page paper describing the details of the physical setup of the laboratory. Several details reveal some of what the conditions for science were in 1894:

- A focus on natural sunlight, which was needed to do good microscope work in 1894. "It is lighted by four windows, having an entirely unobstructed view, and so giving ample light for microscope work."
- There were no Powerpoint presentations back then, but they did have a lantern projector. "The windows are all fitted with heavy shades working in grooves, enabling one to darken the room very easily and quickly when the lantern is to be used for illustration. The views are projected on a screen of tracing cloth, which is mounted on a common spring-roller and is ordinarily rolled up out of the way."
- The dark room had "ruby glass" to allow red filtered sunlight in instead of using a red light for use when developing photographic film, and yes they used film.

The laboratory also had collections of the organisms that produced the injuries, the host of the diseases, and a collection of the symptoms. They also had the beginnings of a "cryptogamic herbarium" (spore collection) and a collection of "material medica" (treatments).[216]

Experiments in Winter Spraying of Pears and Apples (1894)

C.W. published a twenty page summary paper that provides the results of a systematic exploration of various techniques of winter spraying in pear and apple orchards. The paper starts:

> "The ranch of a generation ago in becoming the farm or orchard of today retains its old name and to a considerable extent its old practices. As the sheep began to be replaced by fruit trees the old sheep-dip became the tree-wash. This is the pedigree of one of our standard washes, the lime, salt, and sulphur mixture, and in this case it has proven itself a very useful remedy. The present article is written as a protest against the blind use of this and other washes inherited from other days, for as the sheep were all regularly dipped, so it is the common practice in this State to apply a wash of some kind, upon general principles, each winter or spring, while the tree is dormant, with no regard to the condition or need of the tree. Vendors of patent washes and often horticultural commissioners advocate this practice, and many among the most progressive fruit-growers consider it safer to follow the custom, though orchardists are by no means unanimous in their approval of it."[217]

This paper is very modern in its use of a sub-divided orchard to run a series of experiments matched up with control trees, all on the Cal campus. Twelve different treatments plus a control were made on the pear trees. Nine different treatments plus a control were made on the apple trees. Measurements on subjective scales were made in the spring of 1892, 1893 and 1894 on the growth of the trees, the fruit yield, the abundance of greedy scale on the pears, and the abundance of wooly aphids on the apples. Objective measurements were made on the mortality of the trees. The orchard contained many varieties of apple and pear trees.

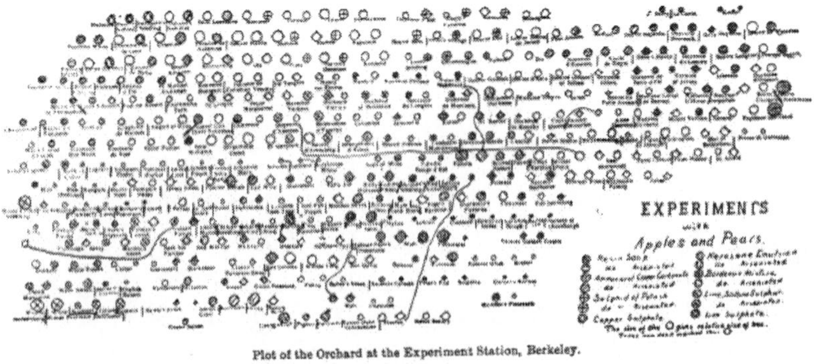

Figure 55 Plot of orchard used in winter spraying experiments

The results were published in tabular form and some conclusions were gathered. This was long before the regular use of confidence intervals and other similar statistical measurements were common, but the systematic nature of the experiment was ahead of its time in entomology.

Root Knots on Fruit Trees and Vines (1894)

C.W. published a five-page paper about root knots that was his most pure plant pathology paper. This paper starts:

> "There is no one thing about which so many inquiries have been received as a peculiar form of root knot or gall on a number of plants, chiefly grape and apricot. It seems to be much more injurious in this State and in Arizona than elsewhere, though it occurs in all parts of the country and in Europe, more or less abundantly."

He then describes how the crown gall is the focus of his investigation and identifies eight other kinds of galls that should not be confused with the crown gall and how they each can be distinguished from a crown gall.

He identifies four theories that have been suggested for the formation of crown galls.

> "Finally, as has become quite the fashion of late years, the bacteria have been charged with the injury. I myself have succeeded in getting pure cultures of a micrococcus from the inside of some of the knots, after taking all of the usual precautions to prevent accidental contamination. This, however, is by no means conclusive, but there is a great deal of evidence that the gall is an infectious disease of the plant."

Finally, C.W. describes how to respond to an infection, which was to identify the affected trees, remove them, burn them, and let the ground lie fallow for a year or two. He then advises orchardists to inspect all incoming stock and dip all trees in Bordeaux mixture.[218]

The infectious agent of crown gall was later identified as *Agrobacterium tumefaciens*, a species of rod-shaped, gram-negative soil bacterium and not the micrococcus that C.W. had identified. Micrococcus is a genus of spherical shaped gram-negative bacteria that live in soil and other locations. One possibility is that he was using the term micrococcus in a generic sense to refer to soil bacteria.

Two Rejected Patent Applications (1895 and 1897)

On August 16, 1895, C.W. applied for a patent entitled "Plows", which was rejected by the U.S. Patent Office. On January 13, 1897, he applied for a patent entitled "Process of Packing and Preserving Food Products", which was also rejected due to the lack of "patentable merit".[219]

[Author's note: I have 18 U.S. patents myself and know that it takes practice to get something through the US patent office. The patent office typically initially rejects all applications. You then negotiate with them by steadily shrinking your claims over the next couple of years.]

These early rejections probably helped him get the two patents though that he did later in life.

Remedies for Insects and Fungi (1897)

C.W. published a twenty-one page paper that delivers the state of the art of 1897 in bug and fungus killing in plain and direct language to farmers and orchardists. The paper reviews six common mistakes in pest control, reviews seven basic categories of pests, and the best approaches to handling each. A short excerpt from the paper is:

> "The yellow-jacket, our common wasp, which is so injurious to fruit, and which makes its nest in the ground, is easily killed by this substance. The nest is located, and about dark, when the wasps are all in, about an ounce of carbon bisulphid is poured down the hole and a handful of earth thrown over it to keep the vapor in. By morning all will be found to be dead. Ants' nests can be destroyed in the same way."[220]

[Author's note: I have used a similar technique several times on yellow-jacket nests near my home, although I use a little malathion instead of carbon bisulphid.]

Orchard Fumigation (1899)

C.W. published bulletin 122 in 1899 that comprehensively reviewed the topic of orchard fumigation. In 1946, Ralph E. Smith wrote about this bulletin:

> "Early in his career in California, Woodworth investigated fumigation; he published a comprehensive bulletin in 1899. At this time it was well established that hydrocyanic acid was the most satisfactory fumigant, that tents in the form of sheets were the most practical, and that the work was best done at night to avoid injury to the tree. Woodworth was the first to stress the importance of determining accurately the proper gas dosage for each tree, and later was the first to recommend a dosage system based on the dimensions of the tent over the tree."[221]

Sprays and Washes (1899)

C.W. published a two-page update of seven recipes for sprays and washes in the annual report of the experiment station. This list shows how few tools they actually had at their disposal in 1899. The paper gives the recipes for sprays and washes of Paris green, Kerosene Emulsion, Rosin Soap, Lime-Salt and Sulfur, Sulfid of Potash, Bordeaux mixture, and Ammonia-Copper Carbonate.[222]

That is all the sprays and washes that there were at the disposal of the economic entomologist in 1899. Good luck with those bugs!

A List of the Insects of California (1903)

This paper was listed by E.O. Essig in C.W.'s Science obituary as one of his outstanding publications. This also served as a prototype for his 1913 textbook "A Guide to California Insects."

Recent Work in Entomology (1905)

This paper is a general overview of the state of entomology in the United States with its application to California. It surveys work done by C.V. Riley's laboratory at the U.S. Division of Entomology as well as other work. He stressed the value of Lime-Sulphur mixes as well as mentioning that the quality of petroleum distillates was lacking. This paper illustrates C.W.'s knowledge of what was happening across all of economic entomology.[223]

The Wing Veins of Insects (1906)

(See the Chapter 2 section entitled C.W.'s Doctoral Dissertation for an extensive discussion of this work.)

This monograph was listed by E.O. Essig in C.W.'s Science obituary as one of his outstanding publications. See the next section for C.W.'s editorial role in the publication series that published it.

University of California Publications in Entomology (1906)

He was the first editor and first contributor to the University of California Publications in Entomology. This monograph series is still going strong. There were nine titles published between 2004 and 2011. Philip S. Ward is the current editorial chair.[224] The series is described as:

> "The University of California Publications in Entomology is a monographic series devoted to the biology of insects and other terrestrial arthropods. The series has traditionally emphasized insect systematics, but monographs on biogeography, evolution, population biology, behavioral ecology and comparative biology are also welcome."[225]

Publication number 1 in Volume 1 is C.W.'s 1906 "The Wing Veins of Insects", the publication of C.W.'s 152 page failed Doctoral dissertation. Volume 1 collects the nine monographs published from 1906 to 1922. C.W. and E.C. Van Dyke are listed as co-editors. E.P. Van Duzee wrote three of those monographs, and E.O. Essig wrote one.[226]

A New Spray Nozzle (1914)

His 1914 paper starts out: "A new principle has been discovered in simple construction whereby a flat spray can be produced ..." This paper shows C.W.'s practical side where he would work to solve real problems, and end up discovering something fundamental.

> "When two streams meet across half their section, the resulting sheet of spray will be of practically uniform thickness throughout, occupying a plane 45 degrees from the plane of the streams and finally breaking up into drops of great fineness and uniformity."

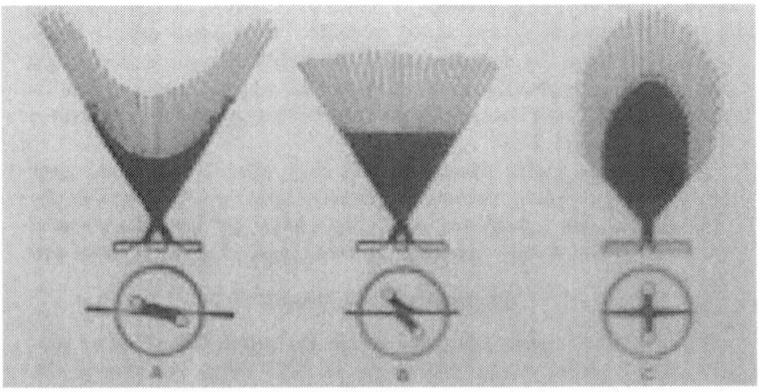

Figure 56 A new spary nozzle - the center drawing shows the deflector position to acheive the flat spray

Most of the flat spray nozzles that are available on the market today do not use C.W.'s design. The typical flat nozzle works by a different method. Rather than having two streams collide as in C.W.'s nozzle, most of the flat spray nozzles on the market have an aperture set back from a flat slot. Other nozzles work by bouncing a stream off of a flat deflector.

The Spraying Systems Washjet product line of nozzles might be of C.W.'s design.[227] A typical example is the Model #23990 "Adjustable Washjet Nozzle" (sold by Windtrax for $21.95).[228]

New Dosage Tables (1915)

His 1915 paper is essentially an applied mathematics paper that derives formulas and tables for pesticide usage considering the size and leakage of the tents used.

A mathematics quote from the paper is:

> "The principle is then that an arithmetical series of leakages is related to a geometrical series of dosages and both correspond to the same complex series of sizes of tents."

He delivers six full-page tables, each with a different dose of sodium cyanide computed with different height and width tents. He says that "The common tables are grossly inaccurate in their method of computation."[229]

Quantitative Entomology (1915)

1915 marks the beginning of a more mathematical portion of C.W.'s career. His paper "New Dosage Tables" in that year has a strong mathematical content. The following few years would see the publishing of the bulk of C.W.'s optics papers, which were intensely mathematic.

This December 1915 paper in the Annals of the Entomology Society of America is a plea for more quantitative research to be done in entomology. Within insect classification, he calls for more explicit and accurate descriptions backed up by quantified measurements.

> "Thus in physics we have ceased to give much prominence to the mere operation of physical laws, but must measure the results with such accuracy that this science has almost become a branch of mathematics. ...
>
> The present paper is intended as suggestions and a plea for the development of a quantitative entomology. Qualitative work must not cease nor be abated, but to it should be added the higher development of the subject which will finally come to be considered the essential portion of the science.

A beginning has already been made in nearly every department of entomology towards this quantitative method of study, enough to give us some idea of the simpler lines of procedure and of the results likely to be secured. Quantitative entomology is not therefore a wholly new idea, but is a great territory, the boundaries only of which have been explored and in the depths of which we may expect to find the chief justification for our endeavors."[230]

He goes on to make specific suggestions as to how to add quantitative elements to each field of entomology. He suggested:

- Focusing on definitive differentiation to systematics – carefully adding variants to insect keys to make them definitive.
- adding measurements of growth to descriptive entomology.
- Adding precise nomenclature systems to descriptive entomology that emphasize the "nature and character of the parts rather than their superficial appearance.
- adding quantitative color measurements across entomology.
- more accurately emphasize the phylogenic differences in classification.
- coordinating the classification systems between different authors.
- more carefully measuring the geographical and seasonal distribution of insects.
- that means be devised to measure food consumption, relative frequency and relative mass of insect populations.

Finally, he suggests that textbooks in economic entomology were wildly out of touch with the real threats in California and provides the following chart:

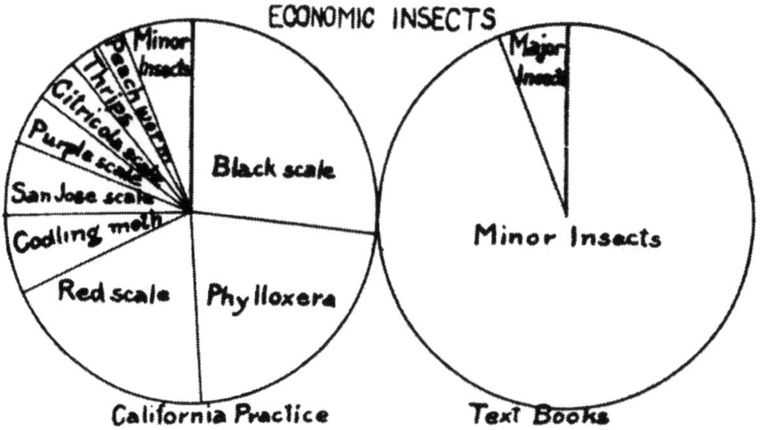

Figure 57 Attention paid to insect species in economic entomology textbooks[231]

He cites this as an example where the lack of quantitative habits by entomologists has led to a misallocation of the available pages in economic entomology texts.

> "This [the chart above] emphasizes in a striking manner the prominence we gave to the occasional and exception matters [over the matters that are central] which will come to take more nearly their proper [smaller] place when this tendency towards quantitative work has progressed further.
>
> I trust while those present may not be ready to adopt all of any of the suggestions of this paper that the underlying idea will meet with your approbation and that perhaps some may be stimulated to take what is here urged as the future progressive work along the lines in which the trend of science must proceed."[232]

This paper seems very modern. He calls for precision across the board and quantitative measurement where it can be had.

His color measurement suggestion is commonplace today. We might say that the colors of the University of California, Berkeley are Yale Blue - RGB (15, 77, 146) and University of California Gold - RGB (183, 135, 39).

Barro Colorado Island – Panama Canal Zone (1925, 1937)

A 1926 article in *Science* reported the visit of C.W. to the Barro Colorado Island Research Station in the Panama Canal Zone.

> "Professor Charles Woodworth, of the University of California, studied several groups of insects in which he is especially interested. In this work he was assisted by his son, Professor Charles E. Woodworth of Modesto Junior College, Modesto, California."[233] Both C.W. and his son C.E. arrived in New Orleans from Havana, Cuba on the S.S. Parismina on August 10, 1925 on the return leg of the journey.[234]

Figure 58 [right] C.W. on a ship with his son Charles[235]

Barro Colorado Island, which means "red clay island", is by far the largest island in Lake Gatun, the lake that forms part of the Panama Canal. Lake Gatun was formed when the Chagres River was dammed as part of the construction of the Panama Canal. Barro Colorado Island was formed from the hills that remained above the level of the newly formed lake. It was set aside as a nature reserve in 1923, "one of the first biological reserves in the New World"[236].

Beginning in the early 1920's, scientists visited the island. The small settlement that contains the research station is on the northeast side of the island. In 1946, the research station became a bureau of the Smithsonian Institute. Today the institute is the centerpiece of the Smithsonian Tropical Research Institute and hosts visits of up to 900 scientists per year.[237] The island "is now the most intensively studied area in the tropics"[238].

Figure 59 Barro Colorado Island in 1920[239]

Figure 60 The Smithsonian Tropical Research Institute on Barro Colorado Island on November 3, 2011, taken by the author from the deck of the cruise ship the Coral Princess during a canal transit

In the 1920's, the island had the advantage of both being a pristine tropical location and being on U.S. soil, fully inside the Canal Zone. C.W. and C.E. visited in 1925, just two years after the reserve was set aside. Today the island is in the nation of Panama.

This trip was close to the end of C.W.'s career at Cal. While C.W. never published any results from his trip to BCI, it is almost certain that the knowledge he gained from his visit was propagated to his colleagues in some manner.

In September 1937, at the age of 72, C.W. returned to Barro Colorado Island. A letter from Dr. James Zetek, founding director of the Canal Zone Biological Area confirmed his travel details. The letter concludes with "Am glad to see you back again.[240]

The Major Orders of Insects (1930)

On March 27, 1921, C.W. gave a speech entitled "The Evolution of the Ancient Orders of Insects" at the California Academy of Sciences in San Francisco.[241]

C.W.'s capstone paper in entomology, which was published just after his retirement in the June 1930 issue of *Psyche*, is a short article which attempts to capture the chronological order of the six major insect orders (other minor orders also exist such as Odonata). For convenience, he assigned a letter to each order. Those are:

- O – Orthoptera (e.g. grasshoppers, locusts and crickets)
- R – Hemiptera (e.g. aphids, cicadias and leafhoppers)
- C – Coleoptera (e.g. beetles)
- D – Diptera (e.g. house fly and mosquitoes)
- H – Hymenoptera (e.g. bees, wasps, sawflies and ants)
- L – Lepidoptera (e.g. moths and butterflies)

These groups split apart from each other during a relatively compact interval in the earth's history between 350 and 250 million years before the present. Some fossil evidence existed in C.W.'s day of the early forms of insects in these orders.

There had been much back and forth between scientists as to the chronological order of the development of these orders. "The six major orders have been arranged in more than thirty different ways and in the last ten years fifteen authors have used ten different arrangements, half of which had not been employed previously."[242] He went on to list the thirty ways and the authors and dates for each. (The 30 used sequences are a significant chunk of the 720 total possibilities.)

The lists were made by various means. The first way was by analyzing the taxonomy of the insects and putting them into groups. This is a famously difficult task due to obstacles such as convergent evolution where the same problem is solved in similar ways by unrelated species.

The first such efforts in C.W.'s list were completed long before Darwin, so the concepts of the chronology of species development and phylogentic trees did not exist for the first authors, and as such were tossed out by C.W. By 1882, half way through C.W.'s list, scientists had stopped proposing new sequences with anything but Orthoptera as the first order in the list by 1882, but many authors were using the old sequences nearly up to the 1930 publishing date of the article. One 1928 author, Leonard, still had Orthoptera as the most recently evolved order.

Modern DNA analysis has allowed the answer to the question of phylogenetic trees to be definitively answered. The correct order is OCRH[DL] where the predecessors of the final two orders, Diptera and Lepidoptera, split from each other, so both OCRHDL and OCRHLD are correct in C.W.'s notation.[243]

In C.W.'s list, the first author to propose the correct first three letters, ORC (also to get any of the first 3 right) was de Hoven in 1856. C.W. had proposed ORCDHL in 1906, had used the reverse of that order as the order of the chapters in his 1913 textbook *Guide to Insects,* and had repeated that proposal in this 1930 paper. The first authors to get the entire sequence correct were Robin Tillyard and a group at the Swammerdam Institute of Life Sciences in 1926.

Figure 61 Robin J. Tillyard[244]

C.W. says:

> "Tillyard, who has most recently proposed an arrangement, differs from my proposal only in the relative position of Hymenoptera and Diptera, which was based on newly discovered ancient fossils which he identified as hymenopterous, perhaps erroneously. Whether he is right or not [he was], there is abundant evidence in the completeness of the differentiation of the families of Diptera in Tertiary times to establish its seniority to the Hymenoptera [all of the orders were actually separated long before the tertiary]. The same kind of evidence makes Lepidoptera the youngest of all."[245]

To be fair to C.W., the orders Hymenoptera, Diptera and Lepidoptera divided from each other during a tight interval of time. There was only a short period between the moment when the ancestor species of Diptera and Lepidoptera split from Hymenoptera and the moment when a descendant of that progenitor species was split itself into what became the final two orders of insects. This sort of fine distinction is difficult to glean from a fossil record. Modern DNA analysis allows this distinction to be made definitively.

Chapter 6 – Species-Specific Entomology and Plant Pathology Research

C.W. spent much of his career leading California agriculture's response to the many insect and fungal pests present. For the duration of his career, agriculture was California's leading industry.

This chapter details C.W.'s species-specific work. For species covered in other chapters see:

- See the Chapter 2 for details on his Master's Thesis work on *Jassidae* (commonly known as leafhoppers, now known scientifically as *Cicadellidae*
  - (See His first publication – Jassidae of Illinois.)
- See Chapter 4 for details on his suggestion of the use of *Drosophila melanogaster*.
  - (See Chapter 4 - *Drosophila melanogaster* (1900).)
- See Chapter 8 for a discussion of his work with the salt-marsh mosquitoes *Culex squmiger* and *Culex currei*
  - (See Chapter 8 - Mosquito Control.)
- See the two Chapter 9 sections for discussion of his work with the silkworm *Bombyx mori.*
  - (See The Wings of *Bombyx mori* (1923).)
  - (See Silkworm research prior to his trips to China.)
- See Chapter 11 for details on his career-long work on the codling moth, *Cydia pomonella* also known as the apple worm.
  - (See Chapter 11 – The Codling Moth and the California Spray Chemical Company – "Ortho".)

This chapter concludes with an account of the four efforts by others to name species after C.W, including one effort that was ultimately successful.

Scale Insects (1893, 1896, 1900 & 1903)

Scale insects are parasites of plants and live by sucking the sap of plants. They are in the Order Hemiptera and live much of lives plastered under a protective waxy scale to the limbs or leaves of plants. Because of this protective scale, they are hard to kill with insecticides. In the typical scale insect life cycle, once a year small crawlers emerge from under the scale and find new homes. They are sexually dimorphic and have a large variation in the details of their reproductive system. The scale insects that you see on the tree are generally female.

Because they are parasitic on plants, there are many scale insects that are primary agricultural pests. Scale insects are in the same Suborder, Sternorrhyncha as other agricultural pests such as aphids, whiteflies and the famous vineyard pest, *phylloxera*. The name Sternorrhyncha refers to the location of their mouth at the bottom of their heads so that they can conveniently eat the plants that they are standing on.

San Jose scale (*Quadraspiiotus perniciosus*) is a major pest of fruit trees. It is native to Northeast Asia and was introduced to San Jose, California on fruit trees imported from China by James Lick, who was also the benefactor of the University of California's Lick Observatory, which C.W. would later help with telescope eyepiece design in the optics part of his career. C.W. worked on control of San Jose scale as well as black scale over his career.

Figure 62 Scale insects (probably Magnolia Scale) infesting a tree at the author's home[246]

[Author's note: Not long after the above photo was taken, my wife and I attempted to clear this tree of its infestation by hand. The next year they returned. A treatment with insecticide the previous summer had failed, as they are only vulnerable during short windows in their annual life cycle. For most of the year they are hunkered down in their protective wax coating living off of the sap of the tree. These scale insects also helped convince a large colony of yellow jackets to make their home nearby, as scale insects are a favorite treat of those predator insects.]

Natural predator effort (1895)

In 1893, L.O. Howard detected an infestation of San José scale, a west coast pest, in Charlottesville, Virginia. Howard wrote a 1895 paper about it entitled "The Eastern Occurrences of the San José Scale". Near the end of the paper, he mentions that: a predator of the San Jose Scale that was found in Charlottesville had been sent to C.W. He says: "Prof. C. W. Woodworth at Berkeley, who wrote that the insects were received in good condition and had been placed upon a well-infested peach tree at Oakland, where they would be kept under observation."[247]

The Black scale (1896)

In 1896, C.W. published a paper about the sin the California Cultivator.

Twelfth Annual Meeting of the Association of Economic Entomologists (1900)

In 1900 C.W. writes: "The San Jose scale (*Aspidiotu pernicionus*) is still with us in California, but is so well in control that it is scarcely ever mentioned when discussing injurious insects in conventions or meetings of farmers. It occurs all over the State, but is chiefly to be found in the great valley. The treatment almost uniformly adopted is winter spraying with lime, salt, and sulphur mixture."[248]

Key to Coccidae of California (1903)

In October of 1903, C.W. self-published "Key to the Coccidae of California". This 42-page document is focused on the species of scale insects that are found in California, including San Jose scale.

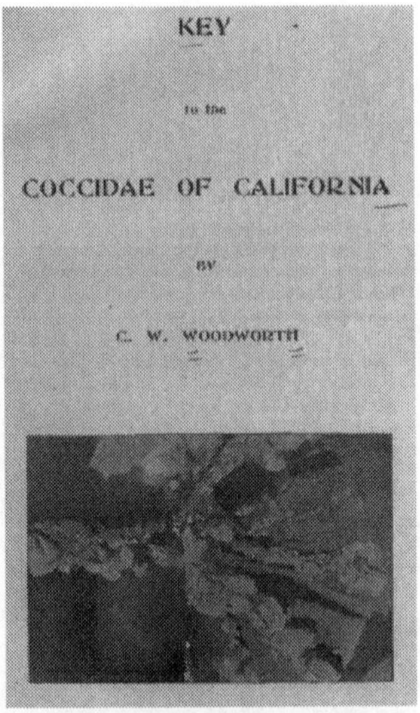

Figure 63 Cover of Key to the Coccidae of California (1903)[249]

The introduction begins:

> "The Scale insects of this State have received a great deal of attention particularly along economic lines. This is the first attempt at making a synopsis for the recognition of our species. The form of the synopsis and of the references is uniform with the author's Key to Orthoptera, in which full explanations will be found.
>
> The study of these insects requires ability to use the compound microscope and considerable microscopic technique. A laboratory guide for the study of scale insects is being prepared for publication for the use of those who may wish to take up the subject by themselves and desire a detailed description of the study methods. …

> The author hopes that this key will stimulate many entomologists on this coast to collect and study in this group."[250]

Crater Blight of Pears (1896, 1900)

A blight was found that affected pear trees. This blight made a mark in the form of a crater on pear trees. C.W. sent a letter to the *Pacific Rural Press* in February 1896 inviting its readers to send samples to him. The treatment he recommended as reprinted in 1900 was to "Cut out the dead and diseased tissue, clean and wash with Bordeaux mixture; cut off all dead and blackened limbs.

He gave an update in a July 1896 issue of the *Pacific Rural Press:*

> "We have made some progress in the study of the disease in that we are uniformly able to obtain pure cultures of a peculiar bacillus. Inoculation experiments have so far given only negative results. The disease occurs on many varieties of pears and only a few apples."[251]

One of C.W.'s advisors at Illinois was Thomas J. Burrill, whose signature achievement in plant pathology was the 1882 determination that fire blight was caused by a bacteria and not a fungus. This was the first determination of a bacterial cause of a plant disease. The relationship of fire blight to crater blight is unclear. The term "crater blight" does not appear in modern literature.

Modern science has identified the fire blight pathogen to be the bacteria *Erwinia amylovora.* It is an infectious disease that can be spread by honey bees, birds, rain, wind and hailstorms. It can be treated with antibiotics, although resistant strains exist. Biological controls as well as copper can also be used.

Hessian Fly (1886, 1891)

The Hessian fly, *Mayetiola destructor,* is a major pest of grains.

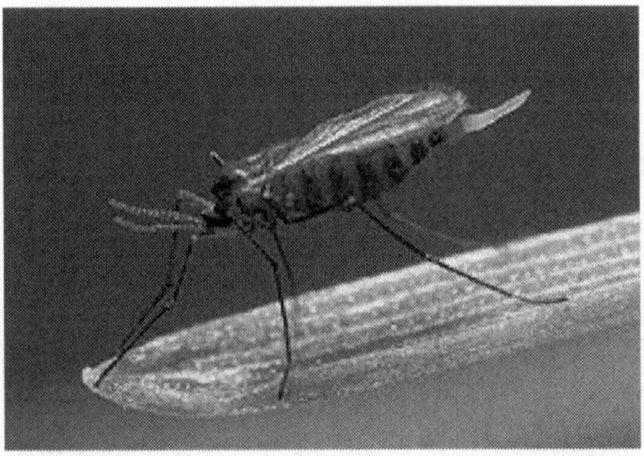

Figure 64 The Hessian fly, Mayetiola destructor[252]

C.W. made a significant series of observations on a university wheat field in Berkeley that had become infested with the Hessian fly. The observations compared the variety of grain with the type and amount of injury that the Hessian fly produced. The field was planted with about 125 different varieties of wheat. He found two varieties that were completely free of injury, eight that were almost free and another 12 that were mostly free.

He also investigated the yield with respect to the varieties. Finally he compared the yield and the crop over the three years of the experiment. "The conclusion to be drawn is that though there may be a decided difference between early and late sowing on a particular year, this difference is due to the peculiar conditions existing on that year; that early planting may be best on one year and late planting on another, and that no rule can be laid down."

Although his results were mixed, this paper showed his early comfort in conducting long, complex and fruitful field experiments. While this study lacks the modern statistical analysis of such studies done in our era, it holds up well 120 years later.

Tarnished Plant Bug (1889)

While at the Arkansas Experiment Station, C.W. wrote about how to use kerosene to control the tarnished plant bug, *Lygus pratensis L.*, in bulletin #10,

Figure 65 Tarnished plant bug[253]

The tarnished plant bug remains a serious pest of small fruits, vegetables, cotton, and seed alfalfa.

The use of kerosene illustrates the limited toolbox that was available to entomologists in this era.

Whiteflies (1900, 1901)

Whiteflies of the family Aleyrodidae are an important threat to agriculture. There are multiple species of whitefly including species that attack citrus trees, grapevines, and tomatoes. They cause damage both directly by feeding and indirectly by serving as the vector of plant viruses. The role of plant viruses was not understood in C.W.'s era.

Florida whitefly investigation (1900)

At the start of C.W.'s second stay at Harvard in June of 1900, he was asked by Henry Arthur Gossard of the Florida Agricultural College and Experiment Station in Lake City, Florida to travel down and stay there for a month or two to help investigate an infestation of the whitefly, *Aleyrodes citri,* on citrus crops there. Florida Agricultural College is one of the four predecessor institutions of the University of Florida. Lake City is about 50 miles northwest of the present campus in Gainesville.

H. A. Gossard was particularly worried that the heavy dews that they have would make the fumigation practices used in other states not practical there. He suggested that they develop a regimen of fumigation during the daytime hours of cloudy winter days under black tents to minimize the injury to the trees.

By July, Gossard had gotten interest from enough orange growers to offer him $150/month for the period of four to six weeks. C.W. got the leave of absence from Harvard on December 6, 1900 and travelled to Florida shortly thereafter.

Grape Whitefly (1901)

In 1901, he published a paper entitled "The White-Flies of California". In this paper he described an unstudied species in great detail that has "proven its ability to damage grapevines in a very serious manner".[254]

He first described where the white fly fits with other families. This is essentially unchanged from its classification today. They are in the suborder Sternorrhyncha, which also contains aphids, phylloxerans, jumping plant lice and scale insects. There are many important agricultural pests in this suborder.

He went on to say:

> "A large number of the species in the colder climates, which live on deciduous trees and on annual herbs, have never been studied in the winter, and their winter history is entirely unknown. It is probable however, that in most cases they had become fully fed before the leaves fall in autumn, but do not transform until the next spring, remaining merely attached to the fallen leaves during winter.*
>
> [A footnote says:] * Since writing the above I learn that my brother, Mr. H. O. Woodworth, has been able to confirm this supposition for a number of species found on deciduous trees in Illinois."

The paper describes the life cycle of the family of whiteflies in great detail. It then describes in detail the otherwise unnamed "White-Fly of the Vine". "This insect has never been described, nor has any mention of it been made, in any publication upon the insects of the vine."[255] He further described how this vine species has a host-alternating, two-brooded life-cycle, meaning that it lived on two types of plants in summer and winter, "the habit, hitherto unknown in this group of transferring their attention, on the approach of winter, to an entirely different plant, the evergreen *Rhamnus californicus* [the coffeeberry plant], and returning to the vine the next spring."[256] He concluded with the suggestion that the best way to manage the White-Fly of the Vine would be the "destruction of the winter-food plant", the other plant that it lives on during the winter. In this way, spraying during the busy season could be avoided. In other words, C.W. suggested that the vineyard owners destroy every coffeeberry plant in the vicinity of the vineyards in an effort to deny the grape whitefly their winter home.

This new species is now known as the grape whitefly, *Trialeurodes vittatas*. It was named by the USDA's Altus Lacy Quaintance in 1900, almost simultaneously to and presumably associated with C.W.'s effort to understand and control this pest.[257] [Presumably, C.W. sent some samples to Quaintance for classification.]

Orange and Lemon Rot (1902)

As part of his work in the Experiment Station, C.W. became involved in several plant pathology efforts, helping farmers handle non-insect pests. In this case, a fungus was attacking oranges and lemons, particularly during transport and causing heavy economic losses.

In 1902, C.W. wrote bulletin #139, *Orange and Lemon Rot* in response to "requests from numerous growers for information on the subject". In this paper, he introduces the nature of the funguses in the *Penicillium* family, particularly *Penicillium digitalum* and *Penicillium crustaceum*. He describes their growth with descriptions such as: "These hyphae penetrate the fruit in much the same way as the root-hairs of higher plants penetrate the soil." He describes their reproduction with descriptions such as "After the vegetative mycelium has somewhat exhausted the substances of the fruit, or if the latter becomes too dry for rapid growth, the fungus prepares to develop a form of fruit of its own." He describes the disease as: "This disease, being entirely a matter of the fruit and belonging particularly to ripe fruit, evidently always gains its entrance to the fruit from the outside and never from the tree."

He then discusses three methods of preventing the germination of the disease with paragraphs on each of refrigeration, ventilation, and wrapping. The following section lays out how to decrease the abundance of the spores in the first place with sections describing the proper disposition of decayed fruit, summer disinfection of the packing houses, and sulfuring of the packing houses. He concludes with a section on the best orchard practice for disposing of decayed fruit. Dr. Hilgard then adds a page describing how to compost decayed fruit with lime and earth to allow its use as fertilizer.[258]

This investigation was 26 years before Alexander Fleming's discovery of the antibiotic properties of *Penicillum notatum*. There is no discussion of the interaction of fungi and bacteria in this paper.

Grasshoppers in California (1902)

(See Chapter 10 for a discussion of the public policy recommendations that he made in this paper.)
(See Grasshoppers in California (1902).)

C.W. published the thirty-six page California State Bulletin number 142 entitled "Grasshoppers in California" in 1902[259]. There had been outbreaks of locust swarms in Roseville, Fair Oaks, and Orangevale, California.

These locusts damaged the fruit trees in these communities. Locusts are the swarming phase of certain grasshoppers. They typically occur when a population of grasshoppers reaches a certain density. Recent research has revealed that when grasshopper's back legs are in frequent contact with other grasshoppers, grasshoppers begin to eat much more, breed much more easily, and become migratory. They can travel great distances, rapidly strip fields, and damage crops.

C.W. described methods of controlling swarms in both their flying and drifting modes. He then described how to control them on their breeding grounds by plowing in the fall or burning over. He also recommended making "a careful survey to determine the breeding grounds of the locusts".

California Peach-Tree Borer (1902)

C.W. published the fifteen-page California State Bulletin number 143 entitled "The California Peach-Tree Borer" in 1902[260]. This insect was then referred to as *Sannioidea opalescens*, but is now called *Synanthedon exitiosa.*

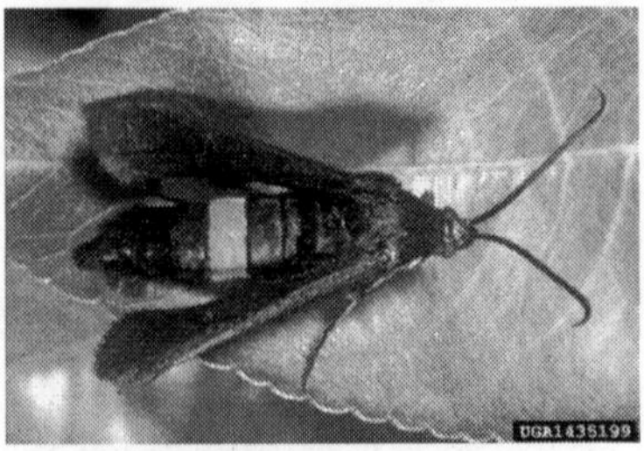

Figure 66 The Peach-Tree Borer[261]

This paper discussed what was known about the "most injurious insect in the Santa Clara Valley". This area is today's Silicon Valley, but in that day it was called "The Valley of Heart's Delight" because its major industry was fruit tree cultivation. The book *Saratoga's First Hundred Years* contains the following captions "The almost unbroken area of many square miles of prune trees comprise comfortable orchard homes of varied sizes from five areas to some of the largest in the world. Viewed from the Saratoga foothills in blossom time, these orchards present a scene unsurpassed in beauty and grandeur.[262] Traces of this legacy remain in the name of a shopping center, The Pruneyard in Campbell, California and in the Orchard Heritage Parks of Sunnyvale and Saratoga, California.

[Author's note: My wife and I live in the town of Monte Sereno in this area and regularly stop by a nearby fruit stand that sells the harvest of one of the few remaining Silicon Valley orchards.]

THE
CALIFORNIA PEACH-TREE BORER.
BY C. W. WOODWORTH.

THE OLD PRACTICE OF DIGGING OUT THE BORERS.

Figure 67 Cover of Bulletin 143, The California Peach Tree Borer[263]

This paper thoroughly presents what was known about the Borer as well as what had been recently learned. He describes the habits of the insect in each of the four seasons in great detail through its egg, worm, pupa and moth life stages. He makes several points:

- While then only infesting the Santa Clara Valley, he asserted that it was likely that it would "suddenly become injurious elsewhere". This has happened per UC ANR Publication 3433.[264]
- He asserted that there was not three distinct broods as was supposed by farmers, but rather a continuum of broods.
- He dispelled the notion that the "gum" was "an unfailing and only sign of the work of the insect" by observing "that the gum has no necessary relationship to the insect at all, but rather represents the evidence of the work of some decay-producing organism which has gained entrance to the tree at the point where it was injured by the feeding of the borer.

- He dispelled the notion that the burrows had a "certain definite arrangement", but rather that the "habits of the worms within the burrow are subject to no recognized rule".
- He pointed out "there is no time during the summer when eggs may not be laid.... It will not be possible ... to mark out any plan of annual treatment which will be equally effective in different years."
- The paper reviews what was known about the life cycle and habits of the borer and how to detect infestations. He then describes the best treatment known, which was treating the tree with carbon disulphide, "By far the best results in fighting the peach-tree borer were obtained from the use of carbon bisulphid." [265] He describes that there is "little or no danger to trees." Finally he shows his ability to find practical solutions by mentioning that "A small can has been devised in which the proper amount may be readily measured ..."
- He also points out the nature of the soil below the tree was critical for selecting the correct dose. If the soil was too loose, a fatal injury to the tree could occur with the same dose that would otherwise be effective. [266]

C.W. also provided an introduction to bulletin, No. 144 by his young assistant, Warren T. Clarke, to the highly successful study economically of a different peach pest, *The Peach Worm.* In this study, Clarke worked in Newcastle, California, which is in the Sierra foothills northeast of Sacramento, for seven months and identified the vulnerable moment in the peach worm's life cycle in the spring when a lime, salt and sulphur treatment could be effective.

Red Spider of Citrus Trees (1902)

On May 10, 1902, the Pacific Rural Press reported that:

> "Prof. C.W. Woodworth of the University, who is now in southern California making a special study of mites on citrus trees, is credited with saying that he is convinced the red spider now proving such a destructive factor among the orange orchards is a new species of the pest, differing in size and especially in the effect of its bite on fruit. The ordinary red spider has been known for some years to orchardists, but they seem easily gotten rid of and are not very destructive. The new species is tenacious of life, and when it bites an orange the fruit decays quickly and will not stand transportation. Professor Woodworth will stay with this issue at the south for several weeks and we hope will strike a settlement of it."[267]

In 1902, C.W. published Bulletin #145, "The Red Spider of Citrus Trees.

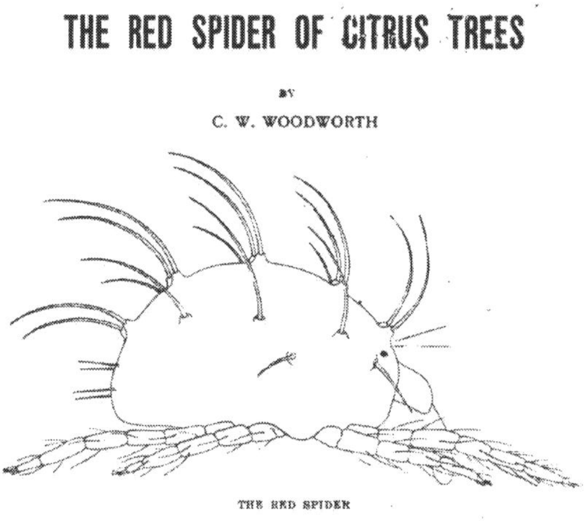

THE RED SPIDER OF CITRUS TREES
BY
C. W. WOODWORTH
THE RED SPIDER

Figure 68 The Red Spider of Citrus Trees[268]

This paper presented the intermediate results of investigations into this pest, largely conducted by one of his students, W. H. Volck, who later would go on to co-found Cal-Spray (Ortho). The red spider is a very small mite that attacks orange and lemon trees and had caused losses.

In this paper, he asserts that[269]:

- The spotting of fruit was not the cause of one of the types of spotting that had been observed. This spotting was instead due to the distillate sprays that had been used.
- The spider was responsible for the "unusual or excessive dropping from the trees".
- The spider was responsible for "the loss which results from the decrease in the size and sugar content of the fruit.
- Since the appearance of the fruit from infested trees was easily recognized, that if the market comes "to recognize and begin to discriminate against the paler fruit … the losses would become very large."
- The insect, *Tetranychus mytilaspidis,* differed from other insects named "red spider", even within California.

He then describes the life cycle of the red spider in great detail and includes a drawing of its egg. He describes them as: "The eggs of the red spider are very peculiar in the possession of a long slender stalk projecting from the middle of the top side, extending upward nearly twice as high again as the egg itself. … The stalk is transparent and surmounted on the top by a very slightly enlarged transverse section, to which is attached, immediately after laying, a series of rather regularly arranged delicate silken threads, about fourteen in number, radiating from this point to the surface of the leaf, forming a series of guys by which the egg is held firmly in position in spite of the fact that otherwise it is very loosely attached to the leaf."

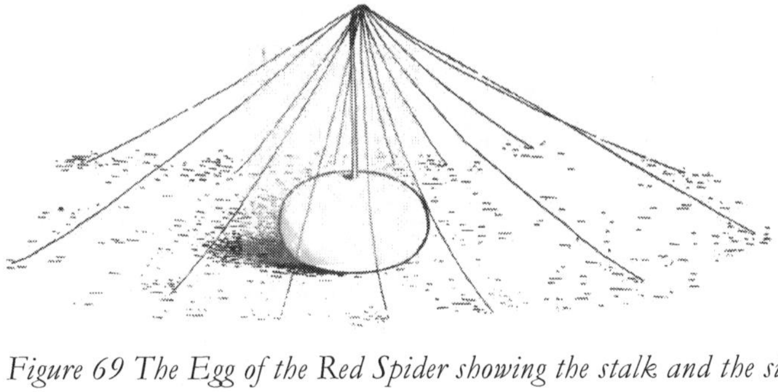

Figure 69 The Egg of the Red Spider showing the stalk and the silken guys[270]

He then describes in detail the natural enemies of the spider including two species of ladybirds, the larvae of a species of lace-winged fly, the *Coniopteryx*, other predaceous mites, and a fungus. He concludes with a discussion of the remedies for the red spider. He makes the following points:

- Cyanide fumigation is "of no value whatsoever as a means of controlling the red spider".
- Sulfuring "cannot be depended on" because the treatment depends "upon the occurrence of hot days."
- That the "only really effective method ... is the use of an insecticide applied as a spray." He also points out that citrus trees are "extremely difficult to spray effectively", and that the "difference between a thorough and careless spraying is very little in time or material but amounts to a great deal in efficiency."

He then gives an elaborate illustrated description of the optimal method for spraying both for the new distillates and for the more established Sulfid of Potash.

Figure 70 Plan for Inside Spraying (note the worker inside of the tree)[271]

Argentine Ants (1908, 1910)

Control of the Argentine Ant (1910)

This extensive 1910 paper analyzes the spread of the Argentine ant, *Linepithema humile,* throughout California. This was an update to a paper written two years before about the ant. At this point, the ants had spread greatly from their initial introduction, but were still relatively contained, with 200 colonies infesting about 5000 acres.

In amongst his collected papers in Cal archive in the Bancroft Library is a map of the Piedmont sewer system with the infested sections colored in.[272]

He suggested using syrup laced with a small amount of arsenic to control ants.

> "We obtained by far the best results by the use of a very weak solution of arsenic and syrup. Most of the commercial ant poisons commonly known as ant pastes consist of arsenic and syrup, but are made very strong in arsenic. This kills the foraging ants almost immediately. We found by reducing the arsenic to between one-fourth and one-eighth of one per cent. They would take large quantities of the material to their nests and feed it to the young, and the whole nest would be killed by a slow poisoning."[273]

Grant's Ant Stakes that you can buy in the grocery store basically use this same formula; they are a solidified sweet mixture laced with just a small amount of arsenic.

Of course, the modern day battle against the invasion of the argentine ant has been completely and definitively lost. The ant is ubiquitous. Happily, there are products like Grant's Ant Stakes to help us control them.

Species named after C.W.

Four species were named after C.W., using *woodworthi* as part of the name. Of these four, one name has been deprecated, one persists as the name of a variety of a species, one exists as a synonym of a species, and one exists, with a different genera name as the species name of *Elidiptera woodworthi.*

Caliothrips woodworthi (1904)

In a 1904 edition of the *Entonomological News*, Miss S.M. Daniel described the male of a new species of thrips and named the species *Caliothrips woodworthi* after C.W. She found the species on pear blossoms in San Leandro, California, not far from Berkeley. She was a Cal undergraduate in the class of 1904 and was the Vice-President of the Cal Agricultural Club.[274] In 1907, Dudley Moulton described this species as a synonym of *Heliothrips fasciatus*.[275]

Figure 71 Susie M. Daniel in the 1904 Cal Blue and Gold Yearbook (aliasing already present in online source image)[276]

This species is now known as *Caliothrips fasciatus* with *Caliothrips woodworthi* as a synonym.[277] Its common name is the California bean thrips. It is known as a pest of bean crops and became invasive and was quarantined in Australia.

San Leandro is now completely developed; its pear orchards are a thing of the past. Berkeley, Oakland, San Leandro, San Lorenzo and Hayward are essentially one continuous urban area.

Figure 72 Female Caliothrips fasciatus[278]

Gypona woodworthi (1914)

In 1914 his future colleague at Cal , Dr. Edward Van Duzee, was working on a catalogue of hemiptera at the Scripps Institute in San Diego and published "Nomenclatural and Critical Notes on Hemiptera" in *Canadian Entomologist*. "He starts with "For the past two years, as many of my correspondents know, I have devoted all my spare moments, which have been all too few to the preparation of a catalogue of the North American Hemiptera"

Later in the paper he says: "Genus Gypona Germ. - *Gypona bimaculata* Woodworth, 1887, is preoccupied by *Gypona bimaculata* Spangberg, 1878, for the former I propose the name woodworthi."[279]

He describes it as "Pale greenish yellow, the scutellar disc creamy, an indefinite smoky band arising on posterior margin of pronotum and extending to apex of elytra."

This is known today as the name of a variety of *Ponana pectoralis*, a type of leafhopper in Cicadellidae, Gyponinae.

Elidiptera woodworthi (1916)

In 1916 his colleague at Cal , Dr. Edward Van Duzee, who would later accompany him to China, named a species of planthopper, *Elidiptera woodworthi* after him. In 1922 this was changed to *Cixidia woodworthi.* A 2002 paper calls it *Epiptera woodworthi.*[280]

Figure 73 Edward P. Van Duzee[281]

Van Duzee's description starts with:

> "***Elidiptera woodworthi,*** new species
>
> Closely allied to *septentrionalis*; broader, more mottled with white; front whitish with its base and the clypeus fulvo-testaceous. Length 7mm.
>
> Vertex a little shorter than in *septentrionalis,* scarcely as long as broad, the impressed median line almost obsolete in the female. Front a little narrower than in the allied species, sides almost rectilinear, at apex curving inward to base of clypeus. …"

He described where he found it as:

> "Described from numerous examples taken on the Jeffrey pine, especially along the southern slope of Mount Tallac,[near the southern end of Fallen Leaf lake at the southern end of the Lake Tahoe basin] after July 19. They were also beaten from cypress bushes growing on this same slope and here the young were taken with the adults. This is of a clearer gray than any of our other species of *Elidiptera*."[282]

A photo of the "closely allied" species *Epiptera septentrionalis* can be found online at:
http://www.pbase.com/tmurray74/image/137792349 .

Myzocallis woodworthi (1917)

In 1917, George O. Shinji named an aphid after C.W. in an article in *Entomological News* Vol. XXVIII entitled "New Aphids from California". The species is light green, 1.2 mm long by 0.5 mm wide. Its abdomen is pale with dusky dorsal bands. It was found on the Cal campus on June 20, 1916 on the host plant *Quercus* [an Oak tree]. Shingi says: "This beautiful aphid is named in honor of Professor Woodworth, of the University of Califonia, with whom the writer has enjoyed studying for more than eight college years."[283]

In 1919, Albert F. Swain mentioned in *Synopsis of the Aphididae of California,* that this was a variety of *Myzocallis quercus, Myzocallis woodworthi* is now listed as a nomen dubium or [deprecated name].[284]

Year	Proposer	Proposed name	Current name	Status
1904	Susie M. Daniel	*Caliothrips woodworthi*	*Caliothrips fasciatus*	Synonym
1914	Edward P. Van	*Gypona woodworthi*	Variety of *Ponana*	Variety name

	Duzee		*pectoralis*	
1916	Edward P. Van Duzee	*Elidiptera woodworthi*	*Epiptera woodworthi*	In use
1917	George O. Shinji	*Myzocallis woodworthi*	Variety of *Myzocallis quercus*	Deprecated name

Table 5 Status of the four attempts to name a species after C.W.

Chapter 7 – Precursors of Integrated Pest Management

While C.W. did not originate the now-central concept in entomology of Integrated Pest Management (IPM), he was an important voice and articulated early versions of some of that field's main concepts.

The Theory of the Parasitic Control of Insect Pests (1908)

C.W. published a paper in *Science* Vol XXVIII, No. 712, page 227 in 1908 that was a central early paper in the development of Integrated Control, which was further developed decades later by others into IPM.

The paper starts with a statement of the complexity of the problem.

> "The conditions determining the life or death of insects are much more complicated than is usually appreciated, and the individual factors in the problem are far from independent. The correct estimation of this interdependence of the causes of death in insects is of vital importance in this connection. The efficiency of each factor is so influenced by the efficiency of the others that the elimination of one cause of death or the addition of an entirely new natural enemy will usually have but a slight effect upon the rate of survival or none at all."

The words used in this paragraph were very advanced for 1908. He talks about both the efficiency of factors and the rates of survival. These are the terms that some modern formulations of Integrated Pest Management are expressed in.

The paper goes on to talk about the economic impacts of pests in very modern terms.

> "The power of an insect to do damage as a rule to the number present during their chief feeding period, and may be quite independent of the numbers that finally come to maturity, and is absolutely independent of the ratio between birth and death rates. A temporary disturbance of this rate produces increase or decrease and may place an insect suddenly in the destructive class or remove it, but while an insect maintains itself in injurious numbers the ratio is an low as though the insect were rare."

He goes on to describe the interplay between the efficiency of an introduced parasite against what it is replacing, again in modern terms.

> "The real question to be settled therefore becomes whether the new insect replaces a more or a less efficient cause of death. The apparent percent of efficiency is really no criterion whatever of the value of the introduction. That which we are desiring to secure is the reduction of the numbers especially during the period of injury, and therefore the only significant datum is the determination of the relative abundance maintained by the injurious species. The numbers of any particular parasite is not even a safe index of its role in the maintenance of this status, unless one were able to accurately weigh its efficiency as contrasted to that which it replaced."

All and all, this paper is decades in advance of the full development of IPM, yet talks about many of concepts that will be formalized later.

Statements about C.W.'s contribution to IPM

Ray F. Smith is called the "Father of Integrated Pest Management" in his U.C. Berkeley obituary.[285] Ray F. Smith was the first recipient of the C.W. Woodworth award, in 1971. In his acceptance speech entitled "Origins of Integrated Control" he is recorded as speaking:

> "In my view, the origins of integrated control and its philosophy can be traced to a very modest and tolerant man [C.W.] who did so much for entomology and ecology at the beginning of this century and for which he has been little credited in recent times".[286]

In 1975, Ray F. Smith also wrote an article for the Pan-Pacific Entomologist, Volume 50(4): 426-29 entitled "The origin of integrated control in California - an account of the contributions of C.W. Woodworth". In a 1978 article entitled "History and Complexity of Integrated Pest Management" he wrote:

> "As the agricultural experiment stations emerged in the United States in the second half of the nineteenth century, entomologists and plant pathologists began to discover biological explanations for the earlier empirically developed pest control methodology, which had been restricted largely to natural and cultural measures, sometimes augmented by minimal use of the earliest insecticides or fungicides. Partly by intuitive insight and partly because there was little choice, leading entomologists advocated an ecological approach to pest control. In the 1880s Stephen A. Forbes, State Entomologist of Illinois and Professor of Zoology and Entomology at the University of Illinois, adopted the word "ecology" and insisted upon the broad application of ecological studies in dealing with insect problems of agricultural crops. A number of others concerned with crop protection also advocated this fundamental approach.

> In spite of this early position by leading entomologists, over the next half-century there was a gradual erosion of the understanding of the importance of ecology in controlling insect pests. There were, of course, exceptions to this, and from time to time a plea was made for the ecological approach. Charles W. Woodworth, Professor of Entomology at the University of California, advocated an ecologically based pest management approach throughout his long career."[287]

In 1982, Carl B. Huffaker, who was the 5th winner of the C.W. Woodworth Award in 1973 wrote a paper entitled "Overall Approach to Insect Problems in Agriculture". In that paper, he wrote:

> "What is IPM? Why so much talk about it? Why did President [Jimmy] Carter request of CEQ [Council of Environmental Quality] a special report on IPM? Rather suddenly, it seemed to promise a panacea for all pest control without conducting extensive new researches - at least to many of the uninformed. But integrated pest management as a concept and discipline is only a more sophisticated version of integrated control. Its origins lie in work in the late 1800's and early 1900's when pesticides where little used. Such greats in entomology as Stephen A. Forbes, C.V. Riley, J.H. Comstock, C.W. Woodworth and W.D. Hunter come to mind. The principles embodied were recommended in the control of boll weevil on U.S. cotton by USDA entomologies W.D. Hunter and B.R. Coad in 1923 (Hunter and Coad, 1923). …

> In the late 1800's, Stephen A. Forbes, of the University of Illinois, had emphasized the application of ecological principles in crop pest control. Yet, through a true pioneer in this respect (and inspiration to C.W. Woodworth who later quietly led California entomologists to develop specific integrated control concepts and methods), Forbes utterly missed the ecological significance of the natural enemies of pests themselves, claiming they had no role in depressing ultimate pest numbers."[288]

In 1985, in their paper "IPM: Definitions and Current Status in U.S. Agriculture", Raymond E. Frisbie and Perry L. Adkisson worte:

> "Integrated Pest Management (IPM) either by chance or circumstance was used as a descriptive term by entomologists as early as 1952. At the time the term commonly used for IPM was integrated control. ... Several scientists used applied ecological means in an attempt to control pests. These included the work by S.A. Forbes in Illinois, and C.W. Woodworth and Harry Smith in California (Metcalf 1930, Smith 1977)."[289]

In 2001, Dr. Frank Zalom, in his C.W. Woodworth Award winner's speech, included the following slide that summarizes some of the points that C.W. made in his 1908 paper as they relate to modern IPM. Dr. Zalom's speech was entitled "IPM, are we there yet? In that speech, he had a slide entitled "C.W. Woodworth as IPM Specialist" that highlighted three sections of C.W.'s paper:

C.W.'s passages in "The Theory of the Parasitic Control of Insect Pests"		**Frank Zalom's annotations to these passages in his C.W. Award speech**
The conditions determining the life or death of insects are much more complicated than is usually appreciated, and the individual factors in the problem are far from independent.		... multiple integrated factors determine the success of insects

The interrelation of factors may be of the most complicated nature; for instance, a parasite which of itself might be wholly inefficient due to its slow rate of reproduction as compared with that of its host, might be rendered very efficient by the cooperation of a contributing factor which could only delay the rate of increase.		... there may be a need for manipulation of the parasitoid, pest or environment to increase its effectiveness
The power of an insect to do damage due as a rule to the number present during their chief feeding period, and may be quite independent of the ratio between birth and death rates. A temporary disturbance of this rate produces increase or decrease and may place an insect suddenly in the destructive class or remove it.		... the presence of a pest doesn't mean that it is causing economic damage

Table 6 Frank Zalom's assessment of C.W.'s IPM contribution

In 2003, G.H. Walter, in Insect Pest Management and Ecological Research said:

> "Inclusion of a profession decision-maker to prevent the indiscriminate use of chemicals was not an innovation of IPM. The idea had been implemented early in the twentieth century, most notably at the hands of C.W. Woodworth in California and D. Isley in Arkansas, who developed the practice of supervised insect control." [290]

Chapter 8 - Mosquito Control

C.W. was a leader in the fight to control mosquitoes in California and later in China. He and members of his department helped free California of the scourge of mosquitoes in general as well as the mosquito-borne illness malaria, which C.W. personally had contracted in Arkansas.

See Chapter 9 for a discussion of his role in mosquito control in the city of Nanjing, China.)

Background of Mosquito Control

In 1900, Major Walter Reed, in a historic and dramatic series of experiments that took place in Havana, Cuba, proved an earlier hypothesis that mosquitoes spread yellow fever. From 1900 to 1901, William Gorgas led a massive effort that managed to partially clear Havana of mosquitoes through the use of oil, insecticide and screens. This reduced the incidence of both yellow fever and malaria there by fifty percent or more. This raised awareness that mosquitos caused disease and that they could be controlled.

William Gorgas also famously led the effort to control mosquitoes during the U.S. portion of the effort to build the Panama Canal, from 1904 to 1914. This effort was central to the success of the U.S. effort.

It had been known for decades that pouring oil on standing bodies of water brought relief from mosquitoes, but there had been almost no scientific study or large-scale experiments done to control them until Leland Howard published in 1900 the USDA's first bulletin focused on mosquito control. Contained in that report were the results of two experiments conducted by John B. Smith on Long Island that used oil to control mosquitoes. In 1901, Leland Howard published an introduction to mosquito control that was widely read.

John B. Smith worked for the Agricultural Experiment Station at Rutgers New Jersey. He began to work on mosquitoes in 1896 while working on an infestation of San Jose Scale in New Jersey. He laid out a plan for a comprehensive mosquito control program in 1901. He was also against the wholesale use of oil to control mosquitoes and determined that the salt marsh mosquitoes found there had a flight range of 30 to 40 miles. He found that the best way to control salt marsh mosquitoes was to eliminate the larval habitats than in trying to kill the mosquitoes. By 1903 he had secured $9,000 for a study. By 1904 he had cleared mosquito larvae from a few limited areas, although the long flying range of the mosquitoes found in the New Jersey marshes meant that many mosquitoes were still to be found. He also had gotten a law passed that allowed local health boards to act against mosquitoes.[291]

Mosquito Control in San Rafael (1903-4)

In his 1906 paper "Mosquito Control" he reports:

> "...only within the last few years has the idea apparently entered into the mind of mankind that mosquitoes need not be accepted, like the sunshine and the rain, as something beyond our control, but that instead a visitation of these swarms is an evidence of our neglect or carelessness. So much effective work has been done during the last two or three years in the control of mosquitoes that I think we are justified in saying that wherever individuals or communities are enough in earnest the mosquitoes can be almost, if not absolutely, controlled." [292]

His paper started by describing a highly successful mosquito control effort that he led. There were infestations of salt marsh mosquitos in San Rafael, California, *Culex squmiger* in the spring and *Culex currei* later in the year. San Rafael is in Marin County North of San Francisco. The region had "been infested more or less by mosquitoes as long as the town has been in existence."[293] The local Improvement Club [in 1904] was focused on improving the situation. Students from the Entomology Department visited the region repeatedly and made observations as to the distribution, collected specimens, and bred the mosquitoes so that the species could be determined. The result of this was that the range of the breeding ground was accurately determined. This enabled a single person, a Mr. Ashmun, to apply oil to the marsh area at right moments. The result was that when "twelve months from the date of my first visit I made a careful search of the town with an insect net, spending a half a day in hard collecting work, I was able to find less than a score of mosquitoes of any species."[294]

While John B. Smith had been able to control salt marsh mosquitoes in limited areas in New Jersey in the previous few years, the long flying range and tremendous extent of the salt marshes there prevented a successful result for many years. This effort in San Rafael was thus the first successful city-scale effort to control salt marsh mosquitoes.

Mosquito Control in Burlingame (1904-5)

C.W.'s 1906 paper further describes a second mosquito control effort in Burlingame in 1904 and 1905. Burlingame is on the San Francisco peninsula, with its marsh area located just South of the present San Francisco International Airport. In this case, the species was *Culex currei.* He and Henry Quayle worked with the local Improvement Club "to make permanent improvements instead of simply using oil on the marshes as had been done in San Rafael". These mosquitoes lay their eggs once a month on the monthly high tide. "It was observed both at San Rafael and at Burlingame that in no case where the tides had free access to a pool were mosquitoes produced, and an attempt was therefore made to connect every pool by means of a ditch with the channels up which the tide came."[295] The marsh "extended from South San Francisco to Coyote point ... nearly ten miles". His assistant "was enabled to keep so well ahead of the insect that throughout the season not a single specimen of *Culex currei* was observed in Burlingame or San Mateo."[296]

The progress on mosquito control in California languished in 1906 for two reasons. The first was the departure of Henry Qualye from the Agricultural Experiment Station in late 1905 for the Southern California Plant Pathology Laboratory, and the second was the aftermath of the April, 1906 San Francisco Earthquake. In 1908 after a three year search, C.W. hired William Herms as Quayle's replacement.

C.W.'s son, Harold Woodworth, worked on mosquito abatement in Burlingame in the 1912-1914 period.
(See the Chapter 14 section entitled Harold Woodworth.)

The Report of the Agricultural Experiment Station for 1912-1913 says:

> "A very extensive and successful mosquito campaign has been carried on under the department's direction by the cities of San Mateo, Burlingame and Hillsborough."[297]

Speech in Santa Rosa (1905)

On 12/6/1905 the following was reported in the *San Francisco Call*:

> Fruitmen to Hear Address
> BERKELEY, Dec 5. - A delegation of prominent University officials, including President Wheeler and Professors E.J. Wickson, W.T. Clarke and C.W. Woodworth, have gone to Santa Rosa, where they will deliver address at the meeting of the State Fruit Growers' Association. The work of the University's experiment stations, with respect to the fruit industry of the State, will be discussed by President Wheeler.
>
> Luther Burbank is expected to be an attendant at the meeting and he will be the subject of an address by Professor Wickson, a friend and admirer of the great wonder worker with plants, vines and trees. Professor Woodworth and Professor Clark are to talk of the pests which trouble the fruit growers of California, and will suggest methods for the destruction of the pests. The work done by the University entomologists in fighting the mosquito plague at Burlingame will be told of by Professor Woodworth."[298]

Malaria control in the Central Valley and foothills (1906-1910)

He concluded his 1906 paper with a discussion of the malaria-causing mosquito *Culex anopheles* in the delta of the Sacramento River and in the Sierra Nevada foothills.

> "From these observations I am not inclined to consider that the *anopheles*, which is the name of the malaria-carrying mosquito, presents any special difficulties. In this State are two regions particularly infested with mosquitoes that need special study; the overflowed lands along the Sacramento River, and the foothill country of the Sierra Nevadas. In both cases the prevailing mosquito is the *anopheles*, and all through that country malaria is common. Members of the entomological department have already given considerable attention to the subject in both these regions, but as yet we have not attempted any practical control work. I can not think that anywhere the problem is more difficult to handle than in the two regions in which such striking results have already been obtained." [299]

C.W.'s colleague William B. Herms was the principal driver of this malaria control effort, but C.W. certainly had a role to play in hiring Herms and helping him behind the scenes. Herms' signature achievement was to succeed, after a four-year effort, in 1915 to get The Mosquito Abatement Districts Act passed in California. This established mosquito control districts. In order to do this, Herms had to establish a coalition between those who sought to control mosquito borne disease and those who wished to exterminate the mosquito.[300]

Alameda County mosquito control records

Alameda County is the county in which both Berkeley and Oakland are located. Some of the first entries on the "District History" on the website of the Alameda County Mosquito Control District read:

> 1904 - City of Oakland [starts] mosquito control in storm drains. The only record currently available is a photograph of a horse-drawn wagon, inspector and equipment from the W.B. Herms [C.W.'s assistant] collection.

1904 - The San Rafael Improvement Club funds mosquito control work on marshes.

1905 - Burlingame Improvement Club funds mosquito control work on marshes.

July 1906 - Mosquito Control, Bulletin No. 178 by H.J. Quayle was published by the University of California.

1908-1910 - Southern Pacific Railroad sponsored a demonstration train [on general Agricultural topics] carrying Dr. William B. Herms to travel throughout California demonstrating how *anopheline* mosquitoes transmit malaria.

1909 - California reported 6,000 cases of malaria.

1910 - First anti-malaria campaign started in Penryn, California [where an intense malaria outbreak had occurred]. The Penryn Fruit Company, Prof. William B. Herms, and Harold F. Gray involved in formation of the program.

May 25, 1915 - The Mosquito Abatement Districts Act passed and signed by the Governor. The bill authorized the formation of mosquito control districts in the State of California.[301]

Summary of C.W.'s contribution to mosquito control

As documented, both C.W. directly and William Herms, who C.W. had hired and encouraged, played a key role in controlling mosquitos in California.

If the strong Bay Area cities of San Rafael and Burlingame had not had salt marsh mosquito control during their early development, their present economies might not be as vibrant as they are. If California had not controlled malaria effectively in the years following, the State may not have had as vibrant of an economy as it did.

Chapter 9 - China

C.W. spent four years of his life in Nanking, now called Nanjing, China doing many things including helping the residents control mosquitoes for the first time, doing experiments with silk worms, helping with early pesticide production there, and writing a textbook on optics.

Silkworm research prior to his trips to China

C.W. was involved in research into the sericulture of silkworms to some degree for much of his career. C.W. did silkworm experiments during his master's program at Illinois from 1886 to 1888.
(See the Chapter 2 section entitled Silkworm experiments at Illinois.)

Like leather goods, silk goods are a somewhat unusual animal product in that the cost of transportation is minimal as compared to the value of the finished product. Additionally, spoilage of the finished product is not a major issue. These two factors together create a situation where, even in the early 20th century, the silk producing countries of the world compete on a global basis. This is unlike many other animal products such as milk and eggs in which the competition is regional.

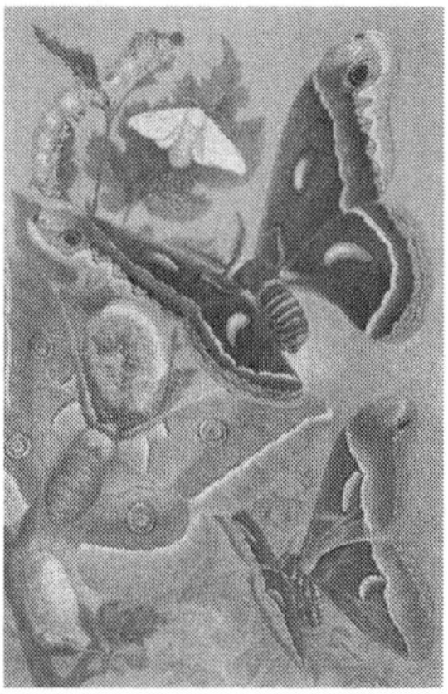

Figure 74 Life stages of Bombyx mori[302]

One impact of C.W.'s research into silkworms must have been for him to make contacts within the California community of Chinese immigrants. This was certainly a contributing factor in leading C.W. to choose to go to Nanking in 1918.

1900

A letter from L.O. Howard of the USDA to C.W. on February 24, 1900 informed him of some silkworm eggs for sale by Mrs. Carrie Williams of San Diego.[303]

Silkworm Circular (1904)

C.W. reported in 1904:

"Attempts are continually being made to revive the growing of silk in California, and the requests for information upon this subject have become so frequent that it seemed desirable to prepare a circular presenting the information in regard to the care of silkworms and to overcome exaggerated ideas as to the profits to be expected from the culture of these insects. This information was therefore prepared and issued as Circular No. 11. Experiments in a small way with silkworms have been under way for two seasons and will be continued on a larger scale in the near future, in the hope that means may be discovered for decreasing the labor item in the production of silk, so that it could be put upon a profitable basis."[304]

Silkworm Experiments (1914)

In 1914, C.W. published a paper laying out an experiment that he wanted help from farmers in conducting. What he was after was to develop a variant of silkworm that could be raised outdoors in California's climate and could be fed with California native plants. The purpose for this was to bring down the cost of silk production in the state so that it could be competitive with that of other countries. He mentions that in some other countries, children provide the labor for silk production.[305]

This effort evidently did not produce the perfect species that would dramatically lower the production costs here. As of now, California does not have a major silk production industry.

First visit to China (1918)

While on sabbatical leave in 1918, he travelled to China and became a lecturer at the University of Nanking (the modern Nanjing) and honorary professor of entomology at the Nanjing University.

The University of Nanking was established in 1911 from a collection of missionary colleges sponsored by American churches. It had about 1000 students at the time. It merged into Nanjing University in 1952.

Figure 75 The University of Nanking in 1920 between C.W.'s assignments there[306]

During his year there he caused mosquitoes to be controlled for the first time in that city's history. Controlling mosquitoes is essential in the battle against mosquito borne illnesses such as malaria and yellow fever. In a short biography in "The Far Eastern Republic" it says: "In one season he cleared the city of Nanking and vicinity of all mosquitoes, a freedom never known before."[307] He also taught courses in silk culture while there and conducted "what is without doubt the largest experiment in sericulture that has ever been carried on in China."[308]

Figure 76 Plaque commemorating C.W.'s first period in China[309]

I have a silver plaque that was given to him. At the top are four large Chinese characters: 金陵大學 or "East direction almost white" or "The sun is about to rise from the East". This is the Chinese name for the University of Nanking, which merged and reorganized with several other institutions in 1952, becoming the modern Nanking University. It says below in Chinese: "Jiang Liang University, entire student body present, Republic of China, year seven, November" (November 1918).[310] Liang Jiang Normal College is the name of an earlier institution that was folded into Nanking University, and may have been retained as the name of a division of the school. Nanking University was recently rated as the #5 university in China.[311]

On his return, a December 23, 1918 Berkeley Gazette article read:

"Professor Woodworth Home From China"

"After spending his sabbatical leave as a member of the faculty of the University of Nanking, China, Professor C.W. Woodworth, on the entomology department at the university, has returned and will resume his work next semester.

In a letter to Dean Thomas Forsyth Hunt of the College of Agriculture, A.J. Bowen of the Chinese university says of Professor Woodworth:

'He has won the hearts of everyone here, Chinese and foreigners. He has been untiring in his work and absolutely unselfish in everything he has done and thought. He has set for us new standards of work and devotion.' "[312]

Lecture series upon his return (1919)

Back home, he gave a lecture series. These speeches were entitled:

March 31, 1919 - "The Educational and Industrial Needs of China"

April 7, 1919 - "The Agriculture of Central China"

April 14, 1919, "Entomological Observations in China"[313][314]

Scholarship founded in his name (1919)

In 1919, one of his former students, E.E. Luther, established a scholarship in C.W.'s honor at the University of Nanking after C.W.'s initial sabbatical there. "Professor Woodworth was formerly connected with the University of Nanking in the department of entomology. He started the summer session in that institution, and was held in high regard by the students. In Chinese, Professor Woodworth will be remembered at the Nanking University as Wu Wai Fu."[315]

E.E. Luther was one of the pair of C.W.'s students that had in 1907 established the Cal Spray Chemical Company, better known by their brand "Ortho".
(See Chapter 11 – The Codling Moth and the California Spray Chemical Company – "Ortho"Ortho".)

China's Greatest Need (1920)

He wrote a paper entitled "China's Greatest Need" that was published in the April 1920 edition of the *Far Eastern Republic*. This was "A monthly Magazine Devoted to the Republic of China By Chinese People, published by the Chinese National Welfare Society in America" in San Francisco, California.

In this paper he argued, "China's greatest need is industrial education." He goes on to say:

> "Another group, including some missionaries and many educated Chinese, give the first lace to the reform of the political situation. The great masses of the Chinese people accept whatever form of government which may be imposed upon them with remarkable docility, and as a natural consequence they are systematically exploited for the enriching of the rulers. Among many of the enlightened this condition has become unbearable, and the political unrest beats itself between the strongly entrenched officialdom and the inertia of the great unthinking masses. Many realize the hopelessness of accomplishing great and permanent reforms until education of the modern practical sort [engineering, scientific agriculture, manual skills and business skills] has permeated and made mobile the great body of the Chinese nation."

He and the others that he was working with had high hopes for the future. He says:

"The plans of the Industrial University include the establishment of branches in all parts of the world because the need of industrial education is not limited to any country but is a universal want which the people of many countries are discussing and endeavoring to meet, though in too small a way. ...

The world is now entering an era of universal intercourse and international relationships making the realization of universal brotherhood essential to the peace and prosperity of the world. This is [a] need of the directing of every influence towards this end."

C.W. took these statements to heart in that he returned to China in 1921 and stayed for three years. The Great Depression, Japan's invasion of Manchuria in 1931, WWII in general, the Chinese Civil War, the Great Leap Forward and the Cultural Revolution all served to slow China's development of effective Industrial education, but China's rise to economic prominence in the 21st century has certainly been driven by the ability of the Chinese people to engage in technological enterprises on the world stage, exactly the thing that C.W. was talking about in 1919.

A tribute to C.W. as he left for China the second time

In 1921, a tribute to C.W. was written by C.W.'s long-time colleague, E.J. Wickson, who was then an editor of The Pacific Rural Press, on the eve of his second journey to China. Dr. Wickson was the agronomy professor that was trying to teach a few entomology classes before C.W. was hired, thirty years before. The article was published on the front page of the *Pacific Rural Press* on October 8, 1921 along with a large photo of him teaching. It is reprinted here in its entirety:

"It is a big idea to do your job in California so well as to unconsciously open a door in China for a most distinguished undertaking in your mature years. It is a big idea to throw yourself into the undertaking of your early manhood with such singleness and sincerity of purpose, to bend all your talent and energy to it and to live such an upright life and thus to conserve all your mental and physical strength, that when the call comes to do something greater when you have just passed fifty years of age, you can enter upon a new task with all the eagerness of your youth and with much greater confidence because of your conscious position of the increased ability to succeed, which comes from experience in conceiving and doing things. Such is the general lesson which we draw, for all men, young and old, for our close personal knowledge of what Professor C.W. Woodworth has done during the last thirty years in the University of California and from what we expect him to do during the next few years as State Entomologist of Kiangsu Province - a position which he has just accepted from the Chinese government - upon the duties of which he will enter next December.

California is full of personal friends of Professor Woodworth – friends from his sunny class-rooms and laboratories; friends from contact with him in field studies from protection of California products; friends from conferences with him at Farmers' Institutes and Fruit-Growers' conventions; friends from reading the lucid and pertinent expositions of the relations of science to practice in the large literature of economic entomology which his pen has created during the last thirty years. To all such we confide our own judgment of him and of his work formed from what we have seen, as it were, from the inside, during the whole period of his activity in this state. Professor Woodworth has the richest and readiest, the most serviceable and fertile mental equipment we ever connected up with. His temperament is the most sanguine and optimistic and his disposition the most uninterruptedly genial that we ever have basked in, and his unselfish devotion to the good, the happiness and the success of others, passes all our experience and observation of the humane attitudes of other men. His capacity for work and the ease and lightness with which he enters upon and discharges it, are only rivaled by the originality and resources of inventive imagination with which he carried work through. He was the first trained entomologist to enter the service of the University in 1891, and during the first decade thereafter the institution was offering more courses and instructing more students in this branch of science than any other institution in the country. He rearranged the course of study in the College of Agriculture and ministered to the first great increase of agricultural students, which appeared about 1900, and for more than a decade the numbers of students in all branches of agricultural science and practice followed the curricular of which he was the great architect. In the planning of research he was similarly resourceful and efficient and the publications of the California Experiment Station about fifteen years ago surpassed those of any other American institution in commanding the attention of authorities on economic entomology everywhere.

> Obviously we have no space for specific references, nor do the friends of Professor Woodworth need them; they know well enough what he is and what he has done in California, and now they send him forth, with regret for their own loss and deprivation, of course, but with confidence and Godspeed, as their gift of one whom they can ill-afford to lose, to lend his aid to the new development and advancement of the oldest and greatest country of the Orient. Associated with his official work for the government which calls him will be the headship of the Division of Entomology in the National Southwestern University, supported by the government and manned chiefly by Chinese professors who are graduates of American colleges. At this institution he will have his headquarters and a Bureau of Entomology.

Second visit to China (1921-24)

He returned for a three-year period in 1921-1924. U.C. granted him a "leave of absence until June 30, 1922, to engage in a campaign against insects in the province of Kiangsu, China."[316] He returned for a period in 1923. He attended a meeting in New York City in April of 1923 and a meeting in Berkeley in August of 1923. His leave was renewed in 1923 with no set end date.[317]

During this period, he organized the Kiangsu Provincial Bureau of Entomology as well as many other things. In the words of the president of the University of Nanking, "He served China in a magnificent way."

A Rockefeller Foundation report summarizing the work of their China Medical Board for the year 1922 says:

"In close association with the University [National Southeastern University in Nanking (Nanjing)] is the Bureau of Entomology of Kiangsu, which has carried on successful work in keeping down flies and mosquitos in various localities, and is planning to deal also with insects which attack field crops and fruit-trees. Dr.[sic] C.W. Woodworth of the University of California, has had charge of this work during the past year and is returning for another year of service."[318]

In historian William J. Haas' biography of the scientist Gist Gee, who worked for the Rockefeller Foundation, is the following description where C.W. stayed in Nanjing:

"Gee and Orrin Smith spent three days in Beijing; ... On 24 October they arrived in Nanjing. Smith was put up with Southeastern's American physical education teacher, McCloy, whose home had become a minor center for Westerners in Nanjing. Besides McCloy's family, there was C.W. Woodworth, a University of California entomologist on leave from Berkeley to head up the new Bureau of Entomology in Nanjing. Hans Driesch and his wife were living with McCloy, too. Like John Dewey and Bertrand Russell, the German biologist was creating a stir in China with his philosophy; .... ."[319]

His colleague at Cal, Dr. Edwin C. Van Dyke, joined C.W. in 1923. A note in a journal says:

"During the year 1923 Dr. Edwin C. Van Dyke's address will be, College of Agriculture, Nanking, China, where he will carry on some of the work already started by Prof. Woodworth. He expects to do some traveling as well in North China and Japan."[320] Dr. Van Dyke was a former medical doctor, who served the University of California from 1913 to 1939 and became an emeritus professor, was joined in China by his wife Mary, who was also interested in natural history. Dr. Van Dyke became a world expert in Coleoptera (beetles).[321]

Fly Swatter Patent (1921, 1923)

While he was in China, on December 14, 1921, C.W. applied for a patent on a fly swatter. Presumably he had worked with his attorneys on the application before he left. The patent was for "an improved fly swatter which is of simple and inexpensive construction and which is devoid of metallic parts, such as are liable to injure curtains and draperies."

> "The present invention contemplates the formation of a fly swatter from a single stalk of bamboo by splitting the end thereof into a large number of fine splints and then spreading the splits apart and fastening them in such position."[322]

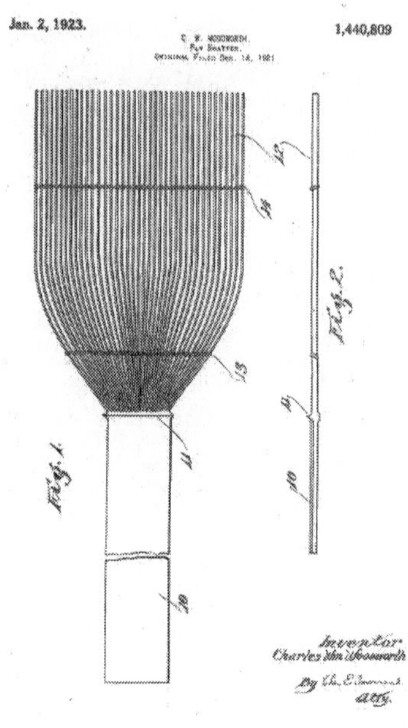

Figure 77 U.S. Patent #1,440,809, Fly Swatter Patent

His niece reported to me that they had a large bag of the fly swatters around their house that C.W. had given to them when she was young. She would sell them to get enough money to go to the movies.[323]

With the advent of plastic, bamboo fly swatters have gone out of fashion. None seem to be available for purchase from any source.

The Wings of *Bombyx mori* (1923)

In February of 1923, he published an anatomical study of the wings of the domesticated silkworm entitled "The Wings of *Bombyx mori*". The paper starts out:

> The comparison of the wild species of mulberry silkworm, *Bombyx mandarina*, and its domesticated descendant, *Bombyx mori*, is of particular interest as showing the effect which selection and forcing (which have increased the size of the body til the wings are well nigh functionless) may have on the structure of the wing.[324]

C.W. had deep knowledge of insect wings following his earlier publication of "The Wing Veins of Insects".

He concluded that domestication had resulted in: "(1) Slightly greater variability, (2) loss of distinctive peculiarities, and (3) a tendency towards extremely primitive conditions of structure."[325]

Speech in NYC about China (1923)

He returned at least once during his time there, travelling in western direction. He arrived in New York on April 5, 1923 on the APL President Roosevelt (there had only been one President Roosevelt at that point, so the name "Theodore" was not necessary.) The ship had sailed from Southampton.[326]

He is recorded as having attended a meeting of the New York Entomological Society at the American Museum of Natural History in New York City on April 17, 1923. The minutes of that meeting record that:

> "Mr. Woodworth gave an interesting account of his efforts to train the Chinese at Nanking in economic entomology, particularly in exterminating flies and mosquitoes and thus reducing the deaths from typhoid, cholera and malaria. Twenty-seven men were used in continuous inspection of possible breeding places, dipping the mosquito larvae out of the pools and destroying the fly larvae by sprinkling with cyanide solution. The control of locusts and of silk worm diseases was also in progress."[327]

Microscope Theory (1924)

He published his book "Microscope Theory" in 1924, during his time there.
(See the Chapter 12 section entitled *Microscope theory (1924)*).

Return in 1924

He departed for home from Shanghai on June 7, 1924 on the American President Lines ship the S.S. President Wilson. He arrived in San Francisco on June 27, 1924. The ship stopped at Kobe, Yokohama, and Honolulu on its journey. The ship's passenger list shows that the ship carried a variety of passengers including many Chinese citizens and some Japanese citizens. A large contingent of U.S. citizens that had been born in the Philippines, then a U.S. Territory, boarded in Honolulu presumably having connected there from another APL ship.[328]

Overall

Many of the details of what he accomplished in China are hidden from view by time and language, yet there does seem to be evidence of a flurry of activity in science around Nanjing during his two periods there. For example, the Science Society of China established its headquarters in Nanjing in 1918 and a major biological laboratory there in 1922.

It is fortunate that he came home before Nanjing was captured by communist forces in March of 1927, just over two and a half years after his return in one of the early engagements of the Chinese Civil War. The Rape of Nanking happened just ten years after that in 1937 during the Second Sino-Japanese War in the build-up to WWII. It is a virtual certainty that some of the people that C.W. worked with there were displaced or killed by the combination of these two events.

His wife's death

Around the time of his return, in September of 1924, C.W.'s beloved wife Leonora died of complications from rheumatoid arthritis and gall bladder surgery. The timing between her death and his return is unclear. His son served as the witness on her death certificate, but that does not necessarily mean that C.W. had not yet returned. (See the Chapter 14 section entitled Leonora's Death.)

What is clear is that C.W. did not engage in any of the advocacy efforts in 1924 or 1925 similar to what he did upon his return from China in 1919, presumably due to the grief of her death.

Letter to his niece (1939)

C.W. enjoyed teaching and liked to teach people about Chinese characters. He wrote to his niece, Celina in 1939, just a year before his death and gave her a lesson in Chinese numbers. His lesson is as good today as it was then.

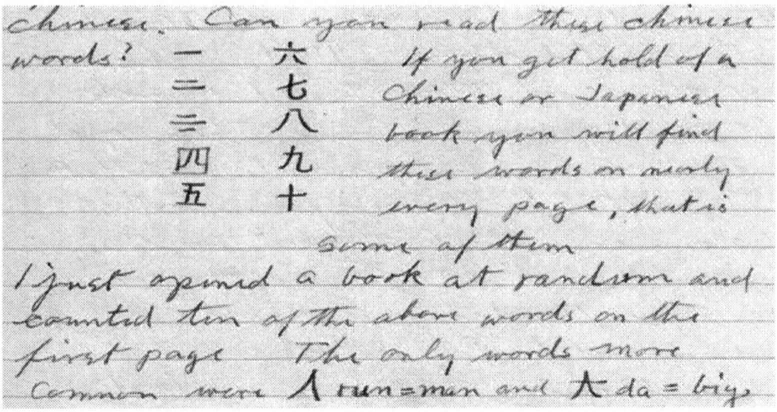
chinese. Can you read these chinese
words? 一 六 If you get hold of a
二 七 Chinese or Japanese
三 八 book you will find
四 九 these words on nearly
五 十 every page, that is
some of them
I just opened a book at random and
counted ten of the above words on the
first page. The only words more
Common were 人 run = man and 大 da = big.

Figure 78 Chinese characters in a 1939 letter to his niece, Celina[329]

Mementos of his China trips

[Author's note: This entire section is an author's note.] He returned with mementos of his journeys to China including a Chinese hat and coat that my mother enjoyed seeing him put on.[330] I have five items from his journeys there: the previously mentioned silver plaque, a small collection of Chinese coins, a small screen, a small green bowl that was a gift to me from his niece Mary, and a large Rose Canton bowl.

Chinese coin collection

Figure 79 Collection of Chinese coins given by C.W. to my mother, Elizabeth Woodworth Holden when she was a child[331]

C.W. gave my mother a small but nice collection of Chinese coins. They are all copper and are all ten fen coins. The four coins in the lower left are from the Republic of China (front and back of two different designs). The coins in the upper left are the fronts and backs of coins issued by three different provinces. The coins in the upper right are the front of coins issued by seven other provinces. In the lower right is the bamboo case that holds the coin collection.

The name of the country during the era of C.W.'s journeys was the Republic of China (which is now the name of the country on Taiwan). During that time there were 28 provinces and 15 other areas, so C.W. managed to collect coins from just under a quarter of them for his granddaughter.

The coins also illustrate a piece of history. The issuance of currency independently by many provinces (and banks) combined with an increase in the price of silver caused a currency crisis and hyperinflation in China in the 1920s and 1930s. There was a major currency reform in 1935 that only partially resolved the situation. China had currency problems for an extended period after this. Even today, China has a manipulated and not fully convertible currency.

Small screen

Figure 80 Small Chinese screen given to Elizabeth Woodworth Holden[332]

Green bowl

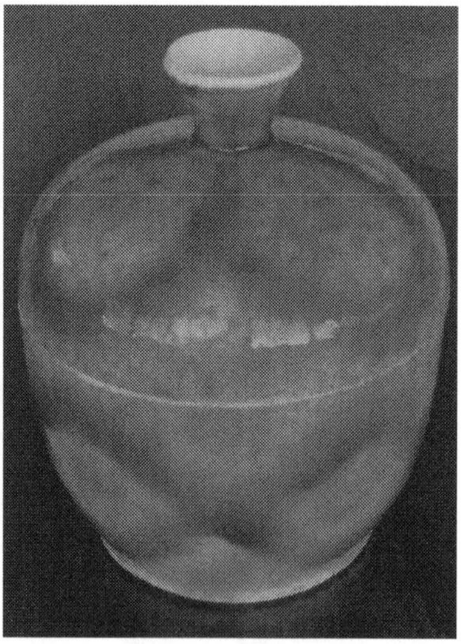

Figure 81 Small green bowl given to me by C.W.'s niece, Mary Detrich[333]

C.W. gave this small bowl to his sister, Minnie Woodworth. Her daughter Mary inherited it from her. In March of 2008, when Mary and her daughters came west to present the C.W. Woodworth Award at the Napa, California PBESA meeting, she gave this bowl to me.

Rose Canton bowl

A large and beautiful "rose canton" bowl was given to my wife Joann and me as a wedding present from my Uncle Jim and Aunt Betty Woodworth in 2002. He had inherited it from C.W.'s daughter, my great Aunt Elizabeth.

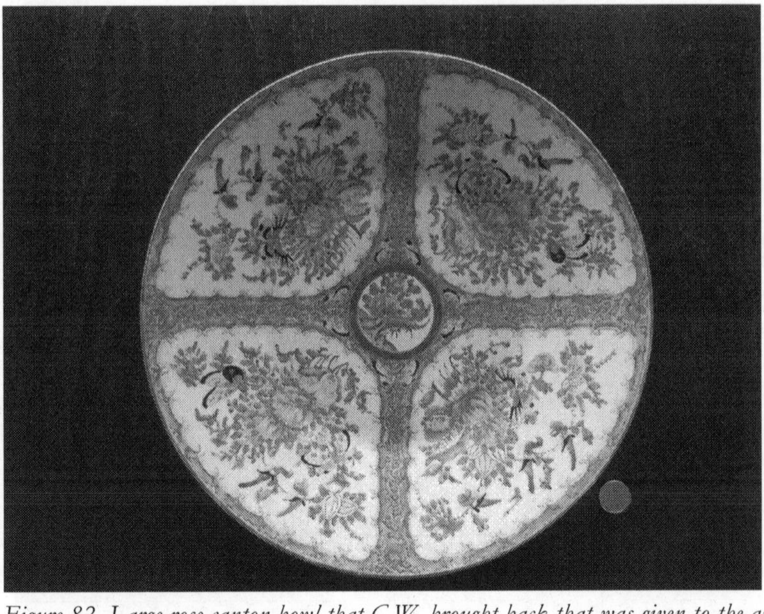

Figure 82 Large rose canton bowl that C.W. brought back that was given to the author and his wife as a wedding present by Uncle Jim and Aunt Betty Woodworth. A quarter is included for size reference.[334]

Chapter 10 - Public Policy Work

Through the course of his career, C.W. became involved in several efforts to influence public policy. He was particularly involved in California's early efforts to pass laws governing the responsible use of insecticides. He also suggested that a law be passed related to emergency powers for county commissioners when faced with locust infestations. He wrote two papers and gave a speech laying out the type of background and experiences that a county commissioner should have. He became involved in an effort to get industrial education on a sound footing in China. Finally, he became involved in two local efforts: the founding of the first public library in Berkeley and the running of the Chung Mei Home for Chinese Boys.

(See the Chapter 9 section entitled China's Greatest Need (1920)).

First public library in Berkeley (1892)

The plaque in front of his landmarked home indicates that C.W. was involved in the establishment of the first public library in Berkeley.[335] He was on the library's board of directors at its initial establishment in 1892.

The library was founded with 264 books in 1893, and buildings were constructed in 1905 and 1931.[336]

The book *History of the Berkeley Schools* has the following account of his involvement, which is itself a condensed version a 1905 Berkeley Daily Gazette article from January 27, 1905:

"Dr. J. Edson Kelsey spoke on "The Beginning" as follows:

In 1892 my brother and I owned a drug store on Shattuck Avenue near Addison Street. At that time there were several students who were making their way through the University by reporting for the San Francisco newspapers. Among the young men who made our store their headquarters was William H. Waster, our Assemblyman. In the fall of that year there was a great sensation when it became known that a number of boys were frequenting a billiard parlor where gambling and drinking were indulged in. As one of the boys who worked for me frequented the place, I became much interested. A letter was written to the Berkeley "Advocate" stating the facts in the case and suggesting the advisability of fitting up a room with books and games, where the boys could have the proper influence about them when away from home. Mrs. Marquand who was then the editor of the "Advocate," became interested and kept the subject before the people by frequent notices.

We interviewed some of the leading citizens and found many who favored the idea. At a mass meeting held in Shattuck Hall, D.L. Bishop was elected temporary chairman and H. Sangster secretary. A permanent organization was formed, with Waste, president, Sangster, secretary, and Kelsey treasurer.

We rented a store in a convenient location on Shattuck Avenue and had it fitted up into two rooms. All helped in getting ready to open - some by gifts of money; some by books and magazines; others by labor, and John Boyd, by giving the use of his horse and wagon for a number of days to bring in he donations. The front room was the library with linoleum on the floor, long tables for magazines, comfortable high-backed chairs, and a desk and table for the librarian. There were also a few book cases, but a sufficient number were soon provided. The rear room, separated from the front room by swinging doors had a Brussels carpet, chairs, a piano, tables, etc. - and was provided with many sorts of games. Both rooms were lighted by oil lanterns.

Miss Lucy W. Luhn was our first librarian. Mr. J.D. Layman, one of the first contributors, gave a full set of the works of Oliver Wendell Holmes, in consideration of which we were to name the library the Holmes Public Library. Mr. Lajonan was at this time one of the assistant librarians at the University. He spoke of "The Struggle" as follows:

The Board of Directors elected on the evening of December third, 1892, when the Holmes Library Association was organized as follows: W.H. Waste, president; J.H. Sangster, secretary; Dr. J.E. Kelsey, treasurer; D.L. Bishop, P.R. Boon, J.I. Logan, E.B. Payne, F.K. Shattuck, S.D. Waterman, E.T. Whittemore, C.W. Woodworth, J.D. Layman, [directors]."[337]

[Author's note: It also seems likely (but with no evidence of it) that C.W. could have been involved with the 1905 library building because John Galen Howard, with whom C.W. collaborated just the year before on the functional requirements for the design of Agricultural Hall, became the architect.]
(See Chapter 15 - Agricultural Hall (Wellman Hall).)

This was the first building for the Berkeley Public Library. Before this time, the library was located in rooms at 2156 Shattuck Avenue.

C.W.'s letter about the Harvard School for Cuban teachers (1900)

The United States obtained the territories of Cuba and the Philippines as a result of the 1898 Spanish-American War. Shortly thereafter, Harvard started an educational program for Cuban teachers. The University of California was contemplating a similar program for teachers from the Philippines. C.W. wrote a letter to U.C. president Benjamin Wheeler about his impressions of the Harvard program.

"I arrived here at Cambridge while the school was in full operation and have been a very interested observer of its closing days. I have taken the trouble to talk with the town people as well as the members of the faculty of the University. It seems to be the uniform opinion that more good has been done than the same amount of effort could have accomplished in any other way. …

I was pleased to see the alertness and interest of the Cubans, of course it would hardly be otherwise given the novelty of everything. They all had the air that the Californian has learned to recognize as characteristic of the tourist. This receptivity of mind just the spirit every teacher strives to awaken, and when awake makes teaching easy and effective."[338]

Grasshoppers in California (1902)

C.W. published the thirty-six page California State Bulletin number 142 entitled "Grasshoppers in California" in 1902[339]. There had been outbreaks of locust swarms in Roseville, Fair Oaks, and Orangevale, California. These communities are now all nice suburbs of Sacramento, but back then they were rural communities on the outskirts of Sacramento filled with orchards and agriculture.

These locusts damaged the fruit trees in these communities. Locusts are the swarming phase of certain grasshoppers. They typically occur when a population of grasshoppers reaches a certain density. Recent research has revealed that when grasshopper's back legs are in frequent contact with other grasshoppers, grasshoppers begin to eat much more, breed much more easily, and become migratory. They can travel great distances, rapidly strip fields and damage crops.

C.W. had trouble inducing the local authorities to destroy the grasshoppers in their breeding grounds "on account of the possibility of local authorities become responsible for damages". He described methods of controlling swarms in both their flying and drifting modes. He then described how to control them in their breeding ground by plowing in the fall or burning over. He also recommended making "a careful survey to determine the breeding grounds of the locusts". He also advised "to secure legislation which will empower the local authorities to carry out the necessary measures for destroying the locusts". This is a sign of his growing awareness of the public policy aspects of entomology. In this particular case, the breeding grounds are not necessarily in the same place or owned by the same people as the fruit trees are, so legislation was needed to allow local authorities to have the right to take significant action, such as plowing a field, potentially causing inconvenience or harm to the landowner of the breeding ground.

Background on Paris green

Paris green, also known as copper (II) arsenite is nasty stuff that kills insects really well because it is a form of arsenic. It is called Paris green because it is green and was used as a paint pigment (color index green 21). It is a pale blue green when finely ground and a deeper true green when coarsely ground. It was used as a pigment for centuries, sometimes poisoning the painter.[340]

Paris green is manufactured by combining the deep blue copper (II) acetate with white arsenic, arsenic trioxide. Copper (II) acetate is one of the forms of verdigris or copper patina that you see on buildings. It is the form produced when copper is weathered in the presence of acetic acid (vinegar). Arsenic trioxide is made from the naturally occurring mineral orpiment, As_2S_3, which is a yellow material that is sometimes found around volcanic fumaroles.

Around the turn of the century, Paris green was being used in large quantities as an insecticide, 1500 to 2000 tons annually in the United States.[341] From today's point of view, dumping many tons of arsenic into the environment every year for decades was a profoundly bad situation. Of course, there was an equally profound lack of knowledge in that era about the effects of such poisoning on humans and on the environment.

The record of a lawsuit in Kentucky from 1902 reads: 'The defendant employed him in July 1901, to scatter and sprinkle paris-green on his potato-vines to kill ladybugs; without warning plaintiff that the paris-green mixture was poisonous; that the weather was hot, and then he, the said plaintiff, left his clothes open, and the flesh of the exposed portions of his person, coming in contact with said paris green, was poisoned, and that he was thereby made sore and caused to suffer for many weeks in body and mind, etc.; all through the gross carelessness and negligence of defendant in failing to give him notice that the said paris-green mixture was poisonous, etc."[342] The lawsuit found against the plaintiff, saying that "The defendant exceeded the scope of his employment in sprinkling paris green elsewhere than on the potato-vines ..." [Author's note: So much for worker safety laws in Kentucky in 1902.]

It turns out the most harmful part of Paris Green is not the copper (II) arsenite itself, although that is still poisonous, but is instead the other forms of arsenic that commonly make their way into real Paris green products. Those other forms include the water-soluble arsenious oxide (without the copper) and white arsenic, which is arsenic trioxide (As_2O_3) from which Paris Green is made.

Louisiana law regulating Paris green (1890)

The first insecticide law was passed by Louisiana in 1890 that regulating the purity of Paris green. This law directed the board of agriculture to distribute circulars detailing the composition of brands of Paris green along with further provisions.

As much of the nation's supply of Paris green was manufactured in New York, the State of New York passed a law regulating the percentages of impurities in Paris green in 1898.[343] The percentages were badly defined in that original law and were revised later.

California law regulating Paris green (1901)

On February 28, 1901, "An Act to prevent fraud in the sale of Paris green used as an insecticide", became law in the State of California. The short and tightly focused law was the first law in California to regulate pesticides and can be considered a key early law in California's strong legacy of environmental leadership. The State of New York had passed a similar law three years before.

Section 3 of that law said that "Paris green, when sold, offered or exposed for sale, as an insecticide, in this State, shall contain at least fifty per centum of arsenious oxid [sic], and shall not contain more than four per centum of the same in the uncombined state.

Section 4 of that law said that "The Director of the California State Agricultural Station at Berkeley shall examine or cause to be examined different brands of paris [sic] green sold, offered or exposed for sale within the State, and cause samples of the same to be analyzed, and shall report results of analyses forthwith to the Secretary of the State Board of Horticulture and to the party or parties submitting said samples, and such report shall be final as regards its quality."[344]

California Insecticide Law (1906, 1912, 1913)

1906 proposal for the First Insecticide Law

C.W. had much to do with the responsible use of pesticides. He became involved in an effort to draft a law which addressed insecticides in a more general way than was done in the 1901 law's narrow focus on Paris green.

He proposed and drafted the first California Insecticide Law in extension bulletin 182 in 1906.

In C.W.'s obituary, E.O. Essig said : "...he drafted the first California Insecticide Law in 1906, was largely instrumental in securing its passage in 1911, and administered the law until July 1, 1923.[345]

The sections of C.W.'s proposal are paraphrased:

1. Every package of insecticide must have a detailed labeled.
2. All insecticides must be registered.
3. Samples of insecticides are taken and tested annually.
4. Additional samples may be taken and tested at any time.
5. The results of the testing are to be published annually.
6. $1800 is appropriated to set up a laboratory.
7. Fee is charged for a certificate.
8. The fees are for the purpose of the testing.
9. There are fines for violating this act.
10. The certificate is the evidence of testing.
11. The act will take effect on 7/1/1907.

C.W.'s proposal may have had an indirect effect on the 1910 Federal Insecticide Act. The key innovation was that C.W.'s proposal treated insecticides generally, rather than focusing on Paris green and lead arsenate, as previous laws had. His proposal does not mention Paris green.

The proposal had a direct impact on the 1911 California Insecticide Law. Numerous sections in that law were taken word-for-word from C.W.'s proposal.

Run-up to the 1910 Federal Insecticide Act

In a the 1917 Proceedings of the Thirty-Fourth Annual Convention of the Association of Official Agricultural Chemists, their president, J.K. Haywood of the Bureau of Chemistry, Washington D.C. said:

"The credit of suggestion Federal legislation relative to this subject is to be given to the Association of Economic Entomologists of the United States, and more especially to Professor E.D. Sanderson of that association. ... On February 3, 1908 professor Sanderson requested that Dr. [H.W.] Wiley formulate a Federal insecticide law. ... The proposed law ... was introduced in the Senate (April 6, 1908) ..., as Senate Bill 6515."[346]

Dr. Harvey W. Wiley was then the Chief of the Bureau, U.S. Department of Agriculture. He is known as the "Father of the Pure Food and Drugs Act". Professor E.D. Sanderson was the Director of the New Hampshire Agricultural Experiment Station.

C.W. and E.D. Sanderson would certainly have been aware of each other. Their writings appear many times in the same publications, and Charles Moores Weed credits them both in the acknowledgements of a textbook. It seems likely that E.D. Sanderson would have read C.W.'s 1906 proposal before his involvement the 1908 Federal law.

The 1910 Federal law does address insecticides in general as C.W.'s proposal did, although it also has text addressing Paris green and lead arsenate specifically.

1910 Federal Insecticide Act

The Federal Insecticide Act of 1910 (FIA) was passed in the immediate wake of the 1906 Pure Food and Drug Act, which was designed to protect American consumers from contaminated food.

FIA focused on ensuring the chemical quality of insecticides. Neither the 1910 Federal law nor the subsequent 1911 California law enacted environmental protections, but instead both laws focused on making sure that the contents of insecticides where known and were unadulterated. FIA was designed to prevent economic exploitation of farmers. There were far fewer insecticides in use during that era, so the regulatory environment was simpler.

In 1947, the FIA was amended by the Federal Insecticide, Rodenticide and Fungicide Act (FIRFA), adding provisions regarding the impact of pesticides on humans. FIRFA has been amended 11 additional times since, adding protection of the environments and assigning enforcement to the Environmental Protection Agency.

FIRFA was called by the historian Christopher J. Bosso "one of the granddaddies of federal regulation".[347] The FIA was 37 years before the FIRFA.

The sections of the 1910 Federal Insecticide Act are paraphrased:

1. Manufacturing adulterated or misbranded insecticides is a crime.
2. Importation of adulterated or misbranded insecticides is a crime.
3. Regulations will be promulgated for this.
4. Authorizes the Dept. of Agriculture to conduct testing
5. District attorneys have the obligation to prosecute reported infractions.
6. Defines terms.
7. Defines adulterated Paris green and lead arsenate and gives a general definition of adulteration for other insecticides.
8. Defines mis-branding in several situations.
9. Gives an exception for wholesalers and dealers of insecticides.
10. Directs the U.S. Treasury to provide samples of imports to the Dept. of Agriculture

11. Defines terms.
12. Names the act.
13. The act will take effect on 4/16/1910.

The following table compares the text of C.W.'s 1906 proposal with the adopted Text of the 1910 FIA.

C.W.'s 1906 Proposal Section	Content of C.W. proposal	Adopted 1910 Federal Insecticide Act
1	Labeling requirement	Sections 1 and 8 have overlap – section 7 has the generalized definition of insecticides beyond just Paris green
2	Registration requirement	Section 11 has overlap
3	Annual samples taken	Sections 3 and 11 have overlap
4	Authorized to take samples	Section 4 and 11 have overlap
5	Publish testing results annually	-
6	Appropriation for testing	-
7	Fees for testing	Section 11 has overlap
8	Use of fees	-
9	Fine for infraction	Sections 1 and 2 has overlap
10	Use of certificate in court	-

Table 7 Comparison of C.W.'s 1906 Proposal with the 1910 Federal Insecticide Law

1911 California Insecticide Law

He writes in his 1912 paper *California Insecticide Industries*[348]:

> "One of the most important results of this affiliation has been the enactment of the [1911] California Insecticide Law, a measure demanded by our leading manufacturers as well as by the fruit growers and which takes advanced ground regarding the guarantee of the quality of the goods offered for sale in this State. This law is sure to have a large influence upon the legislation of other states, and if our prediction of the dominance of California insecticide industries is well founded, it will have a direct and positive influence upon the economic entomology of the Pacific Coast.
>
> The distinctive feature of the California Law is the requirement of the statement on the label of the composition of the insecticide. The manufacturer or dealer must guarantee, and the law requires under severe penalties, that he honestly guarantees, the composition of the insecticide he offers for sale.
>
> ... The great desideratum is the improvement and standardization of the great host of what may be called the minor insecticides. Those that are used in the spraying of orchard trees have been reduced to a good degree of uniformity, due to the work of the economic entomologists and the use of these preparations correspondingly enlarged as the users appreciated more fully their reliability.
>
> The California insecticide law will go far to standardize the other insecticides by giving publicity to their composition, provided that we contribute our share in the study of their relative efficiency."

Details of the 1911 California Insecticide Law

On May 1, 1911, Act 48 of the California Code was approved. It was amended somewhat in 1913. The law is seven pages long and is very direct and understandable.

The first portion of section 11 of the law starts word for word from C.W.'s 1906 proposal. Section 13 of the law has many words from section 4 of C.W.'s proposal. Section 15 of the law is word for word from his proposal. Section 16 appropriates $5,000 per year whereas C.W. just asked for $1,800 one time to equip a laboratory.

C.W. proposed that U.C. test and register pesticides, which was not adopted in the law. The law instead says that it is illegal to manufacture or sell adulterated insecticide and says that U.C. will do the testing in any questionable case. That said, the law provides stiffer penalties that in C.W.'s proposal.

The law's sections are paraphrased:

1. It is unlawful to manufacture adulterated insecticide.
2. It is unlawful to sell adulterated insecticide.
3. The U.C. Agricultural Experiment Station is responsible for examining samples of insecticides.
4. The District Attorneys have the duty to prosecute.
5. The experiment station shall provide certificates of inspection.
6. Definitions are provided of Insecticide, Paris green, Lead Arsenate and Fungicide.
7. A detailed definition is given of adulterated Paris green and Lead Arsenate and a general definition is given for other adulteration.
8. The term "misbranded" is identified.
9. Responsibility was defined in cases with intermediary wholesalers.
10. Responsibility was apportioned between persons and corporations.
11. Proper labeling was defined.
12. Altered but clearly labeled product was allowed and drugs were exempted.
13. The U.C. Agricultural Experiment Station will analyze any sample received together with one dollar.
14. The U.C. Agricultural Experiment Station is authorized to buy a small sample of any lot of insecticide at any time. 14a defines a

series of unregulated products such as fly-paper, borax and moth balls.

15. The U.C. Agricultural Experiment Station shall publish its results.
16. Five thousand dollars per year is allocated for enforcement.
17. Conflict of interest is not allowed.
18. Analytical fees received shall be used for enforcement.
19. This repeals the 1901 law about Paris Green.
20. The law takes effect on July 1, 1911.

The following table compares C.W.'s 1906 proposal with the adopted 1911 law on a section-by-section basis. There are numerous stretches of the law that used C.W.'s words directly.

C.W.'s 1906 Proposal Section	Content of C.W. proposal	Adopted 1911 California Insecticide Law
1	Labeling requirement	Section 11 starts word for word from C.W.'s proposal
2	Registration requirement	(not adopted)
3	Annual samples taken	Section 13 contain many phrases
4	Authorized to take samples	Many phrases used in section 14
5	Publish testing results annually	Section 15 is word for word
6	Appropriation for testing (1,800)	$5,000 appropriated annually
7	Fees for testing	Section 13 has the fee
8	Use of fees	Section 18 is word for word
9	Fine for infraction	Section 1 has stiffer penalties
10	Use of certificate in court	Section 5 is word for word

Table 8 Comparison of C.W.'s 1906 proposal with the 1911 California Insecticide Law

This law was an important measure in helping to ensure that farmers had insecticides that were accurately labeled. If the insecticide was too weak, it would not work right. If it was adulterated, for example if it had too much water-soluble arsenic, their trees could be killed, their workers harmed or the environment could be harmed. This assurance was important enough to C.W. and to the farmers to have them work to get this simple and direct law passed.

As simple as it was, this was an important early step in California's long history of leadership in environmental legislation. This law identified a toxic set of substances and took a key first step in their regulation by making sure that they were at least labeled accurately and that the contents matched the labels. This early success was one of a number of early roots that has led to environmental laws such as California's fuel and lighting efficiency standards.

C.W. would have been pleased that his registration idea was eventually adopted. Section 12811 of California's current Food and Agricultural Code reads:

> "Every manufacturer of, importer of, or dealer in any pesticide, except a person that sells any raw material to a manufacturer of any pesticide or dealer or agent that sells any pesticide that has been registered by the manufacturer or wholesaler shall obtain a certificate of registration from the department before the pesticide is offered for sale."[349]

Requisites of a County Commissioner (1904, 1911)

C.W. wrote two papers that discuss the background and experiences that are needed to be able to do a good job at county commissioner. Those papers are: The Entomological Equipment of the Horticultural Commissioner (1904), and Requisites of a County Commissioner (1911), which was a transcript of a speech.

In December 1911 he gave a speech on this topic to the Fruit Growers' Convention.[350] In this speech, he first praised the new examination requirements for commissioners.

He then illustrated the difficulty with which the commissioners were faced. Commissioners had to sort out whether a given pest arriving at a port should be destroyed based on such factors as the economic harm caused and whether the pest was already completely established. He said:

> "Had it been possible to have drafted laws covering all contingencies in which the horticultural commissioner could have been clearly defined, the answer to the question relative to the commissioner would have been simply that they should enforce the laws. Many commissioners have pretended to assume that their duties were thus limited and prescribe, and have justified arbitrary and vicious acts on the ground that they must carry out the provisions of the law, however unjust and unnecessary the provisions may have been.
>
> The great majority of the commissioners, I am glad to say, have appreciated more clearly the character and purpose of these laws and have tried to apply reason and common sense to their interpretation, and have endeavored to apply the principle that the object of the law was to give them power to serve the people in accordance with wisdom and justice.

An ideal law is one in which the requirements are explicit and definite, but when the horticultural laws were first enacted, the lawmakers where wholly uninformed as to the details which would develop in their administration, and, in consequence, found it necessary to make many of their provisions vague and ambiguous, and even today I doubt if any feel competent to draw up a measure that would be acceptable as meeting all contingencies that might arise."

He later tried to define the questions:

"The two great questions for a horticultural commissioner to answer are, first, what is a pest, and second, what is wise to attempt to do about it?"

He gave the example of the black scale, which was the worst pest then in California. It was a serious pest on lemon and orange trees where it was fought aggressively. It was a widespread but very mild pest on olives and some ornamentals and generally was not treated for on those trees. It was abundant on wild chaparral but only away from the hot interior valleys.

He concluded by suggesting that a committee for the "Unification of Horticultural Inspection" be formed. This committee would:

"consider and report upon all proposed changes in the law; that it gather together all available information concerning similar work in other states and countries and make a special study of the practice of the horticultural commissioners in this State, and that they formulate and submit plans of procedure and draft such amendments to our laws as may see wise. Such a committee carefully selected would seem to be the best means available for improving the character of the work of the office of county horticultural commissioner."

This paper shows that C.W. provided leadership in the public policy domain surrounding county horticultural commissioners, which serve the front line of the law for agriculture.

California Horticultural Quarantine (1909)

C.W. wrote about the failures of agricultural quarantine in 1909 in the *Journal of Economic Entomology*. He provided a list of 11 invasive species that have become established in California, nearly a third of the species that were on a list of insects being watched that was published 13 years before. He concludes with:

> "This list constitutes nearly a third of those mentioned by Craw, and does not by any means include all the species that have become residents of the state during this interval. The horticultural officers were particularly on guard against these scales [after the disastrous importation of San Jose scale from Asia circa 1870], but they nevertheless found admittance. These facts do not reflect upon the care of our horticultural officers because their work has always been most painstaking and earnest, but do seem to indicate the futility of such efforts."[351]

Chung Mei Home for Chinese Boys

Closer to home, C.W. became involved with the Chung Mei Home for Chinese boys in Berkeley.[352][353] This home was later associated with the Minority Adoption Committee of the Children's Home Society.[354]

Charles Shepard founded the Chung Mei Home for homeless Chinese boys in 1923. By the time it closed in 1954 the home had served 800 boys.[355] The home was supported as follows "one third is provided by state and county funds for boys committed by the courts, one third by parents who themselves make commitments, and the remainder by the Baptist denomination and by private donations." [356]

In 1934, the home moved to El Cerrito at the site where the present day Winrush K-8 school is located. There was a remembrance gathering in 2001.

C.W. was a member of the First Baptist Church of Berkeley. C.W. returned from his second journey to China, his three-year stay, in 1924. The exact nature of his involvement with them is not recorded. [Author's note: It seems likely that he became involved with Chung Mei through the combination of his knowledge of China and his attendance at the Baptist Church.]
(See the Chapter 14 section entitled C.W. and Churches.)

[Author's Note: My wife, Joann volunteers at a charity store called the Butter Paddle, which raises funds for a organization that is similar to Chung Mei called EMQ Families First. One of EMQ's two roots was the Ming Quong Children's Center, which started in 1867 to serve at-risk girls in the Chinese community. In 1924, Ming Quong moved into a Julia Morgan designed building in Oakland, next to Berkeley. It seems likely that C.W. would have known a great deal about Ming Quong. EMQ now operates two residential campuses, located in Campbell and Los Gatos, California.]

Chapter 11 – The Codling Moth and the California Spray Chemical Company – "Ortho"

C.W. and two of his students were intensely involved in the work of controlling the codling moth in the apple orchards of the Pajaro Valley and elsewhere. That work led to the founding of the California Spray Chemical Company, known for their brand name "Ortho".

The Codling Moth

The Codling Moth, *Cydia pomonella,* is the classic pest of apple orchards. The larvae of this moth burrow into apples, pome fruits, and walnuts and eat for about three weeks. There are typically two broods per year. The iconic "worm in the apple" is the larva of the codling moth.

Figure 83 Adult codling moth[357]

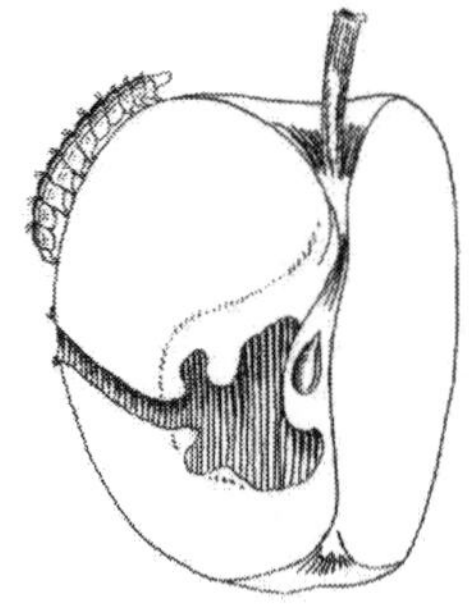

Figure 84 Codling moth larva exiting an apple[358]

Spray and Band Treatment for the Codlin[g] Moth (1890)

In 1890, C.W. published a study comparing the results of spraying three different arsenical compounds. The study also presented the results of a banding operation. The three compounds were white arsenic, Paris green, and London purple. The University Orchard in Berkeley was used (this was long before the University Farm extension in Davis existed).

C.W. indicated that not enough trees were in the white arsenic group to give reliable results. He also noted that the London Purple was used in too high a concentration to be comparable with the good results that he got with Paris green. His result was that "fully one half of the fruit ordinarily eaten by the codlin moth can be saved by spraying."

A second experiment was run by banding the trees. In this treatment a physical barrier of strips cut from old sacks was placed on the trees in various places to prevent the larva from finding a place to nest after they had consumed the fruit. This method had the effect of limiting the population of moths rather than preventing the larva that was present from damaging the fruit. They managed to collect 44% percent of the larvae that they thought was present by counting the damaged fruit. "... still it is not wholly unsatisfactory. Could it be shown that this ratio of destruction was maintained against the first brood, it would probably indicate a large percentage of saving of fruit.[359]"

The research that C.W. did prepared him perfectly to help his students a few years later respond to an infestation with a great invention.

Substitutes for Paris green as insecticides (1899)

In 1899, C.W. presented this essay to the December 9, 1899 Fruit Growers Convention, held at Unitarian Hall, San Jose, California.[360]

New Observations on the Codling-Moth (1903)

In 1903, C.W. presented this essay to the December 10, 1903 Fruit Growers Convention, held in Fresno, California. He presented more detailed observations on the egg-laying process of the moth and on two regions that were found to be immune to the moth due to environmental conditions.

Pajaro Valley infestation

The Pajaro Valley is along the California coast between Santa Cruz and Monterey near the town of Watsonville. The Salinas River cut a low pass through the first ridge of the coast range, and that gap provides a passageway for the marine layer of fog that hangs over the cold water of the Pacific to be pulled inward through the gap towards the Salinas Valley, much in the same way that San Francisco's golden gate brings the marine layer in towards the central valley.

There was a devastating codling moth infestation in the Pajaro Valley in the first few years of the 20th century. The local orchard association raised money to bring in an entomologist. C.W. sent Warren T. Clark, assistant superintendent for the University Extension in Agriculture. copper (II) acetoarsenite, known as Paris green because of its vivid blue green color, was initially used, but the persistent fog of the Pajaro Valley dissolved the Paris green, causing much injury to the foliage of the trees.

Volck and Luther discover that lead arsenate worked

Warren Clark left the project and two of C.W.'s students, William Volck and Ellerslie Luther, took over. They came up with an improved compound, lead arsenate, that was less soluble than Paris green and thus could stand up to the fog. This compound turned out to be better in many other situations. They then started an important company in economic entomology, the California Spray Chemical Company, sometimes referred to as Cal-Spray or CSCC.

The book "Fruits of Natural Advantage: making the industrial countryside in California" summarizes what they did as follows:

"To the reader, such an invention might seem little more interesting than a wormy apple, but it fundamentally changed the insecticide industry. At a time when flimsy companies boasted secret formulas with bogus claims, two university-trained scientists, both fed up with the poor quality of existing insecticides, invented what was assuredly the very best poison of its kind and considered ways of making their discovery public. Presenting growers with a new formula by publishing it in an experiment station bulletin would not put their invention into many hands. Only a factory working under laboratory conditions could manufacture the spray. After consulting with Woodworth and after raising $5,000 from family members and interested investors in Watsonville, Luther and Volck founded California Spray-Chemical in 1907. It was the first insecticide-manufacturing company dedicated to "scientific pest control" and products guaranteed "Correct, Proper, Right, Straight and Pure." California Spray-Chemical, selling under its ORTHO brand, made scientific research the engine of market innovation.[361]"

The Ortho brand

The Ortho brand was included in a book "America's Greatest Brands". In that book it says:

"In 1907, William Volck and Ellerslie Luther formed the California Spray-Chemical Company (Calspray) [sic] to manufacture a product to combat the codling moths that were devastating apple crops in California. They chose the product name Ortho™, from the Greek word orthos, meaning "correct proper, right, straight, and pure.[362]"

The Ortho brand name persists to this day. Ortho's motto, "Always the Right Solution™" captures their legacy of applying knowledge to the problem of pest control.

circa 1947

Figure 85 Logo of the Ortho brand of Cal-Spray[363]

Current day impact

William Hunter Volck and Ellerslie Edgar Luther had been C.W.'s students at Berkeley (Cal). Cal-Spray opened for business and stayed in Watsonville, California for many years. An important apple business in Watsonville was and is Martinelli's. It could be that Martinelli's would not have been as successful as they have without having the effective control of the pests in their apple orchards in those early years. Without CSCC, that bottle of sparkling cider on your holiday table might have been produced by a different company in a different place.

Apples, Codling Moth, and Climate (1910/1912)

A section of a 1910 speech by C.W. was published in 1912. The speech was entitled "The Battle of the Arsenicals" was given at the Watsonville Apple Show in October of 1910. It was published in the *Monthly Weather Review* in October of 1912.

He starts with:

> "It is undoubtedly true that nowhere in the world is there an area planted to any crop of the extent of the apple orchards in this valley [the Pajaro Valley], where spraying is so universally and efficiently done, and there is no similar area where such difficulties have [had] to be surmounted in order to place spraying on a practical basis. The story of the horticultural achievements of the Pajaro Valley will always include the contribution here made to the means of controlling insect pests.
>
> Just a quarter of a century ago I had the privilege of taking part, under the direction of Prof. [Stephen] Forbes in Illinois, in the first thorough scientific experiments made to test the efficiency of arsenicals in the control of the codling moth. This method has gradually extended until now spraying with these substances has become an essential part of the practice of apple growing in every region which figures in the commercial production of this fruit."[364]

C.W. also pointed out the specificity that insecticides need to be applied with.

> "The experience of the past eight years has abundantly proven that to produce the best results we can not follow the practice of other regions. In the Pajaro Valley alone, of all the regions where apples are grown commercially, we have one section where trees need not be sprayed at all for codling moth. The section of the valley toward the sea from Watsonville is a naturally immune area. The immunity is due to the fact that the evening fogs and cold winds from the ocean reach this region so early as to almost invariably prevent the flight of the moth, and, in consequence, the laying of eggs."

The preceding quote also shows that C.W. was intimately involved with the efforts of his former students in controlling the moth.[365]

California Insecticide Industries (1912)

C.W. writes in his 1912 paper *California Insecticide Industries*[366]:

> Next to the cyanide, the arsenicals take the most prominent place among insecticides. Outside of California the arsenicals easily hold first place. The United States insecticide law [of 1910] set definite standards for Paris green and lead arsenate and did not mention by name any other insecticides.
>
> Until within the last five years all the arsenicals used in California came from the East. Now the California Spray Chemical Company manufactures lead arsenate and zinc arsenate and supplies the major part, not only of the California market, but very largely also the Northwest.
>
> The organization of this company came about because of the need of a specially insoluble grade of arsenate of lead, such as none of the Eastern manufacturers would supply, and which they are now only beginning to compete with. In most regions the danger to foliage is not so great as in the Pajaro Valley [the Pajaro Valley has persistent marine layer fog] and therefore does not require this degree of insolubility.
>
> All of the larger Eastern manufacturers of arsenicals still sell their goods in this state, probably in as large quantities as they did before the organization of the California Spray Chemical Company, since there has been a very great increase in the consumption of arsenicals following the Codlin Moth investigation conducted by the University in the Pajaro Valley."

Chief Entomologist

C.W. served as the Chief Entomologist of the California Spray Chemical Company after his retirement from Cal and after the death of his second wife from 1930 to 1933. He travelled on behalf of CSCC to Central and South America. Cal-Spray headquarters was located at 135 Walker Street in Watsonville, California, but C.W. worked at their office at 15 Shattuck Square in downtown Berkeley.

C.W. travelled for CSCC to Mexico, Argentina and Brazil among other places. He arrived on the S.S. Eastern Prince in New York on January 29, 1932, having sailed from Buenos Aires on January 11th.[367]

CSCC corporate history

CSCC was acquired by Chevron's predecessor, Standard Oil of California and was operated as a subsidiary. Its name was changed in 1960 to the California Chemical Company. The Ortho product line was then sold to Monsanto before being purchased by its current owner, the Scotts Company in 1999.

The name of one of CSCC founders and C.W.'s student, William Volck is still honored in Ortho's first home product (which is still sold) "Ortho Volck Oil Spray Dormant Season Insect Killer" ($11.12 on Amazon). You may have some "Ortho Bug-B-Gone Max" or "Ortho Home Defense Max" out in your garage.

In the 1950's, William Volck's widow, Helen Volck Tucker donated her home to be used as the William H. Volck Museum. The museum moved and is now located at 332 East Beach St., Watsonville, CA. This museum contains mementos of Watsonville including a few of Cal-Spray.

Cal-Spray pollution

As with many companies involved with toxic chemicals in that era, CSCC became involved in several environmental lawsuits in later years including at the original site in Watsonville as well as in Omaha.[368] "From 1901 to 1951, 135 Walker St. was home to one of the world's leading chemical pesticide producing facilities. Ortho's Cal-Spray site produced a lead and arsenic-based pesticide dust that was used to battle a codling moth epidemic that was plaguing Pajaro Valley apple growers."[369]

An extensive remediation effort was completed in 2001. This involved removing 270 yards of soil and installing an 11-inch asphalt cap.[370] As of 2003, environmental pollution remained in the vicinity of the site.[371] In 2007, a jury in the case of *Acevedo v. Cal. Spray-Chem. Company* found insufficient evidence that alleged exposure to lead arsenate caused birth defects in three plaintiffs near the site in Watsonville. 200 other plaintiffs had joined in the suit.[372]

The site now contains the outdoor showroom of a store that sells pipe and water tanks.

Chapter 12 - Optics and Machine Calculation Work

In addition to his outstanding work in entomology, C.W. published eleven academic papers in optics as well as on machine calculation topics associated with optics. Aside from his 1893 paper about an enhancement to microscope stages, all of the rest of his work in optics came later in his career, starting in 1916 with his landmark paper "A New Fundamental Equation in Optics". The pinnacle of his professional work in optics came with the publication of his textbook, "Microscope Theory" in 1924 during his three-year period of working in China.

During his retirement, he attempted to build the world's largest telescope in his back yard. This telescope was intended to be an experimental segmented-mirror design. Work stopped on the telescope following the death of his second wife.

Doug Simons, Director of the Gemini Observatory, which operates 8.1 m telescopes on top of both Mauna Kea in Hawaii and Cerro Pachon in the Andes in Chile said that "He was a hell of an optical engineer." When looking at C.W.'s 1924 book "Microscope Theory" he said that "This was state-of-the-art stuff for his time."[373]

A New Idea in Microscope Construction (1893)

C.W.'s first contribution in optics was a paper in *Science* detailing how he had Bausch and Lomb make an enhanced microscope stage. C.W. wanted to be able to rotate the specimen accurately. At the time, Bausch & Lomb made a microscope that allowed the stage to be rotated, but the center of rotation of the stage was hard to align to the center of the optical axis. C.W. came up with an enhancement that allowed the lateral position of the stage mount bar to be adjusted with a rack and pinion so that the two axes could be brought into alignment.[374]

Immediately following his article in that issue of *Science* is an article by W.E. Castle, to whom C.W. would make the suggestion about the use of Drosophila seven years later.

Figure 86 C.W. at a microscope[375]

Display at “San Francisco’s “First World’s Fair”

The microscope was displayed at the California Midwinter International Exposition of 1894 in San Francisco, San Francisco’s first World’s Fair. San Franciscan Harry de Young was the Vice-President of the 1893 Columbian Exhibition, better known as the Chicago World’s Fair. He proposed that a follow-on World’s Fair be held shortly afterwards in San Francisco. Support mushroomed for the fair and the grounds were constructed in what is today’s Music Concourse in Golden Gate Park.[376] One of the buildings from the fair became the home of the M.H. de Young Memorial Museum and stood until it was replaced in 2005. The de Young is the 16th most visited museum in the world. The Japanese Tea Garden is also a legacy of the fair. The original building for the California Academy of Sciences, who published several of C.W.’s papers, was built in 1916 on the site of the fair.

Figure 87 Bird’s-Eye View of the California Midwinter International Exposition[377]

The Association of Agricultural Experiment Stations put together a combined display for the Chicago World's Fair. The University of California contributed sixteen soil samples, about fifty mineral and rock specimens, a mechanical soil analysis apparatus, two dynamos, a dynamo regulator, and a large collection of cereals, grasses & forage plants.[378]

The University of California was allocated a larger space at the subsequent Midwinter Fair, nearly the whole width of the north end of the Liberal Arts Building, which was on the West (panhandle) end of the concourse. Additional exhibits were added including maps and photographs. C.W. was put in charge of the exhibit in entomology.

> It "was designed to show especially the work of instruction in this department. It consisted of a desk of the form used in entomological laboratory, and a set of wall cases, such as used for specimens in the lecture-room. Upon the desk was shown the new orienting microscope, designed and built for our laboratory; a copy of the Laboratory Manual, used in the course in elementary and economic entomology; and a large jar illustrating the transformations of the honey bee. Upon the standard of the wall cases, a set of bottles illustrated the remedies recommended by us; and copies of the formulas were distributed during the fair. One of the wall cases represented the principal kinds of spraying nozzles; another a dissection apparatus; ten were devoted to microscopial preparations of the anatomy of insects; and twelve boxes of beetles gave some idea of the collection of insects used in instruction in systematic and economic entomology."[379]

Some Background on Optics

[Author's note: In order to understand the next few papers, some background in optics and definitions are required.]

General Definitions

Optical Axis: The axis of symmetry of a lens or lens system
Chief Ray: The ray of light from the edge of object that crosses the Optical Axis in the middle of the lens.
Conjugate Foci: old name for the focal point
Focal Point: The point on the far side of a lens where an object comes into focus.

Lens Defect Definitions:

Astigmatism: Every lens has some defects from what would be perfect rotational symmetry around the optical axis. If you imagine a lens made out of gel, the lens becomes astigmatic if you squish it from the side with your fingers. Another way it can become astigmatic is if you pinch one edge of the gel lens so that the "center" of the lens is not quite in the center of the gel anymore. If a + shape is sent through a lens with Astigmatism, the vertical direction of the + will come to focus in front or behind the horizontal direction. You measure astigmatism by measuring half the distance between the planes containing each half of the "+". Eyeglasses that have an astigmatic correction squeeze the image from side to side as you rotate them in front of your eyes.

Coma: Every lens will have small other defects aside from astigmatism or spherical aberration (see the next paragraph), for example if the lens surface is a little wavy. If you press a comb into one of the surfaces of our gel lens, it might have lots of coma for a few minutes. These defects often lead the image to have a little tail that looks like a comet's tail, thus the name coma. A simple way to measure this defect is to send in collimated light and measure the spread of the focal point, front to back. Cheap lenses like those found in toy binoculars have lots of coma.

Spherical Aberration: It is much less expensive to grind glass lenses in the shape of a sphere than any other shape. The middle of a spherical lens has close to the perfect shape for use in magnification, but the edges do not. Cameras that use spherical lenses sometimes block off the light from reaching the "bad" edges of the lens. The measurement of the difference from perfection do to this one defect is called spherical aberration. This defect can be measured in a manner similar to coma, except by excluding from the collimated light the light going through the "good" central part of the lens. Eyeglasses that give distorted images when you look through the edge of the lens probably have some spherical aberration.

A New Fundamental Equation in Optics (1916)

As mentioned earlier, C.W. published what was essentially an applied mathematics entomology paper entitled "New Dosage Tables". That paper derived some formulas and provided some tables to help farmers determine how much hydrogen cyanide to introduce into fumigation tents of various geometries to kill insects without killing the tree. That experience may have emboldened him to increasingly publish mathematics-oriented papers.
(See the Chapter 5 section entitled New Dosage Tables (1915).)

His 1916 paper, "A New Fundamental Equation in Optics" delivers a simple and elegant formula for determining the conjugate foci of a spherical lens. The conjugate foci is the point on the far side where the image of a given object comes back into focus. Previous formulas measured from the surface of the lens. C.W.'s formula measures from the center of curvature of the lens. His paper starts out:

> "All of the elementary text-books in physics are still using an equation for the conjugate foci of spherical lenses which is too inaccurate for the calculation of microscope objectives, applying with approximate accuracy only to very thin lenses. The same equation is all that is given in the more advanced treatises except those securing a closer approximation by the methods of higher mathematics.
>
> It is possible, however, to develop a simple and rigorously accurate equation by geometry applicable to lenses of any thickness by the simple expedient of measuring the focal distances from the center of curvature of the lens instead of measuring it from the surface as has hitherto been the practice.
>
> The equation is
>
> $$n/f + n'/f' = (n - n')/r \cdot \cos(a)/\cos(b')$$
>
> in which n and n′ are the indices of refraction, f and f′ the focal distances of the conjugate foci, r the radius of the lens, a the focal angle and b the radial angle."

This more sophisticated formula gave him the infrastructure to investigate lens aberrations, the subject of his next three optics papers.

> "For the study of aberration the angles a and b can be calculated by solving the two triangles EDO and QDO in which EO and QO remain constant and the other sides vary according to the refractive index of the color of the ray of light investigated in the study of chromatic aberration, or according to the position of Q when studying spherical aberration.
>
> The usual equation found in the books can not be employed for either of the foregoing calculations when more than approximate results are required."

The Astigmatism of Lenses (1917)

This paper, published in the *Journal of the Optical Society of America,* attempted to define precisely what astigmatism meant for spherical lenses. It began:

> "A defect of the eye has probably the prior claim to the term astigmatism, but a defect in the image produced by spherical lenses has long been designated by the same word though having little in common with the former significance.
>
> As applied to spherical lenses more than one conception of the nature of this defect prevails, making it evident that if a rigorous definition of this aberration were formulated it would be necessary to exclude some of the things which are now assembled under this term."

This paper paved the way for his more important 1919 paper.

Astigmatism and Coma (1918)

This paper expands his discussion of astigmatism and coma in his 1917 paper and again builds toward his 1919 paper.

Contribution to the optics of the microscope (1919)

C.W.'s 1919 paper published in the Proceedings of the California Academy of Sciences on July 12, 1919 shows that the existing theory of the five aberrations: distortion, curvature, axial aberration, astigmatism and coma in oblique optical situations do not correspond to some physical measurements that he made. The existing theory had been advanced by J.C.F. Sturm and updated by J.P.C Southall. He included photographs of specific ray tracing experiments.

He then proposes methods of calculating the five distortions by doing ray tracing of specific light paths.

Before this paper, lens design was focused on what happened along the optical axis, the center of the lens system, because it was easy to understand and calculate there. Unfortunately, the rest of the lens is important too and existing calculations fell short of producing good lenses.

The paper begins:

> "A subject which has received as much attention as the optics of the microscope is not liable to offer much that is new except to the delver into the intricacies of its details.
>
> That which follows is not concerned with matters of detail, but instead, is based on a re-examination of some of the fundamental facts from a somewhat different angle than those by which they have usually been approached. This has resulted in the finding of some relationships which appear to have been overlooked and in the perception of the practical importance of some well known relationships in the calculation of lens aberrations.

As a result of these studies a very great simplification of the methods of lens calculation has been evolved, which should prove useful in the design of optical instruments and in the further study of the theory of aberrations by relieving the investigators of these subjects of much of the tedium of the elaborate computations heretofore necessary."

The following diagram presents the five lens aberrations that are visible when using a microscope.

- Distortion – when the image is twisted
- Curvature - when the image cannot be focused simultaneously in both the middle and the edge
- Axial Aberration – when the center or the edge can never be brought into focus
- Astigmatism – when a portion of the image is in focus radially, but not in other directions
- Coma – when one edge of a portion of the image is sharp, but another edge of that portion is not

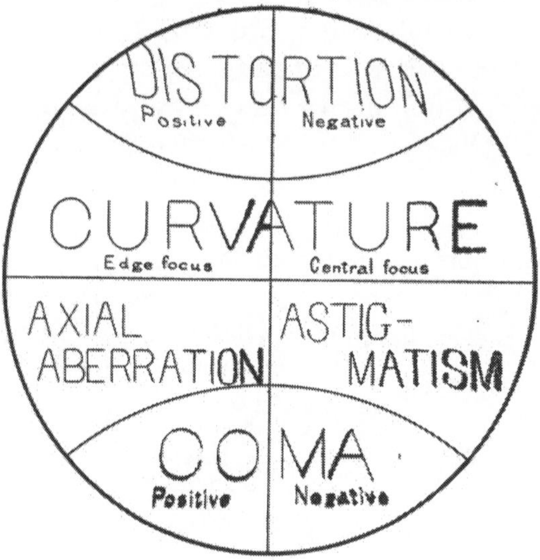

Figure 88 Optical aberrations that can be produced by a microscope[380]

French mathematician Jacques Charles Francois Sturm has been attributed with the early theory of optical perception contained in his study "Ueber die Theorie des Sehens" or "About the Theory of Seeing." Optometrists measure the "Interval of Sturm" when they fit for glasses patients that have astigmatism.

C.W. then delivered a new theory of focus formation in the presence of oblique (off-axis) refraction. He explained his theory by showing how the three classic laws of focus formation along the optical axis could be reinterpreted in terms of oblique refraction.

C.W. had found that the details of Sturm's theory or its update by Southall did not correspond with what he could measure experimentally in an oblique refraction setting. He created an experimental setup where he could test his theory.

> "A very simple and effective way of showing how the reversal is accomplished when a beam of light passes through an oblique locus is by pasting strips of paper on a common reading glass, leaving four equal windows, thus conforming to the diagram used to illustrate Sturm's theory. Supporting the lens obliquely in the sunlight and laying a piece of solio paper [a type of slow gelatin chloride photographic print paper made by Eastman Kodak] in the refracted beam this making a permanent record of the distribution of light at that plane. Repeating this at different planes will enable one to secure a very complete record of the transformation. A few of such records are shown in the accompanying figure."

Figure 89 Photographs of light cones – the letters correspond to the stages in the followng drawings [381]

C.W. then showed that Sturm's mathematical description was not up to the task of handling real lenses that had aberrations, whereas his updated theory could.

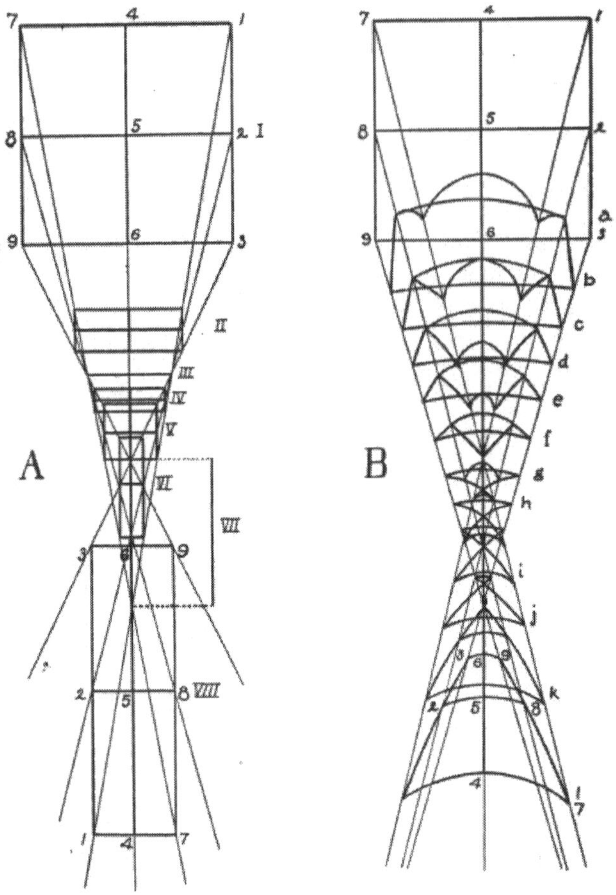

Figure 90 Comparison between A - Sturm's theory and B - C.W.'s theory to show the correspondence to the previous photograph[382]

Finally, he concludes with a graphical and mathematical method of lens calculation that includes measurements of coma and astigmatism. The graphical method is shown below.

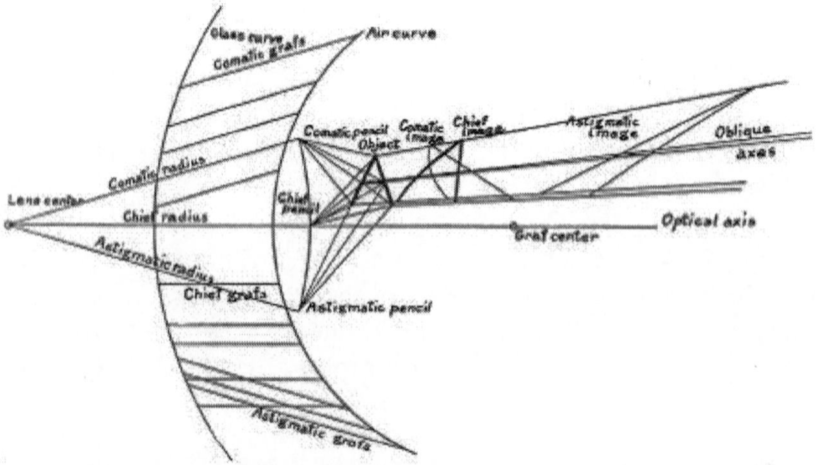

Figure 91 Graphical lens calculation including coma and astigmatism measurement[383]

A Focal-Length Equation (1920)

C.W.'s September 1920 paper, published as the cover article in Vol. IV, Number 5 of the Journal of the Optical Society of America, is entitled "A Focal Length Equation". His paper starts out:

> "No general equation for calculating the focal length of a lens system appears to have been published. The mathematical equivalent of the author's method of calculating paraxial ray courses may be stated in the form of such an equation as follows:
>
> $$J_m = j_{m-1} + i_m\left(1 - \sum_{k=1}^{k=m-1} j_k d_k/(n_k+1)\right)$$"

C.W. then proceeds to re-compute the focal length of a lens system that was defined in the textbook "Principles and Methods of Geometric Optics" by James Southall.

This equation defines an iterative calculation that contains only arithmetic calculations (add, subtract, multiply and divide). Since his formula contains no logarithmic or trigonometric functions, it was ideally suited for the limited computing resources of his day. Expressed in modern terms, this paper is essentially an algorithm development paper in that it transformed a problem into one that could be computed easily.

Following C.W.'s paper in the same issue is "Note on Professor Woodworth's Formula For Focal Length" by James P.C. Southall, a physics professor at Columbia who wrote the textbook containing the lens system for which C.W. recomputed the focal length. He states the Professor Woodworth's formula

> "is extremely compact and convenient and lends itself readily to numerical computation as he shows. So far as I am aware, this formula has never been published before in precisely this form, although it is difficult to see how it could have escaped notice."

He goes on to verify the new formula in two ways.

The Treatment of Certain Special Cases in Lens Calculation (1920)

This very elaborate paper was published in the Journal of the Optical Society of America. This paper is another one of his very modern algorithm development papers that details how to recast certain lens calculations so as not to lose precision due to rounding errors.

One of the examples in his paper is how to run the calculations needed to create a "Huygenian" eyepiece for the James Lick Telescope. Huygenian eyepieces were the first type of compound eyepieces used. They work well with long focal length telescopes. They consist of two plano-convex lenses and are obsolete today, but were state of the art in 1920.

The Lick Observatory sits on Mt. Hamilton above San Jose, California. It has always been associated with the University of California and is today managed by U.C. Santa Cruz. When it was built in 1888, it was the largest refractor telescope in the world. It remains the second largest in operation now. [Author's note: I can see the observatory from a viewpoint a few houses away from my home and often look over at it when I walk my dogs.]

Because of the size of the enormous lens in the James Lick Telescope, several of C.W.'s calculations that were fine with normal sized lenses would lose accuracy because variables with similar values were subtracted from each other. In response to this shortcoming, C.W. created an alternative algorithm that did the needed calculation in a different way. He called his original method the focus method and the new method the intercept method.

[Author's note: If any of you have created digital signal processing algorithms, you will recognize some of these same challenges in keeping the accuracy in calculations.]

Note on T. Smith's method of tracing rays through an optical system (1921)

Starting in August 1915, T. Smith of the UK's National Physical Laboratory published a series of papers collectively entitled "On Tracing Rays through an Optical System." This paper shows how to rearrange the classic trigonometric equations used in lens design into ones suitable for logarithmic calculation so that calculating machines can be used. It also showed the calculations used for paraxial rays (rays fractionally off of the center axis) could be generalized in certain situations for non-paraxial rays through the use of conjugate points. He also published a novel numerical table of "cosines in terms of sines" that saved some steps in the calculation.

In January, 1921, James P. C. Southall of Columbia, author of the landmark 1913 book "The Principles and Methods of Geometrical Optics", commented on T. Smith's paper saying that the new method wasn't really simpler than the other known methods. Dr. Southall then went on to derive another set of formulas for lens calculations. He then showed how one of C.W.'s formulas could be derived.

In July 1921, C.W. commented that T. Smith's method was indeed useful and then proposed a further modification of it. The modification employed a line perpendicular to the axis. He also showed an alternative calculation method for machine calculation.

Methods for machine calculation of rays through a lens system (1923)

C.W. made this submission to the Journal of the Optical Society of America while he was at the National Southeastern University at Nanking, China. In it, he gives a version of the standard lens power calculation that can be accomplished using several forms of machine calculation.

In his day, there were multiple forms of machine calculation. Adding machines were available by this time, which could add and do subtraction through complement addition. Slide rules and variants of slide rules could do logarithms, multiplication, division, and trigonometric functions. Slide rule-inspired specialized instruments such as actinographs for film exposure calculations were also available in this period. Finally, specialized and complex machine computing systems to calculate specific results, such as the tides, were long known. It is unclear which device C.W. had in mind, nor does this paper give a clue.

For paraxial rays, this calculation uses the "paraxial approximation" to simplify the calculation, which is the method of approximating the sine cosine of an angle. For rays which are traced near the axis of a lens, Sin(x) is approximately equal to x (in radians). For the edge rays, he provides another method of approximating the sine and cosine.

[Author's note: In today's world, transforming a problem into one that can be solved conveniently on a computing machine is called algorithm development and is typically accomplished by software engineers. The sort of work that he was undertaking is very modern. C.W. would have fit right into today's world.]

Microscope theory (1924)

C.W. published a 240 page textbook titled "Microscope Theory" in the Transactions of the Science Society of China. It was reprinted by the Commercial Press in Shanghai in 1924.[384]

The introduction of the book reads:

> The most important instrument for biological research is the microscope, and it is also of high importance in near every department of science. The user of this instrument should have a comprehensive understanding of the principles upon which the efficiency of the instrument depends, but such information is not at present available. The object for securing this knowledge is in order that the user may be better able to obtain the highest possible results from the instrument and to enable him to design new instruments to meet new needs that may arise in the course of his research work. The writer's first efforts to secure a better understanding of the theory of the microscope arose from the need of a new kind of microscope for a special investigation in insect pathology.[385]

Of particular interest is C.W.'s focus on wavefront diagrams in his analysis. This technique foreshadows much modern work in optical and antenna design.

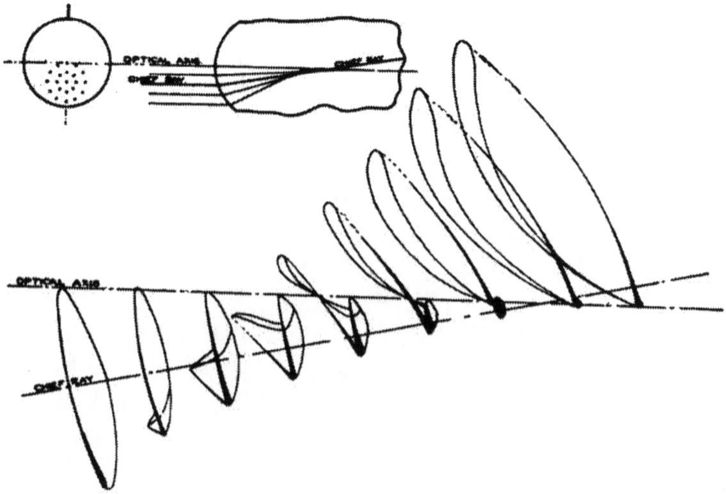

Figure 92 Wavefront diagram from the earlier "The Astigmatism of Lenses – "The shapes assumed when passing through a focus of the wave fronts of a beam of parallel rays after refraction at a single spherical surface upon which the beam is obliquely incident."[386]

The Theory of the Wave Train of Light (1925)

There is a letter from Cal Physics professor Ralph S. Minor that reads as follows:

"I was much interested in your final paper which you submitted on the Theory of the Wave Train of Light. I find that there have been several speculations along a similar line recently in the attempt to apply the quantum theory to optical phenomena. If you attended Professor Milliken's Phi Beta Kappa address you may recall his reference to these attempts. We are apparently some distance from the goal in our attempts to fit the quantum theory into our knowledge of diffraction and interference, and your paper presents an interesting point of view."[387]

[Author's note: This is the only reference to this paper that I could find. It seems likely that it was not published.]

Sine-arc and arc-sine tables for lens Calculation (1930)

This was a booklet of sine-arc and arc-sine values, calculated to four digits. He needed these values for his lens calculations and saw fit to deliver the results to the public. Before the days of computers, tables of values such as these were an important enabler of scientific calculation.

An advertisement in the October 28, 1938 issue of *Science* reads:

> Five-place Arcs Sines and Cosines for Machine Calculation Interpolating to Eight. Price $2.00. Microscopic Theory. Shanghai, 1924. Price $3.00. C.W. Woodworth 2237 Carlton St., Berkeley, CA[388]

Segmented Mirror Telescopes (1928-1930)

C.W. developed an idea for how to construct a "composite-reflector" telescope in the late 1920's. This technique is now known as building a "segmented-mirror" telescope and is a key technique used in the largest telescopes in the world. His telescope mounted 400 small mirrors on a flat wooden frame and can be described as a segmented planar Fresnel reflector array. Today's segmented mirror telescopes have their reflectors mounted on a parabolic surface.

A December 2, 1928 letter from Harlan Shapley of the Harvard College Observatory says:

> "I am glad to hear of your progress in the composite telescope. In these days of bigger and bigger telescopes, it is going to be worthwhile to have all variations from the conventional forms investigated."[389]

As he retired from the University of California approaching his 65th birthday in 1930, C.W. attempted to build the most powerful telescope in the world made up to that point by constructing an experimental segmented-mirror reflecting telescope in his backyard. A March 30, 1930 New York Times article was entitled "Strongest Telescope Sought Through Combining Hundreds".

> "The new telescope may prove to be more powerful than any telescope now in operation, if the 400 small mirrors which will go into its construction can be made to focus their power properly. None of these mirrors will be larger than fifteen square inches, but their combined power will be more than 100 square feet of reflecting surface. The 'eyepiece' of the instrument will be located on top of a garage forty feet high."

An article in "Amateur Telescope Making" similarly describes:

> Professor Charles W. Woodworth of the University of California is making a mosaic type of telescope containing 400 mirrors, each 15 inches in diameter, and all attached to a single rigid backing. Each is to be adjusted, if possible, to the position called for by theory. Dr. Woodworth submitted his idea to this journal a year or more ago and the opinion given through one of its corresponding editor was that the theory was erred but in practice the difficulties would probably prove insuperable (see A.T.M., page 242 near bottom). He is trying it out, and this is the correct procedure in cases where there is any doubt.[390]

C.W.'s telescope would have been approximately 3.4m in diameter. Not until eighteen years later would a larger telescope be built, the 5.08m Hale Telescope at the Palomar Observatory in San Diego County, California.

There is no published report of the results of the telescope, and it is unclear why this is so. He was a published author in optics, and even the knowledge derived from a failed attempt to build the world's largest telescope might have been useful. The death of his second wife is mostly likely the event that put an end to his work on the telescope. Bernice Christopher Woodworth died of heart failure caused by kidney failure on May 6, 1930 just five weeks after the publication of the New York Times article.

The best evidence about this comes from a 1937 letter to his niece Celina in which he relates:

> "Likewise when Bernice passed on and my teaching work was over and my family scattered you can see why I grasped at the opportunity of travelling over Central and South America with a new job [as the Chief Entomologist of the California Spray Chemical Corporation] and the meeting of new people"[391]

Two years later, in 1932, Guido Horn d'Arturo in Italy built a similar telescope and published the results in 1935.[392] It is unclear whether d'Arturo read any of the many press articles written about C.W.'s telescope construction effort just two years earlier. D'Arturo was Jewish, and WWII stopped his efforts. In 1953, d'Arturo completed a 1.8m version of the telescope and made photographs of many new stars. Horn d'Arturo retired in 1954. An observatory and a library in Bologna, Italy are named after him.

Research activity into segmented-mirror telescopes picked up in the 1960's. Today, the largest telescopes in the world use segmented-mirror designs. The 10.4 m Gran Telescopio Canarias in the Canary Islands, the 10m Keck 1 & 2 in Hawaii, and the 0.2 Southern African Large Telescope in South Africa are all segmented mirror telescopes.

Today's segmented-mirror telescopes use hexagonal mirrors mounted on a parabolic frame. This keeps the light from the different mirrors more in phase with each other and maximizes the reflecting area. The incremental steps from C.W.'s telescope to today's telescopes are:

1. Change from a flat substrate to a parabolic substrate.
2. Change from square to hexagonal mirrors.
3. Mount the whole telescope on a movable arm (movable telescope mounts were already widely used in C.W.'s day.)
4. Upgrade the mirrors to highly precise mirrors (requires modern industrial technology.)
5. Add adaptive optics controls to deform each mirror in response to the measured properties of the earth's atmosphere (requires modern measurement, computer, and materials technology.)

Correspondence with Arthur C. Hardy about Ray Tracing (1935)

A letter from MIT physics chair, Arthur C. Hardy exists that was written in response to some criticisms that C.W. made regarding an optics textbook that Dr. Hardy had written. The book referred to is presumably "The Principles of Optics" (1932) by Arthur C. Hardy and Fred H. Perrin. He starts out:

> "I very much appreciate your letter of March 6, [1935] and the only defense I can offer to your valid criticisms is that Mr. Perrin and I were attempting to write a textbook rather than a treatise."

Course in Optical Triangulation (1936)

During the period of his stay at the Temple Institute in Rochester, NY, C.W. gave a course in optical triangulation to some employees of Bausch and Lomb. A January 29, 1936 letter from F.A. Eaton requests that C.W. repeat the course for five employees that could not attend the first time that the course was given.[393] No course materials from these classes survive

Optical triangulation is used in the rangefinders of classic SLR (single lens reflex) cameras as well as in surveying equipment and weapon sights. In the classic SLR camera, the focus ring is turned until the two halves of the image line up in the viewfinder. In the classic stereoscopic weapon sight, the sight is adjusted until the images in each eye from the two lenses overlap. C.W.'s contribution to the science of rangefinders is unclear.

Bausch & Lomb had made rangefinders for the U.S. Navy since before WWI.[394] The U.S. military used many models of Bausch & Lomb range and height finders in WWII.[395] The impact of C.W.'s class for Bausch & Lomb employees to the development of these rangefinders in WWII is unclear.

[Author's note: It is easy to imagine that C.W.'s expertise in lenses may have allowed Bausch & Lomb to produce stereoscopic range finders for weapon sights during WWII with clearer and more precise images.]

Image Point Equations and Machine Calculation (1937)

In a December, 1937 letter to his niece, the 72 year old, retired C.W. describes some work he was doing on two fronts during his retirement, on optical image point equations and on the machine calculation of mathematical problems associated with the correction of lenses. A section of that letter reads:

> "Here in Jacksonville I have sightseeing as one motive when I am taking my exercises and I have walked all over town. Then I was writing an article on image point equations based on the fact that recent authors have opposite ideas as to which directions the light rays follow. This I have now finished and sent copies to four leading authorities to get their reactions.
>
> A third thing has been the making of a machine for doing the mathematical problems concerned with the correction of lenses. When I was in Cambridge I studied all the mathematical machines at the Mass. Inst. of Technology and when in Washington I went into the construction of the tide predicting machine in the Coast and Geodetic Survey. And on the way down here I worked over my ideas and thought I was ready to build my machine so I hunted around and found a machine shop where they could make the principal parts. They allowed me to work there also myself. Now I have it nearly assembled. It is perhaps too much to expect to have it work right off as I have built it. It will at least show me what needs to be changed."[396]

In the late twenties and early thirties of the twentieth century, the famous "differential analyzer" mechanical analog computer was built in the laboratory of Vannevar Bush at MIT. The differential analyzer weighed 100 tons or so, was the size of a room and could calculate differential equations. In 1936, a young Claude Shannon was hired by Bush as a research assistant to run the differential analyzer.[397]

Figure 93 Vannevar Bush during WWII[398]

[Author's note: Given C.W.'s statement shown above "When I was in Cambridge [probably sometime in 1937], I studied all the mathematical machines at the Mass. Inst. of Technology …", it seems likely that he may have met both Vannevar Bush and Claude Shannon during this visit. Shannon is, of course, the father of Information Theory, which he published eleven years later in 1948. Shannon's theory underlies the design of every modern communication link, from cell phones to high-speed backplane links.

There are some nice photos of the differential analyzer along with Vannevar Bush and Claude Shannon at the MIT museum website at http://web.mit.edu/museum/]

Chapter 13 - Distillate Chemistry

During his retirement, C.W. was granted a patent entitled "Low Temperature Oil Refining Process". This patent was a state-of-the-art apparatus that made use of two techniques that had been recently developed by others. These techniques are known as thin-film distillation and short-path distillation. The apparatus that C.W. invented was a clever combination of these, but does appear to have been utilized in industrial operations, possibly because C.W. died only 16 months after his patent had been granted.

These two techniques are important today in situations where the compounds to be processed are fragile, notably the preparation of certain pharmaceuticals and food products such as fish oil capsules that have been processed to deliver triple-strength omega 3 compounds.

A primer on distillation

Distillation is an important chemical process in many industries. The most familiar form of distillation is used in the production of spirits such as whiskey or vodka. In order to produce one of these spirits you follow this basic method:

1. Prepare a liquid containing chopped up and cooked grain or starchy vegetables.
2. Allow yeast to eat the sugars in that liquid producing a mixture with a modest percentage of alcohol.
3. Boil the liquid and collect the vapor that comes off, cooling that vapor back into a liquid that has a higher percentage of alcohol.
4. Repeat step 3 with the liquid that you have collected until the result is strong enough for your taste.

This method of producing spirits relies on the fact that alcohol has lower boiling temperature (78° C) than water (100° C). When you boil the fermented mixture of water, alcohol and other chemicals, much more alcohol boils off than water. Each time the process is repeated the alcohol becomes more concentrated up to a limit of about 95.6 percent. The "relative volatility" of the various compounds determines how easy it is to separate them.

Distillation is also central to the process of refining oil. Crude oil, as it comes from the ground, is a mixture of many chemicals ranging from light compounds such as pentane to heavy compounds such as hexadecane. Large refineries use sophisticated versions of distillation such as fractional distillation carried out under high pressures in industrial settings to produce many products central to our daily lives including gasoline, diesel fuel, and lubricating oil. Many forms of plastic are also made from crude oil by further processing some of the components that have been separated out by fractional distillation.

Thin-film distillation

In conventional distillation, a vessel of liquid is boiled, and the vapor is collected with a condenser. In thin-film distillation, a thin film of liquid is introduced on a heated surface by techniques such as wicking, wiping, pouring or spraying. The vapor rising from that thin film is then collected. This technique allows more control of the distillation.

The great advantage of thin-film distillation over conventional distillation is the decreased "residence" of the substance in the distiller. In conventional distillation, a large batch of the substance is boiled in a liquid, potentially for many hours. This extended heating may destroy or degrade fragile compounds. In thin-film distillation, a potentially cooled liquid is wicked, wiped, poured or sprayed onto the distillation surface and is quickly heated. The resulting vapor is collected and rapidly cooled. The entire process can be completed in seconds, protecting fragile compounds.

The original patent on thin-film distillation was issued as patent #2,040,837 on May 19, 1936 to Edward C. D'Yarmett, just 15 months before C.W. applied for his patent, which will be described later in this chapter. In D'Yarmett's patent, a metal brush spinning inside a cylinder wipes a film of oil on the inside of that cylinder. Heat is applied to the outside of the cylinder and the vapor escapes out the top.

Partial-vacuum distillation

Distillation has also been extended through the use of a partial vacuum above the distillation vessel or surface. The boiling temperature of a liquid is dependent on the pressure of the gas above it. Fragile compounds can be further protected by distilling them in near-vacuum, at a much lower temperature than would be otherwise needed. The typical result is that the deeper the partial vacuum that can be produced in the apparatus, the lower the temperature of the distillation, and the better that fragile compounds can be protected.

The first patent on vacuum distillation, #1,972,157 was issued to Stuart Fannelee Miller on September 4, 1934.

Short-path distillation

In conventional distillation, liquid is boiled in a large boiler, and pipes carry the vapor over to a condenser, which cools the vapor back into a liquid. This works great for distilling vodka, but has two disadvantages in the handling of fragile compounds:

- The first disadvantage is that the compound has a higher "residence" because it must traverse the piping between the boiler and the condenser. The compound is held in the heated state for a longer period, potentially degrading it.
- The second disadvantage is that it is hard to pull a deep partial vacuum on an apparatus that is composed of many parts or is physically large.

Short-path distillation apparatuses have been produced that put the condenser immediately above a thin-film distillation surface. This allows both of the above disadvantages to be addressed. The compounds have a short residence in the apparatus, because they only need to fly a very short distance from the (heated) distillation surface over to the (cooled) condensing surface. The apparatus can be made physically very compact, since the two surfaces are near each other. This has led to modern day designs that are capable of being pulled to a deep partial vacuum.

An important early patent, #2,073,202 "Vacuum Distillation" that includes short-path distillation as well as vacuum distillation was issued on March 9, 1937 to John Lewis McCowen, just 5 months before C.W. applied for his patent (described later in this chapter).

A New Self-Regulating Parafin Bath (1914)

C.W. published one of the steps that he made along the path towards his patent in the middle of his career with the 1914 paper "A New Self-Regulating Parafin Bath".

[Author's note: I had the pleasure of presenting this paper as a historic paper to the plenary of the 2006 meeting of the PBESA in Maui as a part of the C.W. Woodworth Award presentation. Since I am an engineer by training, I selected this paper as it describes a laboratory apparatus that was easy for me to understand and articulate.]

The problem that C.W. was trying to solve was to have a convenient way of melting paraffin. Paraffin wax was used to mount insects. This was in the days before thermostatically controlled heaters. Today we would simply turn the dial on our digitally controlled heater to 58 degrees C, the melting point of paraffin. In 1914, you could try to carefully adjust a Bunsen burner to get the wax to melt, however, it must have been almost impossible to get the wax to stay at exactly the right temperature for a long period.

C.W. had a glass blower create a special flask that had a depression in the top of it, a very long spout that came off of the side and pointed up, and a small bowl at the end of the spout that was open at the end. Liquid chloroform was poured into the open end and a light bulb was placed under the flask. It turns out that chloroform boils at exactly the right temperature, 58 degrees C to melt the paraffin wax, and a "sixteen candle power" [~20W incandescent[399]] light bulb provided just enough heat. The long spout and bowl allowed the chloroform vapor to cool on the way up and condense back into liquid before much escaped.

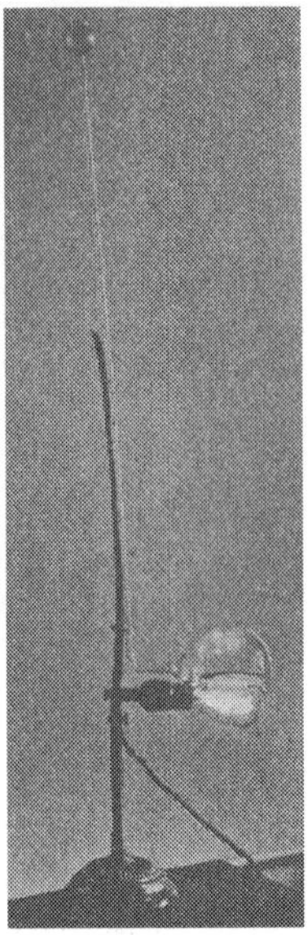

Figure 94 Apparatus for a "New Self-Regulating Paraffin Bath" [400]

[Author's note: I'm not sure what OSHA would have thought about boiling chloroform in a workplace, but apparently it worked well. Inevitably, some of the chloroform vapor must have escaped out of the end of the spout, but presumably they just opened the window.

This paper illustrates how difficult it was to do science in that era. C.W. had to invent an apparatus to serve as a simple thermostat, "thermo" meaning heat, "stat" meaning same, or "stay the same heat". Today's thermostats are off-the-shelf and do not require boiling chloroform.]

C.W.'s experience with this apparatus is clearly one of the contributing factors toward the development of his patent. In both this apparatus and in his oil-refining patent, a moderate temperature energy source evaporates an organic chemical.

Low Temperature Oil Refining Process (1937)

On August 16, 1937 C.W. filed for a patent on a "Low Temperature Oil Refining Process". The patent was granted on July 18, 1939 as U.S. patent number 2,166,193 with ten claims. The patent articulates a method that makes use of recently developed techniques in both thin-film distillation and short-path distillation, two important and frequently used methods.

His invention allows some of the lighter components of crude oil "in the paraffin series [kerosene is one of these]" to be directly distilled off in an air-oil emulsion form without the need for high temperatures or high pressures and operating at atmospheric pressure. It used a low energy heat source (item 11 in the drawing) to create an air-oil emulsion fog above a thin oil soaked wick (item 9) on a surface above the heat source (item 10).

> "As the film of crude oil travels upwardly along the wick and is affected by the heat source, small droplets appear on the surface of the wick, which droplets are constantly in motion, dancing or bouncing away from the wick surface and falling back thereupon. As heat is absorbed by the oil film, the dancing motion of the small droplets becomes more and more extensive until the droplets spring away from the wick to such an extent as to contact the inner surface of the collecting hood ..."

The oil fog settles on an upper surface (item 12), runs down, and is collected in a channel (item 13). The operation of his invention is improved by applying a positive electrical change to the collector surface (item 12).

This invention is an instance of single step-distillation as described in the primer above, but carried out on a thin film of liquid that has been wicked onto a surface, without the need to raise the bulk of the liquid to boiling.

Thin-film distillation is conducted by the use of a thin wick over a heated surface (item 9 over item 10).

Short-path distillation is shown by the close proximity of the condenser to the heated surface (item 12 being close to item 10).

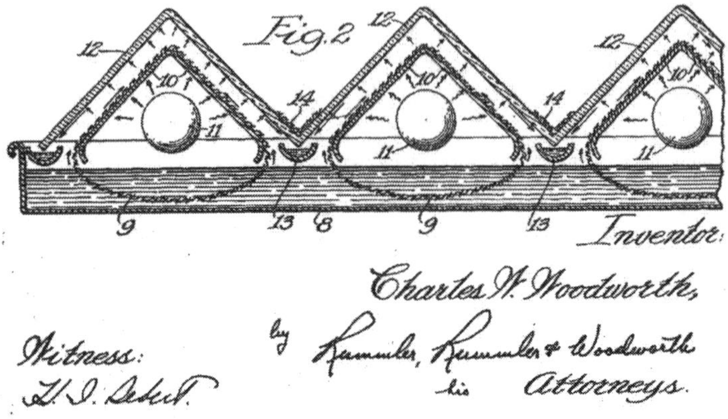

Figure 95 Low Temperate Oil Refining Process Patent[401]

The use of film-boiling to create an air-oil emulsion fog and having that fog carry the distillate over to the condenser in a liquid form seems unique to this process. In most applications of distillation, you only want the vapor to reach the condenser and not any micro-droplets of liquid, since the micro-droplets contain the original liquid, thus defeating the purpose of the distillation.

[Author's note: My guess is that in C.W.'s apparatus, kerosene vapor is actually distilled from the crude oil, but that vapor immediately condensed back into small droplets of liquid kerosene once away from the heated surface. These small and very light droplets then bounce around in the flow of vapor leaving the heated surface until they hit the condenser. I say this because it says in the patent that the apparatus worked really well, that it yielded "an extraordinarily high production of an oil of a uniform grade." If droplets had been directly transferred from the heated surface to the condenser, his apparatus probably would not have worked as well because distillation depends on the differential evaporation rates of the compounds.

My mother lamented to me on multiple occasions that if he had just had *"six more months* to work on this that we *could have been millionaires"*.[402] Whether this is true or not is impossible to know, and alas, his patent has long since expired.]

This invention is certainly not appropriate for classical oil refining. Even in his day, the oil refining industry was already sophisticated, running complex industrial-scale operations. Refineries use fractional distillation, which allows the lighter components to be refined out into a much purer form by distilling the liquid many times as the liquid condenses and re-evaporates as it travels up a column that is filled with beads or other surfaces. The oil industry also layers catalytic cracking on top of fractional distillation to change the chemical mix of the output oil components, as there is typically not the right mix of the lighter and more valuable chemicals that the market demands in crude oil. Catalytic cracking breaks up some of the heavier components through the use of special catalysts and heat prior to distillation. C.W.'s process does not seem to fit the bill in terms of allowing fractional distillation, supporting catalytic cracking, or allowing high throughput.

However, separate from oil refining, there is a related field of thin-film short-path distillation of fragile compounds in the pharmaceutical and food preparation fields. Although C.W.'s patent discussion only talks about its use with crude oil, it does seem to be a very early use of thin-film and short-path distillation. C.W. did not invent either of these two processes, but he created a clever apparatus that used both techniques, not long after both had been invented.

Two examples where thin-film short-path distillation, like C.W. made use of are when creating omega-3 concentrated fish oil from regular fish oil and when recovering pharmaceutical grade glycerin from biodiesel.

Natural fish oil has a mixture of omega-3 and omega-6 compounds. omega-3 compounds are better for you than omega-6 compounds. There is a market for a variety of fish oil that has a concentrated amount of omega-3 compounds. Because the fish oil is minimally heated in a thin-film short-path distillation process, it is not damaged during the distillation. The companies Incon Processing, LLC, Pfaudler Reactor Systems & GEA Niro all make products that use this sort of distillation.[403]

Chapter 14 – His family and personal life

Although he became a widower twice, C.W. was happily married and raised four accomplished children.

Marriage to Leonora Stern

On September 4, 1889, C.W. married Leonora Stern in Rolla, Missouri, the city where her parents, Edward Stern and Lizzie Hardin Evans Stern, lived.

Leonora's father, Edward Stern, was from Bavaria. Edward was born in 1834 and moved from Bavaria to Tazewell, Tennessee before 1860 along with three brothers or cousins. The 1860 U.S. census shows him in Tazewell. He is recorded there as a merchant in 1870 U.S. Census. Edward was Jewish.[404] (The curly hair of my younger days may well have come from Edward.)

Tazewell is a town in Northeastern Tennessee, very near the Virginia/Tennessee (eastern) side of the Cumberland Gap. The Cumberland Gap is a historically important pass over the Appalachian Mountains and is associated with Daniel Boone. The gap changed hands three times during the Civil War, not long after Edward's arrival.

Figure 96 Lizzie Harden Evans Stern with Elizabeth Woodworth in 1908 by the Russian River in Montesano, California[405]

Leonora's mother, Elizabeth "Lizzie" Hardin Evans, was a product of the American South. She was also born in Tazewell, Tennessee.[406] Her family had deep roots in Virginia, Tennessee and Kentucky. One part of her family was descended from a first cousin of author Jonathan Swift and a second cousin of poet John Dryden. Lizzie and Edward were married in 1867 in Tazewell. Their daughter, Leonora was born on August 7, 1869 in Tazewell. They had sons Walter in 1875 and Joseph in 1881. By 1880, the family had moved to Rolla, Missouri where Edward is recorded as a merchant and Lizzie as "keeping house" in the U.S. Census. An 1881 business directory records her father Edward as having a millinery (a hat making shop).[407]

C.W. and Leonora were married in 1889 in Rolla, Missouri, after he got his first professor job in Fayetteville, Arkansas in 1888. C.W.'s sister Metta said that Leonora was C.W.'s student in Fayetteville.[408] Their marriage license was issued on 2 PM, September 4, 1889 by Circuit Clerk, David E. Conan. It is signed by B.G. Manord, Pastor of the 1st Baptist Church of Fayetteville, Arkansas in his role as officiant.[409] [Author's note: I have the original of the certificate.]

Fayetteville is in Northwest Arkansas, only 251 miles from Rolla in central Missouri. A reasonable guess is that they met in Fayetteville and then took the train up to Rolla to get married with her parents. The fact that the officiant for the wedding was from Fayetteville is another clue. One interpretation of that is that the pastor may have ministered to them both. C.W. was twenty-four years and four months old and a new professor; Leonora was eighteen years and one month old at the time of their marriage.

The St. Louis-San Francisco Railroad had tracks that follow a path similar to the modern Interstate 44 from Oklahoma City and Tulsa to St. Louis.[410] These tracks passed right through Rolla. They also had a feeder line that headed south to Fayetteville. Although this railroad had San Francisco in its name and was nicknamed "Frisco", it never operated west of Texas. C.W., Leonora, and pastor Manord would have taken the train north from Fayetteville and changed trains in Monett in southwestern Missouri.[411] Later in the century, the passenger train from OKC to St. Louis would be called the "Meteor".[412] The mainline tracks are still in service and are now operated by the BNSF.

Figure 97 Train Station in Monett, Missouri where they would have changed trains on the way to their wedding[413]

Rolla, like Fayetteville, was and is a university town. It was then home to the Missouri School of Mines and Metallurgy, now known as Missouri S&T, the first technological learning institution west of the Mississippi.

Charles and Leonora had four children: Lawrence in 1890 in Fayetteville, AR, Harold in 1894 in Berkeley, CA, Charles in 1898 in Berkeley, CA, and Elizabeth in 1901 in Boston, MA.

Figure 98 Leonora Stern with caption saying "Those Dimples!" from Elizabeth Woodworth's photo album[414]

Leonora is listed as being an honorary member of the Prytanean Society at the University of California in 1924.[415] The Prytanean Society is a women's honor society that was founded at Cal in 1900.[416]

She became an invalid at some point in her life with "arthritis deformans", which is now known as rheumatoid arthritis. She is seated in every photograph that exists of her. The large first floor of their home in Berkeley was organized to allow her to get around in a wheelchair.

Leonora's siblings

Her brother Walter died young in 1895 around the age of 20.

The WWI draft record for her brother Joseph Stern shows their mother Elizabeth living at 1712 Greenwich Street in San Francisco.[417] Joseph is recorded in 1918 as living in Seattle and working as a travelling salesman for the N.K. Fairbank, Co. of 461 Market St. San Francisco.[418] In January of 1920, her mother Elizabeth and brother Joseph are recorded in the U.S. census as living in San Francisco. Sometime later that year, a voter registration record shows them living in Berkeley, just two blocks away from C.W. and Leonora, at 2224 Blake Street.[419]

Group photos of their family over time

Figure 99 C.W., C.E. (in front), Harold, Lawrence, Leonora circa 1900[420]

Figure 100 Lawrence, Charles E. (my Grandfather), Leonora, Charles W., Harold, Elizabeth Woodworth in Berkeley, CA circa 1916[421]

Figure 101 (Back Row) Lawrence, Mamie, Charles. E., Louise, C.W, Ray & Elizabeth Plass, & Harold; (Front Row) Jim & Elizabeth at home in Berkeley circa 1937[422]

Lawrence Woodworth

Lawrence Ariel Woodworth, the oldest son of Charles W. and Leonora Stern Woodworth was born on June 8, 1890 in Fayetteville Arkansas during the time of C.W.'s employment at Arkansas Industrial University. His birth date is just one week short of nine months after his parent's wedding day!

In 1909 at Berkeley High School, he is recorded as playing the role of the Count de Camembert in a production of "The Artist's Dream."[423] He graduated from the University of California with a degree in mining engineering.

Before WWI, he worked for two companies in the mining industry as an engineer: the North California Mining Company in Oroville, California and the L.T. Allen International Examination Assays. He is recorded as single on his 1917-18 WWI draft registration card, where he is given an occupational exemption as a mining engineer. From 1917 to 1919, he served in the Aviation Section and Engineering Corps of the U.S. Army. After the war he worked as an engineer for the A.G. Suydam Co., the Reorganized United Mines Co., and the Magnesite Reduction Corporation.[424]

Figure 102 Lawrence Woodworth in Nevada[425]

He married Theo Severence sometime between 1917 and 1920. No pictures survive of her. She immigrated with her father and three sisters on a ship from Liverpool, England through Canada, passing through the St. Albans, VT U.S. rail border crossing in 1910. (This was not an uncommon immigration route into the United States.) Unfortunately, the 1920 census records him back home at his parent's house in Berkeley as a widower. There is a photo missing from about this period in Lawrence's sister Elizabeth Woodworth's childhood photo album captioned "Scarlet Fever, Letterman General Hospital" with Lawrence's photo below it. The Spanish Flu epidemic of 1918-1919 is another possibility for causing her death, but there is no compelling evidence for or against either of these ideas. Elizabeth's photo album also has a photo of her and some friends wearing quarantine masks during this period.

In the 1930 U.S. Census, he is recorded living in Berkeley with C.W. and C.W.'s second wife Bernice and working as an engineer in the mining industry.[426] Later, he worked for Standard Oil (the present-day Chevron) in San Francisco.

In 1939, he is listed in several Oakland Tribune articles as serving as a geologist for the Tassajara Dome Oil Company of Oakland, California. In 1944, he was living on 228 Redwood Street in Vallejo, Solano County, California. The Tassajara Dome Oil Company unsuccessfully explored some oil fields in the Contra Costa portion of the San Francisco Bay Area. In 1941, he is listed as living at 338 First Street, in Pleasanton, CA.[427]

C.W. wrote in a November 1939 letter to his sister Minnie: "I am glad you are all well as is my family, even Lawrence is better and has gone to work for an oil company that is starting to bore a well in the field discovered by Prof. Clarke and which Lawrence helped him to study."[428]

He later married a woman named Cecil. They lived together on Redwood Street in Vallejo.[429] He died on August 26, 1949 in Solano County, California. He never had any children. Lawrence's sister Elizabeth kept in contact with Cecil after his death, and Cecil gave some china to her, apparently from C.W.'s trip to China. Elizabeth mailed the china to C.W.'s grandson Jim Woodworth, but the china broke in transit.

Harold Woodworth

Figure 103 Harold Woodworth, circa 1920[430]

Harold Evans Woodworth, the second son of C.W. and Leonora, was born on May 30, 1894 in California, likely in Berkeley or thereabout. Evans was his maternal grandmother's maiden name.

Harold got a B.S. in entomology from the College of Agriculture of the University of California (now U.C. Berkeley) in 1917.[431]

In 1912 and 1913 he was involved with mosquito control in San Mateo County, California.

In 1915 he wrote a paper entitled "Mosquito Control in the Vicinity of San Mateo 1904-1915" (Berkeley, California: Agricultural Experiment Station, College of Agriculture, University of California). He writes about the late spring of 1912 "people who had to go out on the marsh wore nets, tied ropes or strings around their ankles and wrists, wore gloves and even then were bitten."[432] By midsummer of 1912, "the mosquitoes migrated to town in a dark cloud for three days. Everybody who was not held in some way or another left town. It greatly affected property values and so it was seen that something radical must be done."[433] By 1913, the situation was better. An oiling campaign had reduced the problem. He reports: "For the small sum of about $5,500, these cities were freed of the pest which practically drove them from their homes the previous year."[434]

> "In July [1916] the supervisors of Kern County, CA approved the formation of the Dr. Morris Mosquito Abatement District (MAD). Named for a respected local physician who had led the fight against malaria, the Dr. Morris MAD was the state's first inland MAD formed to fight malaria. The Kern County trustees recruited Harold Woodworth, Charles Woodworth's son, to serve as the district's superintendent."[435]

In 1919 he was listed as being a faculty member of the Sigma Pi fraternity at the University of California.[436] In 1920, he was listed in the U.S. census as living in Redwood City, California on the San Francisco peninsula, working as a horticultural commissioner for San Mateo County.

A record of the University of the Philippines says: "... Mr. HAROLD E. WOODWORTH, a young graduate of the University of California, was appointed professor of entomology and head of the Department. Professor Woodworth returned to the United States in 1922."[437][438]

In 1925, he married Mamie Barlow, the adopted stepdaughter of former U.S. Congressman Charles Averill Barlow (1858-1927), who had represented San Luis Obispo in Congress between 1897 and 1899 and Julia Lillis Caldwell. After moving to Kern County, Charles Barlow became a principal in the Barlow and Hill Law Firm. The Barlow and Hill firm was associated with helping to set up numerous of the Kern County oil firms. It also produced maps of the Kern County oil tracts. Charles Barlow was also one of the most successful growers of citrus fruit in the area.[439]

His entry in a 1911 "History of Kern County: starts out:

> "No industry has contributed in greater degree to the wealth of Kern county than that of oil development and probably no firm has been identified more intimately with the advancement of the industry during the past decade than that of Barlow and Hill, a title familiar to all who have kept in touch with local progress. Since the organization of the firm in 1902 they have organized many companies, all of which have been successful, and the six which they now operate have shares of stock that are quoted as gilt-edged security with a continuous tendency to rise in public and private markets."[440]

In 1930, Harold and Mamie are recorded in the U.S. census as living at 1905 18th Street in Bakersfield, CA with Harold working as the manager of a farm. They never had children.

In 1941, Harold is recorded as receiving $26,458 as the sole heir of the remainder of C.W.'s estate. C.W. had written in his will that he had given "my other children their share in my property and I therefore name my son Harold Evans Woodworth, my sole heir to the property yet remaining in my possession."[441]

At some point, oil was discovered on their land and they did well. They had land near Arvin, California. In 1953, he and two others got a zoning variance to build an office building at 2201 F St. in Bakersfield.[442] Between 1956 and 1958 they moved to the house [that I remember visiting] at 2800 22nd Street in Bakersfield, California. He died in Kern County when I was eleven on August 25 1971[443].

[Author's note: I remember Harold as a kind and warm-hearted man. He had a big Cadillac and liked to take us to his favorite restaurant near the Bakersfield airport when we visited.

I remember his wife, my Great-Aunt Mamie as always having a wonderful twinkle in her eye. They were well travelled and had many stories about visiting one place or another. On their many journeys, they liked to travel with a private guide rather than on a tour. They enjoyed visiting San Francisco, particularly when their nephew Jim was as Intern at French Hospital there. Jim and Betty followed their advice of employing private guides on many trips.[444]

I also remember Mamie's mother, Charles Averill Barlow's wife Julia Caldwell Barlow. She outlived her husband by over 50 years. We referred to her as "Mrs. Barlow". She reached her 100th birthday and died about 1980. She lived with Harold and Mamie in Bakersfield. Mamie died in 1991 at the age of 94.]

Estate of Woodworth

A long legal saga ensued after Mamie died. Since Harold and Mamie did not have children, the proceeds of Harold's life remainder trust for Mamie was to be divided amongst the heirs, Elizabeth Woodworth and the two children of the late Charles E. Woodworth: my Uncle Jim and my mother. However, both Elizabeth Woodworth Plass and her husband Raymond Plass died between Harold's death and Mamie's death. Elizabeth's will bequeathed everything to Ray. Ray's will bequeathed his estate to the University of California, Berkeley. Harold and Mamie's trust was stuck in legal limbo because it was unclear whether the terms of the original estate held or whether Raymond Plass' will held.

The issue had to do with whether U.C. got a half (one of the two sibling's share) or a third (one of the three heir's share) of the estate. The case went all of the way to the California Supreme Court where the University of California won. The case is called *Estate of Woodworth.* A Google search on the term gives 670 hits. The case is discussed in law books and shows up on the syllabus of Wills & Trusts classes in some law schools. [Author's note: I still have a pile of the paperwork from the case.]

The www.ecasebriefs.com law website describes the issue that the California Supreme Case resolved as: "Whether a determination of the term "heirs at law" should be determined as of the date of the death of the named ancestor who predeceased the life tenant." The holding of the court was that: "The term "heirs at law" must be determined as of the date of the named ancestor who predeceased the life tenant and not at the death of the life tenant. The grantor did not manifest any other intent and the terms of the will do not express a meaning of futurity. None of the specific terms of the words include a reference to the future and the words "pay to" do not mean vest or otherwise constitute an expression of futurity. The intent of the testator as to when the heirs of law should be determined is not evident in the will and it would be speculative to try and discern such intent. The court must implement rules of construction to insure uniformity and predictability in the law."[445]

[Author's note: After my mother's death, I inherited some oil and gas rights to some Kern County property from Harold and Mamie's estate that had been adjudicated in *Estate of Woodworth*. My mother actually received some small oil rights lease checks from Enron before that company's demise. Unfortunately for me, all oil production has ceased on this property. (If anyone is in the market for some depleted fractional oil and gas rights on a few hundred acres in Kern County, let me know.)]

Charles E. Woodworth

Charles Edward Woodworth was born in Berkeley, California on September 25, 1898. His younger sister, Elizabeth called him by the nickname of "Chick". He was known as "Charles" in adulthood.

Figure 104 Charles E. Woodworth, circa 1919[446]

Charles graduated with a BS and an MS from the University of California, Berkeley. His May 1923 86-page master's thesis was entitled "The Sawflies of California.[447] He was a member of the Sigma Pi fraternity while at Cal.[448] He took a job as a Professor at Modesto Junior College in Modesto in California's Central Valley. The college had been established only two years earlier in 1921 and is the oldest Junior College in California.[449]

Figure 105 1925 image of South Hall of Modesto Junior College[450]

He is mentioned in the May 14, 1926 issue of *Science* as having assisted his father on a research effort at the Barro Colorado Island Research Station in the Panama Canal Zone.[451] He is on the manifest of the S.S. Parismina, arriving with his father in New Orleans from Havana, Cuba on August 10, 1925.

Figure 106 C.W.'s son Charles E. Woodworth circa 1927[452]

Marriage to Louise Nelson

In Modesto he met and married one of his fellow teachers at the college, the widow, Sarah Louise "Louise" Nelson Vickers. She was the daughter of early Methodist Amazon missionaries, Justus Henry Nelson and Fannie Bishop Capen. They established the first Protestant Church in the Amazon Basin in Belém, Para, Brazil, near the mouth of the Amazon. Charles' bride Louise was born in Belém. Justus lived as a self-supporting missionary there for 45 years. Fannie Nelson lived in Belém for some years and then returned to Boston to raise their children, all four of which graduated from Boston University.

Louise Nelson attended Boston Girls Latin School, now named Boston Latin Academy. It was established in 1877 and was the first college preparatory school for girls in the United States. She attended the historically Methodist (now nonsectarian) Boston University, as did her Methodist missionary father and her siblings. She graduated in 1910 with a degree in chemistry. It was rare during that era for a woman to graduate with a degree in science.

Figure 107 1905 graduation photo for two of Louise Nelson's brothers from Boston University[453]

Justus presided over Charles and Louise's June 20, 1926 Berkeley, California wedding. The wedding was at the First Congregational Church near the Cal campus and the reception was at C.W. and Leonora's house a few blocks away. A Modesto Herald-News article says:

> "The wedding of Mrs. Louise Nelson Vickers and Charles Edward Woodworth was solemnized Sunday afternoon, June 20, at 2 o'clock, at the First Congregational Church at Berkeley.

> Rev. Justus H. Nelson, father of the bride and returned missionary from Brazil, was the officiating minister. Preceding the ceremony, Miss Erma Stern, a cousin of the bridegroom, sang "I Love You Truly" and "Oh, Promise Me.
>
> The bride was charmingly gowned in a lavender georgette, trimmed in crème lace. She carried a shower bouquet of pink roses, white sweetpeas and lily of the valley. Miss Ellen Bibens, the maid of honor, wore a peach georgette and carried an arm bouquet of maidenhair fern.
>
> Lawrence Woodworth, brother of the groom was the best man. …
> Mrs. Woodworth is the daughter of Rev. J. H. Nelson, who returned in December from a life spent as a missionary in Brazil. She has been a member of the faculty at the Modesto college during the last year, and occupied the position as the head of the Home Economics Department. She is a charming young woman, and during her year in Modesto has succeeded in endearing herself to the students and faculty of the college and all others with whom she has come in contact. …
>
> Prof. Charles E. Woodworth has been a member of the faculty of the Modesto College during the past two years, and is a young man of high character, and has made an enviable place for himself in the Modesto educational world. …"[454]

Louise was the first cousin of Thomas Sterling North, Newbery Honor winning author, under the name Sterling North, of many children's books. Two of his books, *Rascal* and *Midnight and Jeremiah,* were made into the Disney movies *Rascal (1969)* and *So Dear to My Heart (1949)*. His home has been preserved as a museum in Edgerton, Wisconsin. Louise was also the first cousin of poet and *Poetry* magazine editor Jessica Nelson North.

Charles adopted Louise's son, James Vickers Woodworth. While in Modesto, they had a daughter, my mother, Elizabeth Louise Woodworth. She was born very premature, but survived. A newspaper article entitled "35 Ounce Baby in Modesto - Kept Alive In Electric Incubator - She's Fed With Eye Dropper"[455] about her survival detailed how "she could be put in a cigar box" and was picked up by the Associated Press. They lived at 322 Johnson Street in Modesto.

Figure 108 C.W., C.E. and Elizabeth Woodworth in Modesto, CA, 1927[456]

Ph.D. in Wisconsin

Charles and Louise then moved to Madison, Wisconsin where he attended the University of Wisconsin and received a Ph.D. in entomology. His 1930 122-page Ph.D. thesis was entitled "The effect of reduced pressure on the respiration of the honey bee."[457]

Figure 109 Christmas 1928 from Madison, Wisconsin[458]

Military service

During World War I, he entered the United States Army and was in training when the armistice was declared.

In World War II, during a twenty six month period in the Bismarck Archipelago, Luzon, the Southern Philippines, [459]Burma and China, he was commanding officer of the Army's 33rd Mosquito Control Unit. Their job was to find the breeding place of the mosquitoes and eradicate them as well as teaching the soldiers how to protect themselves. He received special citations and ended his service as a major. The control of insect borne-disease in the South Pacific during WWII through the use of DDT and other agents was a significant factor in the allied victory there.

Figure 110 Charles E. Woodworth in WWII[460]

He returned from war in October 1945. His lungs were significantly damaged during this service. He had to hang upside down on numerous occasions for the rest of his life to drain them.[461] This service injury also contributed to his somewhat early death of a respiratory ailment in 1964.

Career with the USDA

He had a long career with the USDA Agricultural Research Service. He was a leader of the Vegetable Insects Laboratory in the Blalock Tracks at College Place, Washington. In 1947 he worked in the Truck Crop and Garden Insect Laboratory there.[462] His principal research was into the wireworm, although he worked on many other things during his long career. The fact that the wireworm lives underground makes them difficult to exterminate. Much of his work had to do with techniques to allow reasonable crop yield in the presence of wireworms. He also did work on controlling onion maggot flies. Walla Walla sweet onions are the most famous agricultural product of Southeast Washington State where they lived.

Thirty-one insect specimens that were collected by him are in the Essig Museum of Entomology at the University of California, Berkeley.[463] All of the specimens are from Order Hemiptera, Family Aphididae (aphids) and were collected in either Walla Walla, WA or Saint Helena, CA from 1937 to 1951.

A 1941 USDA publication lists him working in the Walla Walla office of the ARS where the topics of research are the wireworm and the pea weevil. He and his co-workers are listed as: Merton C. Lane, B.S., Entomologist in charge of wireworm investigations, Charles E. Woodworth, Ph.D., Associate Entomologist, Edward W. Jones, M.A. Assistant Entomologist, Russell S. Lehman, M.S. Assistant Entomologist, Kenneth E. Gibson, M.S., Assistant Entomologist, Horace P. Lanchester, M.S. Jr. Entomologist, and Walter E. Peay, M.S., Jr. Entomologist (seasonal headquarters, pea weevil investigation).[464]

In 1947 he spent 2 ½ months in Washington, D.C., Beltsville, MD, and Moorestown, PA studying the latest techniques in analysis for DDT and other related compounds.[465] In 1948, he was burned in the arms and face in a laboratory explosion[466], but made a full recovery.

The 1961 Washington State University Bulletin, the course catalog for the University, lists him as a "Collaborator in Entomology".[467] Pullman is a 117-mile journey from College Place.

His Entomology publications include:

- The Sawflies of California (May, 1923), University of California Press, 192 pages
- The Effect of Reduced Pressure on the Respiration of the Honey Bee (1930), Madison, 244 pages (his doctoral dissertation)
- The Reactions of Wireworms to Arsenicals (1938), U.S. Government Printing Office, Reprinted from the Journal of Agricultural Research. Vol. 57, no. 3, August 1, 1938

Community service

He was listed in "Who's Who in the West" and "Who's Who in Washington". He was a charter member of the College Place Kiwanis Club and was its secretary for its first 15 years. He led several Community Chest drives. He was also a member of the First Congregational Church of Walla Walla, Washington where he was elected Deacon in January of 1947.[468][469] He was the scoutmaster of Troop 11 in College Place in 1946, despite the fact that his son James was twenty-five by then.[470]

Shortly after his death in 1966, the Kiwanis Club renamed the softball field in Kiwanis Park, College Place as the "Charles E. Woodworth Memorial Ball Field." The diamond is still there. [Author's note: When I look at it on Google Earth, it appears to have seen better days.]

Memories of Charles E. Woodworth

Figure 111 Charles E. Woodworth circa 1960[471]

His granddaughters Gail, Vicki and Linda would spend a week with their grandparents in College Place. When Gail was old enough, she would go with him to his office. There she counted worms and also helped develop the weather reports, measuring the amount of rain or adding information to the graphs.[472]

[Author's note: He died when I was six, but I have a distinct memory of their home in College Place, near Walla Walla. They had a large rose garden behind their house with an archway entrance to it. I remember running around the garden with my brother. I also have a good memory of being "polished" with a towel by my grandfather after a bath. He would dry us by moving the towel quickly as if he were putting the final polish on a pair of shoes.]

Elizabeth Woodworth Plass

Figure 112 Young Elizabeth and Charles Woodworth circa 1903, caption by Elizabeth Woodworth in her photo album[473]

C.W.'s youngest child, Mary Elizabeth "Elizabeth" was born on February 7, 1901 in Boston, Massachusetts, during the second time that C.W. was at Harvard. She graduated from the University of California in about 1922. In 1924, she is recorded as being a stenographer.

In 1927, she married Raymond "Ray" Plass. Uncle Ray was born in Rhode Island in 1898. His family had lived in and around Providence for many generations. He was an electrical engineer (as am I) who worked at the Ray Oil Burner Company in San Francisco for virtually all his career. (The company was named after a different Ray.) His specialty was the control of industrial burners. He received three U.S. patents for his work there, all having to do with controlling burners. One of the patents is entitled "Viscosity compensating oil burner control system".

Elizabeth and Ray lived at 1934 Hopkins St., Berkeley, about a mile north of the Cal Campus in May of 1930. They lived at 1803 Oxford St, just north of the northwest corner of the Cal campus in 1944.[474] His mother, Jessie Charlotte Wheeler lived with them for a while. They eventually built a beautiful home in Piedmont, in the East Bay hills near Oakland. Elizabeth became interested in Asian art. She would find pieces, paintings, anything artistic even though it was in poor shape, and Ray would refurbish the item to its original splendor.[475]

Elizabeth volunteered many hours at Merritt Hospital in Oakland. She was the president of the volunteers for at least two years.[476]

[Author's note: Into his eighties, Ray would drive down the hill and take BART into his work in San Francisco. He had a spring in his step and was a joy. He could also whittle well; he once whittled me a clever wooden puzzle with about ten pieces. I gave a short eulogy for him at his 1988 funeral.]

Elizabeth's Photo Album

[Author's note: During the research for this book, something amazing happened. The C.W. Woodworth house in Berkeley came on the market in October of 2011. At the first open house, I met Tim Lundgren of the Berkeley Historical Society.[477] In the mid-90's he had purchased a photo album at a flea market. Inside the front cover of the photo album was Elizabeth's name and address of the house. Tim got an email from the Berkeley Architectural Heritage Association (BAHA) that the Woodworth House was open and remembered that he had bought that photo album some fifteen years before. He brought the album to the open house. We just missed each other at first, but he had given his name to the realtor and wasn't far away when she called him. With that, I was reunited with my great-aunt Elizabeth's photo album. The album contains her pictures from age eight through 24 or so. It includes by far the best photos of my great-grandmother, Leonora Stern as well as the only known photos of Leonora's mother, Lizzie Hardin Evans Stern.]

Figure 113 Tim Lundgren with Elizabeth Woodworth's photo album in the "Big Room" at 2237 Carleton[478]

"Bobby the family dog

Elizabeth's photo album has many loving photos of Bobby, their family dog.

Figure 114 C.W. and Bobby[479]

Foresters

C.W. is recorded as serving as the "Grand Chief Ranger" of the Companion Court, a social organization associated with Independent Order of Foresters (IOF) in an Oakland Tribune article on July 20, 1904. He delivered the address of welcome at a social occasion.[480]

The Independent Order of Foresters is a fraternal benefit society that is today headquartered in Toronto and promotes activities associated with children's health including the Children's Miracle Network. They also sell a series of life insurance products.[481]

Commons Club

Commons clubs were fraternal organizations that had open memberships. They were common at colleges and universities in the late 19th and early 20th centuries.

In a letter to his niece on May 18, 1940 he mentions:

> "You may be interested in learning that a short time ago we had Mr. Streit lecture to us at a dinner meeting of the Commons Club to which I belong. He made a very good impression. He is a very convincing speaker. His plans seemed sound but the inertia to be overcome may require the effects of the present war to accomplish it. I have little doubt that when peace finally comes his work will be a very important contribution to the organization of the future world."[482]

The Commons Club in Berkeley still exists and is now known as the City Commons Club after a merger with another club.[483]

This speaker was undoubtedly Clarence Streit promoting his book "Union Now" who urged the allies to form a political union of democratic nations with a common foreign policy and defense force. Streit's organization, the Federal Union, played a role in the creation of the Marshall Plan and the formation of NATO as well as some other transnational organizations. A group called the Streit Council is still around today.[484]

Leonora's Death

Leonora died on September 7, 1924, just three days after their 35th anniversary. Her funeral was held at 2 PM on September 10th at their home.[485]

Her September 7, 1924 death certificate lists her cause of death as "arthritis deformans" with a contributing factor of "acute nephritis following operation". The certificate goes on to say that a cholecystectomy was done as part of the autopsy, that she died at Merritt Hospital in Oakland, and that she was cremated.

My interpretation of the certificate is that she had been greatly weakened by her decades with rheumatoid arthritis. At some point she needed a gall bladder operation from which she got a kidney infection and died. This was before both penicillin and kidney dialysis, so if you had an operation you might get a bacterial infection, and if your kidneys shut down due to that infection your electrolytes might get out of balance causing your heart to stop.

In a December 24, 1937 letter to his niece Celina who had lamented the loss of a baby in a letter to him, C.W. related what Leonora had said to him:

"I received two letters which made me feel sad. One was from Howard and Elsie whose hearts are sore from the loss of Alvin, the other was yours. Both are courageously accepting the situation. It would have been much worse if courage was also lost. You know how much Leonora had to suffer and how bravely she lived. She said 'she had to grin and bear it or bear it without grinning.' …

I know something of the sorrow of the loss of someone we have come to think of as part of our own life. When Leonora died the foundations seemed fallen from beneath me but I had to hang on to my work and I had my family and I came to see that she had done her work and that she had left me memories to cherish."[486]

Marriage to Bernice Christopher

On April 4, 1926, at 823 Waterloo St. in Los Angeles, CA, C.W. married Bernice Christopher, his first cousin once removed. She was born in Michigan on July 31, 1881[487] and was sixteen years younger than C.W. She was 44 and he was 60. The 1930 U.S. census has her mistakenly 4 years younger.[488] She was the daughter of John Inslee Christopher and Mary Elizabeth Woodworth, who was the daughter of Stephen Elias Woodworth and Ann Gilbert. Her mother Mary was C.W.'s step-sister and first cousin, but was nearly a full generation older than C.W. and was raised in a different household, that of her grandparents after her mother's death. Both of Bernice's parents had been raised in Michigan.[489] Bernice was the niece of Mary Gilbert, one of the signers of the Declaration of Sentiments.

As the result of these interconnections, C.W. was Bernice's first cousin once removed. Bernice was also his much-older step-sister's daughter.

To make things less complicated, it was a later-in-life, post child-bearing-years, find-someone-to-be-happy-with as-we-grow-older marriage for both of them. It was the first marriage for her.

Unfortunately, she died at home just four years later, on May 6, 1930 at 10 AM of "acute dilation of heart myocardial failure" (heart failure) with the contributing factor of "chronic parenchymatous nephritis" (kidney disease). C.W.'s daughter Elizabeth was the witness on the death certificate.[490]

My assumption is that what that means is that she really died of kidney failure. Back in the days before dialysis machines, if your kidneys stopped working, your electrolytes would get severely out of balance. This would interfere with the electrical activity of the heart and stop it.

C.W. did not remarry after this in his ten remaining years. In the same 1937 letter to his niece Celina as mentioned in the previous section, he relates:

> "Likewise when Bernice passed on and my teaching work was over and my family scattered you can see why I grasped at the opportunity of travelling over Central and South America with a new job and the meeting of new people. I could finally think of the loving nature in all its manifestations as the permanent thing in our lives together."[491]

Figure 115 C.W.'s sister Minnie, Bernice, C.W. and niece Celina at 823 Waterloo St., Los Angeles, CA[492]

If you look at the Google Street-view image of the house at 823 Waterloo Street, Los Angeles, CA, it has not changed much since this photograph was taken. The curved arch over the window is easily seen.

Christmas Card 1926

sent to Aunt Metta and Uncle Henry Burkhart farm in Potomac IL

Figure 116 Holiday Card 1925 – this is a photo of their home - note the stamp with their picture and the number "2" drawn around as well as the drawn postmark with the dates of both Christmas and New Years on it[493]

Figure 117 Three snapshots – Bernice and C.W., C.W. with his car, Memorial Stadium during a football game from the southern part of tightwad hill[494]

C.W.'s Grandchildren

Although C.W. and Leonora had four children, they ended up with only one biological grandchild, my mother, and one adopted grandchild, my Uncle Jim. Of C.W. and Leonora's children:

- Lawrence was widowed early, never had children, and died at age 59
- Harold married once for life, never had children, and died at age 77
- Charles E. married once for life to a widow, legally adopted her son Jim, had my mother, Elizabeth L., and died at age 66.

- (Mary) Elizabeth married once for life, never had children, and died at age 84.

All four of their children lived healthy & reasonably long lives and were educated. There is no evidence that their father's occupation (with its exposure to pesticides) had any bearing on their relative lack of children.

Figure 118 C.W.'s grandchildren Elizabeth and Jim Woodworth[495]

James Vickers Woodworth

The first was my Uncle Jim. James Nelson Vickers was born of Hazzlett (spelled Hazlitt on some documents) Vickers and Sarah Louise "Louise" Nelson Vickers on August 27, 1921 in Dover, New Hampshire. His father had a B.S. from the Oregon State Agricultural College and another degree from University of Arkansas. He served as the Business Secretary of the University of New Hampshire. His father died on August 22, 1923, a week before Jim's second birthday of acute bacterial endocarditis, which is a bacterial infection of the heart.

His mother moved to Portland, Oregon where her brother Luther was living and then attended Oregon State University. In 1925, she started a job teaching home economics at Modesto Junior College in Modesto, California. In June of 1926, she married Charles E. Woodworth, who was also a teacher at the College. Charles legally adopted Jim, who was renamed James Vickers Woodworth.

In 1939, their family visited the Bay Area, staying at C.W.'s home. They visited the World's Fair on Treasure Island. Teenage Jim had a long busy day and was so tired that he fell asleep without undressing on the couch in the study, where he had his room.[496]

Jim went to Whitman College in Walla Walla, Washington and received an M.D. from the University of Oregon Medical School in 1946 under the sponsorship of the U.S. Army. He did his internship in San Francisco. He married Cara Elisabeth "Betty" Davis, whom he had met at Whitman.

Figure 119 Jim Woodworth in Medical School[497]

He became an Internist and had a successful medical practice in Portland, Oregon. They had three girls, Gail, Vicki, and Linda and have three grandchildren and a great-grandchild.

Elizabeth Louise Woodworth

My mother, Elizabeth Louise Woodworth was born on June 6, 1927 in Modesto, California of Charles E. Woodworth and Sarah Louise Nelson Woodworth. She was born prematurely and was so small that she "fit into a cigar box". An Associated Press story reported on her survival.

Figure 120 Charles E., Elizabeth, Charles W. Woodworth, circa 1931[498]

She attended Whitman College and graduated from Lewis and Clark College in Portland, Oregon. She got a master's degree in Christian education from the Pacific School of Religion in Berkeley. In 1955, she married my father Norman Bill "Bill" Holden in Sacramento.

She returned to what is now called California State University, Sacramento and received a Masters in Counseling in the 1970's. She worked as a counselor and adult education teacher. She had two children, my brother Craig and me, and four grandchildren.

[Author's note: Because my mother only knew her grandfather, C.W. as a child and was not overly interested in science, she never conveyed to me any of the details of C.W.'s career. I attended U.C. Davis without knowing that my great-grandfather is considered the founder of the Davis' Entomology department. I even took a class in Briggs Hall where the department is located. I have had to rediscover most of the information in this book through careful research as well as through interactions with the PBESA members during my annual visits starting in 2004 to their meetings to present the C.W. Woodworth Award.
(See *Chapter 17 – The C.W. Woodworth Award*.)]

Political Leanings

The California voter registration records of C.W. and his wife & family list them all as Republicans [even though they were living in Berkeley]. His mother-in-law and brother-in-law were also recorded as Republicans in 1920. My mother, C.W.'s granddaughter, was a lifelong Democrat [as am I]. In C.W.'s era, the Republican Party was the party of civil rights.

In his correspondence there is an August through October 1934 exchange of letters with a Reverend John Thomas James, STM that discusses various issues related to the Great Depression. In these letters, his political views seem to be conservative leaning, but reasonably centrist and clear thinking. C.W. writes:

"What I called the first plan was to maintain markets by giving credit. When these creditors could not pay, naturally, production had to stop and so we have unemployment. You say our 'leaders collapsed spiritually.' I have heard this often, but no one can name these leaders. Our Mr. Harris says it was [former Secretary of the Treasury Andrew] Mellon and [banker J.P. 'Jack'] Morgan [Jr.]. Some of the Democrats say it was [President Herbert] Hoover. Others say it was the majority in Congress who tried to corner wheat. You evidently don't mean any of these and what you say about them does not describe any of them or any other man or group I know anything about. I do not know anyone in the world whose duty is to correlate production and distribution. President Roosevelt and the last Congress may say they are trying to do this now, but I cannot see that they [the National Recovery Administration] have not done more harm than good. I believe you are echoing an incorrect diagnosis.

I have recognized the necessity of charity at the present time to feed those who are hungry. If the cause of the present condition is 'hatred', why not try to find out who does the hating and who is being hated? I do not know anyone who hates those out of work. The only reason I know why employers do not hire men is that they do not know how to do so without a loss.

I did not particularly raise the question whether so much had been spent for charity, but I did try to point out that with all the spending we are worse off today economically than ever before in our history. The enormous expenditures have not made any progress towards recovery and that they cannot contribute towards it. The best that this kind of effort can accomplish is to skid us down to a lower standard of living than this generation has ever seen. What it seems destined to bring about is the destruction of the middle class leaving only the rich and poor, and if we follow Russia killing off the rich, leaving only the poor.

I have no method for the whole nation. I see no hope for them except the indirect help of trying to decrease the competition for the jobs that will be available. I hope for the creation of a new middle class of relatively wealthy people to whom wealth is not the goal of their lives nor the means of living on the labors of a servant class. This great mass who seem to prefer to be laborers and servants can only be helped I believe by this indirect method. I do not want to discourage any who try to help them but I do think we should look the situation squarely in the face and recognize that the present methods can have no other effect than to make things worse for all except the extremes, of the poor with nothing to lose and the rich who have the ability to prosper under any condition.

In conclusion, I should perhaps point out why the present methods can only lower our standards.

1. It now costs more to run the government than to feed the population. Can the body politic be healthy with such a host of parasites?
2. The NRA [National Recovery Administration] increases the outgo and decreases the income of the middle class. Laborers may have a temporary advantage but it cannot continue.
3. The AAA [Agricultural Adjustment Act of 1933] taxes New York for the benefit of Texas and starts Argentina raising more wheat and Brazil more cotton all to the injury of the American middle class.
4. The tinkering with the currency [there was complex interplay of money supply and gold reserve actions between nations during this period] has already destroyed a third of my life's savings. This [his life's savings] has not been great but enough to save me from having to accept charity in my old age. This trip I am making will cost me a half more than it should.
5. The various relief measures have all tended to destroy independence and created an ever increasing class of people who do not want to support themselves.
6. There has been just three items in the moral breakdown (a) we returned to legalized murder when we entered the war

[he must be referring to WWI] (b) we departed from business honesty in repudiating debts [the depression led to many bank failures, bankruptcies, and a credit crisis], and (c) we have lost our self-respect when we seek to receive that which we have not earned.

Yours, C.W. Woodworth"

In a November, 1939 letter to his sister Minnie he writes:

"We had an election here in California Tuesday as I suppose you saw by the papers. We were awfully afraid that the state finances would be wrecked, but a 2-1 vote turned down the measure."[499]

The only tax-related California ballot proposition that failed in 1939 was entitled "Retirement Warrants". This defeated measure would have instituted a 3% state income tax among other things.[500]

Avocations

He had many avocations. These included genealogy, chess, shorthand, and prohibition.

Genealogy

Among the many things C.W. was good at, he was an excellent genealogist. [Author's note: I have his original genealogical records. They are systematic and well documented. The most precious is a 250 page leather-bound, small three-ring binder full of yellowed type-written and hand-annotated pages of records detailing each family group and his wife's extended families. There is also a section detailing his daughter-in-law's (my grand-mother's) family.]

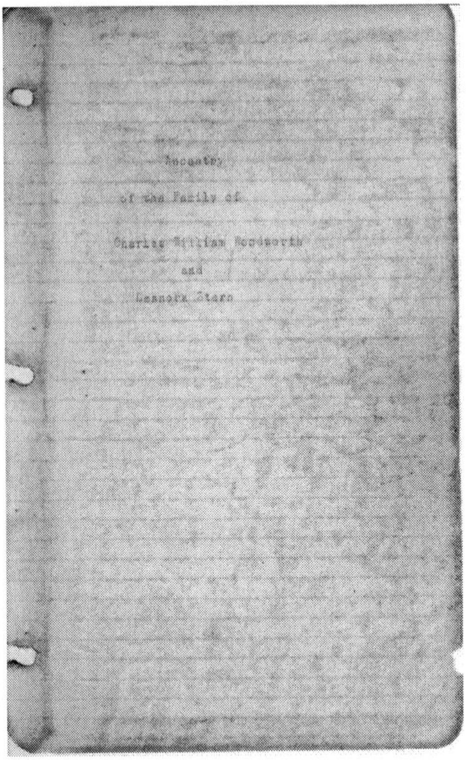

Ancestry

of the Family of

Charles William Woodworth

and

Leonora Stern

Figure 121 Cover page of his book of genealogy research[501]

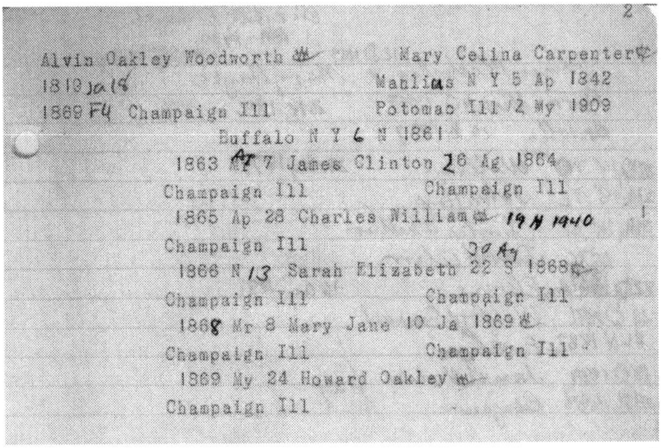

2

Alvin Oakley Woodworth Mary Celina Carpenter
1819 Ja 19 Manlius N Y 5 Ap 1842
1869 F4 Champaign Ill Potomac Ill 2 My 1909
Buffalo N Y 6 N 1861
1863 Ap 7 James Clinton 26 Ag 1864
Champaign Ill Champaign Ill
1865 Ap 28 Charles William 19 N 1940
Champaign Ill 30 Ag
1866 N 13 Sarah Elizabeth 22 S 1868
Champaign Ill Champaign Ill
1868 Mr 8 Mary Jane 10 Ja 1869
Champaign Ill Champaign Ill
1869 My 24 Howard Oakley
Champaign Ill

Figure 122 Page for his immediate family in C.W.'s genealogy book[502]

Chess

He studied chess mathematically and analyzed 30,000 games.[503] He was a founding member of the Berkeley College Chess Club in 1897. The club played matches against the U.C. Chess Club.[504]

In a 1939 letter to his sister Minnie, the 74 year old C.W. was describing a "church night" event that he attended, he says: "I went to the second [room] and played chess and won every game."[505]

Prohibition

He was interested in prohibition and attended at least two state conventions on it.[506] One was on August 27, 1892 in Los Angeles[507] and another was in 1902.[508]

Once when C.W. was visiting College Place (Walla Walla) where his son Charles E. lived, C.W. and his grandson Jim went to town on the bus. While waiting for the return bus, C.W. offered his grandson a cold drink. Jim asked for a root beer, but grandfather said "no, not anything with beer". He was a teetotaler in every respect.[509]

Shorthand

He perfected an extensive new system of shorthand.[510] In his correspondence is an October 19, 1924 letter from Cal English Professor Cornelius Bradley giving some critique of his system. A particular complaint is that C.W.'s system conflated the sounds for "ah" and "awe". Professor Bradley jokingly called that "yoking an ox with an ass". He also suggested paying more attention to words with double meanings and pronunciations like "lead" and omitting foreign words from the system. It is unclear if anything came of C.W.'s shorthand system, and no record of the system itself seems to exist. Of course, the development of Stenotype machines, dictation machines, and word processors have diminished the role of shorthand.

Religious beliefs

Some sense of C.W.'s religious beliefs and how they may have evolved through his life can be gathered from his writings.

His parent's religion

C.W's parents were likely Christian. Their November 6, 1861 marriage certificate from Buffalo, NY has a drawing of the biblical scene entitled "Marriage in Cana of Galiliee" [the water into wine story] in the background. [The most famous painting of this scene is by Veronese, but the artist who made the drawing on the certificate was not as talented as Veronese.] Given his family's origins in upstate New York, it seems highly like that they were Protestant. Given C.W.'s Baptist religion, it seems likely that they were Baptist.

1893 Endowment effort

In C.W.'s collected correspondence is a letter that indicates that someone in C.W.'s religious community made an offer to endow the University of California in some manner, but with a religious restriction. C.W. passed that offer onto Cal President Kellogg. On October 16, 1893 President Kellogg responded:

> "I have consulted our Law Professor as to the point contained in your letter. He thinks that our Board of Regents can not accept an endowment with the condition you name. If such an endowment were offered, all we could do would be respectfully to decline it."[511]

1911 speech

One little snippet from the transcript of a speech he gave in 1911 is hard to interpret with what it says about his beliefs. It might mean that he believed in the classic story of St. Peter or it might be that he was just using that story as a metaphor in his speech. It reads:

> "If all insects could be classified as saints or sinners, the horticultural commissioner could stand as St. Peter at the gate separating the good from the bad and condemning the latter class to destruction."[512]

1920 writings

Some sense of his religious beliefs can be gathered from two snippets from his article "China's Greatest Need".[513] In this paper, he argues for the establishment of an Industrial University in China. He says: "The fundamental principle of the Industrial University is that our duty to God is to make of our lives the greatest success in every particular, and to aid others to obtain the same success."[514] In the conclusion of the same paper he says:

> "While the stress is thus laid on things that can be measured with money, we believe that this is the best way to lead to the higher and finer things of life. After the material things are conquered, after one has leaned efficiency in earning his daily bread, he will have the time and power and the inclination to also pursue those things which are more than bread. We believe that this follows from the natural God-given instincts of man; that it is the natural reaction which will follow from the self-wrought relief from the limiting environment we which to ameliorate. We believe that this Industrial University will not be built upon the sands but on the firm foundation of the wisest and truest philanthropy, contributing in a most effective way to the abundance of life eternal."[515]

1930 Writing

C.W. wrote a little piece in *Science* titled "What is Control?" about the use of the phrase "natural control" in some entomology publications.

"The term control carries the thought of definite conscious action of a rational being, something done by man for his own benefit. It may be indirect through a mechanism he has set up, but it is always something that carries out his will. According to the older thinking [religious thinking], certain actions of nature were also conceived as controlled by an intelligence who ordered everything for the benefit of man and of individual men, and thus we had natural remedies administered by this higher power who used parasites and predators as his agents. Either the retention of this conception of nature, or more likely, the unthinking retention of this form of statement gives us now [the term] natural control.

Contrasted with this is the use of the work un-controlled, which is almost universally expressive of the action of nature where a control by man is not exercised. Natural control is thus a contradiction of terms, because it is equivalent to non-control, and should disappear from the literature of entomology."[516]

1937 Letter to his niece

More evidence of his evolving thinking is found in his December 24, 1937 letter to his niece Celina who had lamented the loss of a baby in a letter to him.

"Perhaps one of the first questions that will to us is 'why' and in most cases we will have to leave the question unanswered but after [a] while we can see that the answer to that question is of no real significance to us. Very few of the accidents of life are anything we could have avoided and any way if they were our fault it is a past fault that we can do nothing now to prevent. There is a sense in which fatalism is right but fatalism stops with this very unsatisfying answer to the question 'why'. The real question is what are we going to do about it. Its answer is in the now and in the time to come. Someone has likened our life to a play. We each have our part to play. We may be a prince or a pauper. That does not really matter. The real question is how we play our part. If the part is hard the more reason to play it well.

I am proud of you because I know you are playing your part well. Your going back to work I think was fine of you. The passing on of the things you had made for your own to the other baby was fine. The continuing of your church work again shows your spirit and the fact that you carry on even from you[r] sick room still more emphacises [sic] the fact.

These are only the fragments that reach me over a thousand miles of separation. I know if I were there I would have many others to record. Otherwise I know there must be times of discouragement, of deep sorrow, of weeping. But these things pass away, they are of the moment. They perhaps have their function to perform, provided we do not let them keep us down in the valley but rather to stimulate us to climb upwards toward the heights."[517]

Despite the loss of her child, his letter to her has no reference to the will of God or of any sort of personal God. He refers to church, but only in the context of her church work. His advice to his niece is secular, practical and wonderfully comforting.

C.W. and Churches

He was a member of the Baptist Church. In Fayetteville, Arkansas, he almost certainly belonged to the First Baptist Church of Fayetteville since he was married by its Pastor in 1889.[518] This congregation is still in existence. At the time it was located in a white frame building on College Avenue, just one block south of its current location at 20 East Dickson Street in Fayetteville.[519]

In Berkeley, he belonged to the First Baptist Church of Berkeley and was involved in its activities. In November 1939 the 74 year old C.W. wrote to his sister:

> "We are to have a celebration next month of the 50th anniversary of the Baptist Church. I am in my 49th year so you see I am near the beginning of the church. I am chairman of the program committee so I shall have my hands full for a month or so. I may develop some dramatic features in connection with this affair. We have the first committee meeting tomorrow night and then things will begin to happen".[520]

The First Baptist Church of Berkeley was established in 1889, which is 50 years before 1939.[521] This church is at 2345 Channing Way in Berkeley, in between his house and campus and is today a part of the Association of Welcoming and Affirming Baptist Churches, which basically means that they fully support LGBT rights including marriage equality.[522]

The present-day openness of this church does not mean that it was always so. C.W. was a scientist who did not believe in the Genesis story of creation. A transcript of a speech he gave to the Cambridge Entomological Club reads:

> "An example of the far reaching character of a fact is that of the origin of species through evolution. When Darwin established the truth of this fact it soon came to be recognized that this basal fact of evolution was a fundamental principal of almost every other science which had occupied the attention of man."[523]

My mother reported to me that "He was thrown out of a church because he believed in evolution."[524] She was religious herself, received a master's degree in Christian education, and was not trained in biological science so she always told me this with mixed emotion. The March 1895 edition of the Pacific Unitarian reports:

> The Baptist Church of Berkeley has expelled for heresy, Mr. W.C. Maxwell, a student of the University, and Professor C.W. Woodworth, who came to his defense. A considerable number of the church opposed the action, but the strait-laced are in the majority, and the believers in rationalistic Christianity were turned out. Mr. Maxwell admits that he has become a Unitarian. Professor Woodworth considers himself still a Baptist.[525]

Given that C.W. chaired the 50th anniversary celebration committee of the First Baptist Church in 1939, they must have changed their mind at some point. His expulsion happened just 35 ½ years after the publication of the Origin of Species. By then, evolution's place as the central unifying concept of biology must have been clear to C.W. In our era, the subject of biology is simply not understandable without a clear understanding of evolution. To a trained biologist in 1895, the same was undoubtedly true. It shows something of his nature as a teacher and his character that he patiently stayed with this church until they readmitted him.

Conclusions

[Author's note: my guess as to his underlying belief system from the evidence given is that he was perhaps a deist who did not believe in a personal God, but who enjoyed attending church and believed in life after death. He did not take the bible literally and believed in evolution with possibly some initial input from a "creator". There is no compelling evidence regarding his views about whether the events of Christ's life as recorded in the Bible happened that way.]

His family's religion (or lack thereof)

C.W.'s wife Leonora was the daughter of a German-Jewish heritage father and an English heritage, non-Jewish, presumably Christian mother, both from Tennessee.

C.W.'s son Charles E. was married in the First Congregational Church in Berkeley[526], just a few blocks from C.W.'s home (and 2 ½ blocks from Sproul Plaza on the campus). His bride, my grandmother Louise Nelson, was the daughter of Methodist missionaries, so it is unclear how they both changed to being Congregationalists. When my grandparents lived in the Walla Walla, WA area, a newspaper article has my grandmother reviewing a book at the Mission Study Group of the First Congregational Church there.[527] My mother, C.W.'s granddaughter, was also a Congregationalist.

Figure 123 First Congregational Church in Berkeley where C.W's son was married (my grandparents)

[Author's note: Along with many other science-oriented people, I became an atheist as a young adult. The exact moment came during an embryology lab exercise at U.C. Davis when I looked at a slide of a human embryo and saw the gill slits that form at an early stage of human development. I assume that Christ was a real person who lived an admirable but regular life, the story of which was recast many decades after his death into something that it was not. I also assume that God is a human construct. However, since so many people believe in Christ and God, both are central to human history as well as the functioning of today's society. While I am slightly disappointed that C.W. did not become an atheist, I am very happy that he was thrown out of a church for believing in evolution.]

Retirement

On January 28, 1930, C.W. took a final three-month sabbatical leave from the University before retiring on April 28, 1930 on his 65th birthday.[528]

His second wife, Bernice Christopher Woodworth, died on May 6, 1930, just 8 days after his retirement.

Sometime later in 1930, he accepted a job as the Chief Entomologist of Cal-Spray. He travelled for them to "South America in 1930-32, during which time he took a trip around the world."[529]

Figure 124 C.W. in later years[530]

He wrote to his niece in 1937:

> "Many of my colleagues find a crisis in their lives when they reach the age of retirement. They have lived in the classroom. When that door is shut so many of them cannot find themselves. Perhaps it is particularly difficult at their time of life.

I have been fortunate in my many interests. I am always at work at one thing or another. When the day is dull I have often thought what a dreary day this would be if I did not have a very interesting thing that I wanted to do today. If I only had one interest I can see that often I would get where I was not accomplishing much, where I needed a vacation from that particular work. then another of my interests would offer an attractive door."[531]

Figure 125 C.W. in 1938[532]

Figure 126 C.W. in 1938[533]

Death

C.W. died of prostate cancer on November 19, 1940 in Berkeley. His U.C. Berkeley obituary says that he died "after a long and painful illness which he endured with characteristic fortitude."[534]

His *Science* magazine obituary was written by his colleague, Edward O. Essig, who was also the author of "A History of Entomology" (1931). It was published on December 20, 1940.

Chapter 15 - Agricultural Hall (Wellman Hall)

A July 25, 1904 Oakland Tribune article entitled "Order Plans For College Building" talks about the progress toward securing a new agricultural building on the Berkeley campus. This building was constructed in 1912 and was called Agricultural Hall. This building was renamed Wellman Hall in 1967. It was designed by John Galen Howard[535] and added to the National Register of Historic Places in 1982.

Figure 127 John Galen Howard in 1886[536]

Wellman Hall now houses the Department of Environmental Science, Policy and Management as well as the Essig Museum of Entomology. The article reads:

> "**Order Plans For College Building, New Structure the Agricultural Department is Wanted at the State University**
> Berkeley, July 25. – Steps toward securing a new agricultural building for the University of California have progressed so far that John Galen Howard, the supervising architect of the university, has been instructed to prepare plans for the proposed structure. The designs will be finished before the next session of the Legislature opens for it is intended at that time to make a hard fight for an appropriation.

The task of securing the money for the building, which is greatly needed at the university, has been entrusted to Assemblyman William H. Waste.

He will frame the bill carrying the appropriation and in the event of his return to the Legislature will introduce it in one of the houses.

Superficial plans for the proposed new structure have been prepared by Professor C.W. Woodworth of the department of agriculture. The designs embody the most modern ideas to be found in agricultural buildings and will be used as a basis by Architect Howard.

The agricultural building is one of the most needed structures on the campus at the present time and for that reason was picked out for the first appropriation to be next asked by the university from the lawmakers of the State."[537]

Figure 128 Agriculture Hall in 1913, C.W.'s office was on the left end on the middle level (the lowest visible level)[538]

Figure 129 Wellman Hall (formerly Agricultural Hall) 2011[539]

The long central skylight of Wellman Hall has a resemblance to the central skylight in C.W.'s home that he designed and had built in 1906, almost at the same time. Unfortunately, ventilation and acoustic ceiling retrofits have blocked some of the light from this skylight.

(See the Chapter 16 section entitled *The big room.*)

His office in Agriculture Hall

The Catalog of Officers and Students from February 1921 lists his office as 201 Agriculture Hall.[540]

Figure 130 The door of C.W.'s office in 201 Wellman Hall (formerly Agriculture Hall) in 2011[541]

Chapter 16 - His Landmarked Home

C.W. designed and had built two homes in Berkeley, one of which would become a Berkeley architectural landmark.

Earlier residences

During his time at Harvard, letters from C.W. in 1887 and 1888 have his return address at 27 Irving St. in Cambridge, just two blocks east of campus.[542] The current apartment building at that address does not appear to be from that era.

During his time at Arkansas Industrial University, C.W. appears to have rented in Fayetteville both before and after his wedding. The property archives in Washington County, Arkansas, where Fayetteville is located, have no record of his owning a home during that period.[543]

After the move to Berkeley, the family lived in an unknown location, presumably renting.

During his second time at Harvard in 1900, the family is recorded in "The Harvard Index" at 58 Winthrop Street in Cambridge, just two and a half blocks southwest of campus.[544] This address looks to be combined into the property of the University Lutheran Church at 66 Winthrop. This church was built in 1951, so whatever he lived in there is long gone.[545]

2043 Lincoln Street

In 1903, they built a 4-bedroom, 2-bath house at 2043 Lincoln Street in Berkeley.[546] He apparently designed this home, but few details are known.[547] The house has two stories and nine rooms and is just a regular house. It has a one-car garage and stairs up to the second story entrance. It shares one aspect with his later home in that it has a complex roof, with three dormer windows.

The location of this house is the last house next to a business that is on busy Shattuck Avenue. Today that business is "Virginia Cleaners", which has a drive-thru lane. The location is two blocks west and four blocks north of the Northwest corner of campus. The Agricultural Extension Building where he worked is close to the Northwest corner of campus. The house was sold in 2003 for $750,000.

Sometime, presumably shortly after this home was designed, C.W.'s wife Leonora Stern came down with a case, or had her case worsen, of arthritis deformans, what is today called rheumatoid arthritis. The design of 2043 Lincoln, a two-story house with the entrance up a stair way is certainly not suitable for someone who has difficulty standing. It is a reasonable supposition that her condition is what drove the design of their home at 2237 Carleton, where they would both live out the rest of their lives. C.W. also got promoted from Assistant to Associate Professor in 1904.
(See the Chapter 14 section entitled *Leonora's* Death.)

2237 Carleton

On June 30, 1905, C.W. was issued building permit number 512 by the Town of Berkeley. It was for a 1-½ story frame building on the North side of Carlton just below Ellsworth. The architect was listed as "Same" and the contractor as 'Same". The building was to be used as a dwelling and the cost was estimated to be $2500.[548]

The current name of the street is Carleton Street. However, its name is written as Carlton Street on the original plat maps as well as the 1905 building permit.[549]

Shortly thereafter they built a nineteen-room, six-bedroom, three-bath, 3997 square foot home at 2237 Carleton Street in Berkeley, California, which C.W. had designed. It is in the "Berkeley Brown Shingle" style. In 1993, it was designated Berkeley Landmark #180, due to the diligence of the owners John Stone and Peggy Wilson.[550] The final building is certainly not a 1-½ story building, so perhaps the plans changed between the issuance of the permit and the time of construction. Presumably the Berkeley city inspectors were a little more lenient back then than they probably are now.

Although the house does have six levels, the large main level would have been highly suited to Leonora's rheumatoid arthritis. There is a bath and a large room, marked as the "Meeting Room" in the floor plan below, which could have served as their bedroom.

"THE BUNGALOW"

Charles W. Woodworth house Berkley, Ca

Figure 131 The Charles W. Woodworth house in Berkeley, California circa 1906[551]

[Author's note: In 2008, my cousin Kathy set up a tour with the owners for she, my wife Joann, I, and C.W.'s niece Mary. It was a treat to meet them, see the house, and have a nice dinner all together at the Claremont Hotel. My mother (C.W.'s granddaughter) and father honeymooned at the Claremont in 1955.

The house was put up for sale in October of 2011. I was able to attend two open houses of the home and take many photographs.]

Figure 132 The author, my wife Joann, C.W.'s Great-Neice Kathy Detrich, and C.W.'s Neice Mary Detrich (seated) in front of C.W.'s house in Berkeley in 2008 [552]

Figure 133 The C.W. Woodworth house in 2008 [553]

Architectural influences

C.W. was the architect of the home, which has many unique features. The home has elements of the style of Bernard Maybeck, who was a friend of C.W.'s, was active in Berkeley in that period, and was also a professor at Cal.

With its use of shingle siding set in trees, the home has some resemblance to the 1903 Bernard Maybeck designed (Men's) Faculty Club and the 1920 John Galen Howard designed Dwinelle Annex buildings on the Cal campus. There are visual connections to a number of other Maybeck homes including the Cubby House, the McGrew house, and a series of Maybeck's homes in La Loma Park.

BAHA Inventory

The Berkeley Architecture Heritage Association (BAHA) did a "Historic Resource Inventory" of the house in September 29, 1977. The survey, conducted by Fillmore Eisenmeyer, included as a source C.W.'s daughter and my great-aunt Elizabeth. The text is:

> "This house is a fine and original example of the Berkeley Shingle Style. It was designed by Charles Woodworth, professor of entomology at U.C. He also designed his previous residence at 2043 Lincoln Street, and in 1904 assisted John Galen Howard in the design of the University Entomology Building. Woodworth was a friend of Bernard Maybeck, and it could be speculated that Maybeck might have encouraged or assisted Woodworth in his architectural achievements."
>
> "Woodworth helped found the first public library in Berkeley, the first Baptist Church, and the Chung Mei Home for Chinese Boys."[554]

Architectural details

Six levels

One of the unique features of the home is the fact that it has six levels. The front two-thirds of the house contains the two largest levels. The back one-third of the house contains the other two main levels, offset by a half of a floor downward.

The additional two levels are a partial basement under the front portion of the house and a small attic off of the top level that is open to the big room. In the floor plan below, the attic is shown in the "Top Floor" diagram. The stairs leading to the basement are shown in the "Lower Level" diagram.

Five flights of stairs connect the six levels. All five flights are shown on the floor plan below. Each of the six levels is reached in succession as you ascend the stairwell clockwise. Light from the windows of the smaller back levels bathes the middle flights of the stairwell. Light from the 60 square foot skylight in the big room bathes the top two flights.

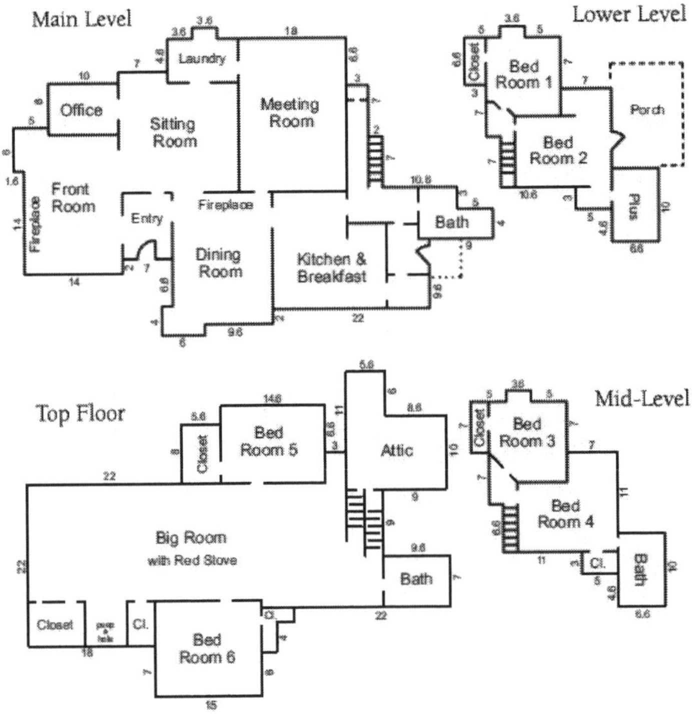

Figure 134 Floor plan of his house from the 2011 sale brochure[555]

The big room

The front upper level contains "The Big Room". This 20′ x 45′ (900 square foot) room encompasses over half of the upper floor. The Southern portion (away from the street) of the big room has a 12′ x 5′ (60 square foot) skylight that allows natural light to permeate the top level. Two bedrooms, a bathroom, and an attic come off of the big room. Closets that utilize the space under the roof line the sides of the front part of the great room. The room is heated with a stove in the middle of the room.
(See Chapter 15 - Agricultural Hall (Wellman Hall) for a discussion about skylights.)

The big room is large enough to allow distinct sub-uses of it. The Stone's sub-divided the big room into two separate rooms. Their bedroom was on the South (street) end and a TV plus sitting plus garden area was on the North end. They used the West upper level bedroom as a painting studio. The attic area held books and a chair for reading.

Originally what you saw when looking up were the ceiling joists holding up the wood slats of the roof. In 2010-11, wood planks were added by the Stones to the bottom of the ceiling joists in big room in a decorative pattern (presumably hiding some insulation). They also removed the partitions that sub-divided the big room. Apparently the finish carpentry effort involved a good deal of puzzle-solving to cover the three dimensional surface. [Author's note: This change is a good improvement to the look of the big room and should also make the room warmer in the winter and cooler in the summer.]

Figure 135 The Great Room, taken from the small adjoining attic[556]

Figure 136 C.W.'s desk in the big room with the looking glass below it[557]

Complex roof

As a result of the complex layout, the roof has twelve hips and five valleys as well as four subsidiary sections and a skylight. [Author's note: I'm sure the roofer's bill is very high.]

Finish details

The house has a number of distinctive finishing details. Some of these are:

- Much of the lower floor is finished with built-in wood cabinets and detail.
- There is a built-in high-backed breakfast nook.
- The downstairs hardwood floor has a woven detail in the corners.
- There are five built-in window seats and one window desk.
- The mailbox has a beveled glass window on the inside so that you can see if the mail has arrived.
- Many of the downstairs rooms have plaster coved ceilings with large radius coving.
- Two of the three bathrooms have pull-chain, overhead-tank toilets.
- The windows are composed of small-paned leaded glass.

Figure 137 Woven floor woodwork detail[558]

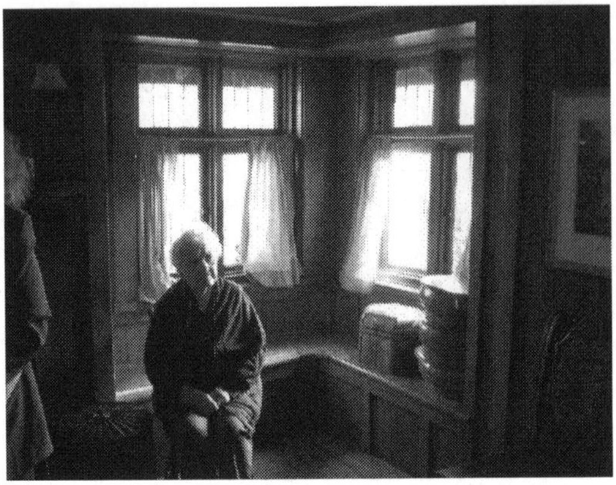

Figure 138 C.W.'s niece Mary sitting in a wooden window seat in the front room[559]

The looking glass

[Author's note: My mother repeated to me several times a story about how she loved to look through the looking glass from his upper floor office to the front door. When we toured the house and asked about it, sure enough the looking glass was still there under the desk in the big room. Since the house is large, it is a pretty good walk from the desk to front door. This looking glass might have been helpful in minimizing C.W.'s distractions.]

Figure 139 The looking glass in the floor under the desk in the big room[560]

Double fireplace

The sitting room and the dining room have an unusual double fireplace that is separated by a pocket door.

Figure 140 Double fireplace separated by a pocket door

On the sitting room side (left in the picture above), an inscription formed in the bricks across the top quotes the first two lines of the poem "Song" written by Henry Wadsworth Longfellow. The poem in its entirety is:

Stay, stay at home my heart and rest;
Home-keeping hearts are the happiest,
For those that wander they know not where
Are full of trouble and full of care;
To stay at home is best.

Weary and homesick and distressed,
They wander east, they wander west,
And are baffled and beaten and blown about
By the winds of the wilderness of doubt;
To stay at home is best.

Then stay at home my heart, and rest;
The bird is safest in its nest;
O'er all that flutter their wings and fly
A hawk is hovering in the sky;
To stay at home is best.

The bricks look as if they were a commercial product, made with the inscription already formed, perhaps in a special mold. It is unclear if this decoration was a little ode by C.W. to his wife who worked in the home, a statement by her about the joy of being at home, or an expression of the happiness of their marriage.

Figure 141 Longfellow inscription above the sitting room fireplace[561]

Clinker brick chimney

The front of the house was modified during C.W.'s time there to add the clinker brick chimney and to change the corner window (to the left in the picture). The front room of the house did not have a fireplace originally and may have been a bit cold in the winter. Andrew at BAHA told me that corner windows like that were unusual at the time. He also speculated that one reason to change the window was to strengthen the corner. [Author's note: I looked for present day evidence of the window modification, but could find none. The carpenters must have been skilled.]

Clinker bricks are bricks that have been heated to an excessive temperature either accidentally or intentionally. They are denser, more brittle and make a distinctive clink when two are hit against each other. They are often discolored and/or disfigured due to the excessive heat and were often discarded. Clinker bricks became popular as a distinctive architectural element during the Arts & Crafts movement.[562]

Figure 142 Top of the clinker brick chimney

The lower portion of the clinker brick chimney has some unusual detail. Two flutes of brick taper into the wall. This detail can be seen as the backdrop in many family photos.

Figure 143 Middle of the clinker brick chimney

A 2011 seismic report prepared as a part of the attempt to sell the house determined that this chimney is structurally unsound and would likely topple in the case of an earthquake. The large Hayward Fault is about 0.9 miles away from the house. The closest point of the fault is very near the point where the fault splits the uprights in Cal's Memorial Stadium, which was built in the valley created by the fault. As of 2011, seismologists have repeatedly declared that the Hayward Fault is overdue to slip. The same structural report indicated that the chimney could be rebuilt to have largely the same appearance.

The workshop/barn

A photograph of his 1930 Segmented Telescope [I was not able to get permission to use it in the book.] shows the telescope against the house and C.W. on top of another large building where the eyepiece was to be. That article refers to the building as his "workshop" and another calls it his "barn".
(See the Chapter 12 section entitled Segmented Mirror Telescopes (1928-1930).)

Measuring the photograph, the eyepiece looks to be about 35′ high. The plane of the lenses looks to slope away from the building at about 40 degrees or so. The frame is mentioned to be 100 square feet or 10 feet per side. Doing some math, that puts the eyepiece about 40 to 45 feet behind of the house horizontally. The house is about 40 feet from the rear property line. There is no record of C.W. having owned the property behind his house. My guess is that he must have leased that property and put up a simple workshop building on the back property line. That building does not exist today; the building and parking lot for the Berkeley Seventh Day Adventist Church at 2236 Parker Street is in its place.

Landmark Designation

Figure 144 City of Berkeley Landmark demarcation[563]

In 1993, the owners John Stone and Peggy Wilson were able to get the home listed as a City of Berkeley Landmark number 180. [Author's note: I am thankful for their efforts.]

Events and Occurrences in his home

In 1911, a birthday party for neighbor Lola Blankenship was held at the house. The Blankenship's lived on the northeast corner of Ellsworth and Carlton, at 2619 Ellsworth. The party was recorded in a picture. The photo shows the home with the original corner window and without the chimney.[564]

Figure 145 Birthday party for neighbor Lola Blankenship - C.W.'s daughter Elizabeth on left, his son Lawrence in center[565]

On June 23, 1923, a wedding reception was held at the house to celebrate the wedding of his son Charles to Sarah Louise Nelson Vickers (my grandparents). A newspaper account reads:

> "Following the impressive marriage service, the bridal party adjourned to the home of the groom's father, Prof. Charles W. Woodworth, where the reception was held. The home was attractively decorated with potted ferns and red dahlias. Over one hundred relatives and friends of the young couple attended the wedding and reception."[566]

On September 10, 1924, the funeral for C.W.'s wife Leonora was held in the home.

In 1930, C.W. attempted to build an experimental multi-segment telescope in the backyard that was far ahead of its time. [Author's note: All traces of this telescope construction effort have unfortunately been removed, apparently long ago. I looked around the backyard thoroughly.]
(See the Chapter 12 section entitled Segmented Mirror Telescopes (1928-1930).

In 1972, a man named Bill Jackson was married in the living room.[567]

On September 29, 1996, it was a shown as part of the Berkeley Architectural Heritage Association Arts and Crafts Home Tour.

His feelings about his home

C.W. wrote in a May 1940 letter to his niece Celina about his feelings towards the house. A pair of illnesses including prostate cancer had restricted his movement, but he wrote: "Fortunately, I was at home in the best place in the world to live when this curtailment of my movements came about."[568]

Owners and Residents

The owners reported that the house has had a number of interesting owners or residents over the years. Hervey Voge, who bought the house in 1959 with Rhea Voge edited the book "A Climbers Guide to the High Sierra" in 1954. The "About the Editor" section of a later edition of that book reads:

> "Hervey Harper Voge was born June 29, 1910. He earned his Ph.D. in chemistry from University of California, then received a chemistry fellowship in 1935 from the National Academy of Sciences. Voge was a Sierra Club member and mountaineer and started climbing in the early 1930s while he was a student at Berkeley, California. Voge made first ascents of multiple peaks, including Washington Column from below. He climbed with other well-known area climbers of the day, including David Brower, Norman Clyde, Bestor Robinson, Dick Leonard, and Jules Eichorn. Fellow student David Brower joined the Sierra Club in 1933 at the suggestion of Voge. In 1934, Voge and Brower traversed the High Sierra from Kearsarge Pass area to Yosemite, climbing 59 peaks in 69 days. Voge named two peaks, Norman Clyde Peak and Muriel Peak. While climbing peaks, he made an effort to preserve peak registers and record first ascents.
>
> Dr. Voge lived in Berkeley, California. He married and had at least one daughter, Tamara. Professionally, Voge was a chemical engineer for Shell Development. His work includes heading a team that developed a rocket fuel for use in the vacuum of outer space. Voge was issued 25 US patents for his research work. He died in the Caribbean Islands on June 20, 1990."[569]

At some point, the developer of the Transcendental Meditation method, Maharishi Mahesh Yogi, apparently stayed in the house.[570]

In the late 1970's, the anti-nuclear energy organization, the Abalone Alliance was headquartered or had a presence there. The Abalone Alliance is most famous for spearheading the opposition to PG&E's Diablo Canyon nuclear power plant.[571]

Howard and Alice Barney lived there in the 1980's. They ran a firm known as "Barneyscan Corporation" for at least some period from the house and were involved in the development of various aspects of scanning technology.[572] He is listed as an inventor on seven patents. Three of the patents were filed with Howard living in Berkeley, two with the address of the CWW House. Those two were the "Slide Scanner", filed July 22, 1987 and the "Image Scanner with Calibration Mechanism to Obtain Full Dynamic Range and Compensated Linear Output, filed February 20, 1991.[573]

The "Pocket Guide to Digital Prepress" says: "The first color CCD scanner, the Barneyscanner, was invented by Howard Barney in 1986. It was the first color scanner to attach to a PC or Macintosh. It scanned 35mm color slides."[574] They were also the first company to bundle Adobe Photoshop with a scanner. The first commercially available version of Photoshop shipped with their scanner. They received a $5.5M venture capital investment during this period, in 1990.[575]

Table of owners and residents

I put together the following table from the real estate records kept by the Berkeley Architectural Heritage Association together with the records from the County Recorder and the recollection of the realtors associated with the 2012 sale.[576]

Owner(s)	Date	Purchase Price
C.W. & Leonora, then C.W., then C.W. & Bernice, then C.W. Woodworth	1905-1940	$2,500 estimated cost on the building permit
His son, Lawrence Woodworth, transferred from	2/18/1941	none

estate		
Mary E. and Amy K Wolfe	7/11/1941	$5,500
Charles L. Jr. & Virginia Haynes	12/28/1955	$13,500
Hervey A. & Rhea B. Voge	1/5/1959	Listed for $25,000
Rhea B. Voge	8/3/1972	Not listed
Patricia O. Ough, Anne Ough (Anne is living elsewhere in Sept. 1977, presumably renting the house out)	9/3/1974	Not listed
Someone associated with the Abalone Alliance	Late 1970's	Probably renters
Howard H. & Alice Barney	1980's	Possibly renters
John Stone & Peggy Wilson	7/1/1992-present	$365,000 [577]
Current owners	12/30/2011	$930,000

Table 9 List of owners of 2237 Carleton Avenue, Berkeley, CA

Additional real estate investments

On February 20, 1906, they took out a $3,000 mortgage with the Homestead Loan Association against "N Carlton 425, E Fulton, E 50 x N 135, log 26, block 1455, Berkeley property maps 1 and 2, Blake Tract, Berkeley."[578] This was likely a bank loan on the completed home. On June 16, 1906 with these proceeds they bought some additional property in Berkeley, a portion of lots 17, 18 & 19 of block A of the Golden Gate Homestead in Berkeley for $3300.[579] This tract was bounded by Shattuck, Milvia, Viginia & Cedar[580], 5 blocks North of University and was presumably an investment. Today the tract contains a series of business along Shattuck, the Berkeley Arts Magnet School and some houses. It is unclear when they sold this property, but it was not part of his estate.[581]

Chapter 17 – The C.W. Woodworth Award

C.W. was a charter member and founding president of the Pacific Branch of the American Association of Economic Entomologists. He is shown as the president of the association in the proceedings of the first three meetings.

The American Association of Economic Entomologists (AAEE) was founded in 1889 by the group of entomologists hired after the passage of the Hatch Act, which founded the Agricultural Experiment Stations at the land grant institutions that had earlier been founded by the 1862 Morrill Act. In 1953, the AAEE merged with the Entomological Society of America (ESA), which had been founded 1906. This is the reference for the dates that are found on the old logo of the ESA (shown below). The modern ESA uses 1889 as its founding date.

Figure 146 Old logo of the Entomological Society of America[582]

The Pacific Branch of the ESA (PBESA) gives an annual award for achievement in entomology in the Pacific region of the U.S. over the previous ten years called the C.W. Woodworth Award. The decision to give out the award was made on June 25, 1968 and the meeting of the PBESA.[583] It was first given out in 1969.

[Author's note: This award has been sponsored since 2004 by my wife, Joann Wilfert, and I, with additional support by Dr. Craig and Kathryn Holden, and Dr. Jim and Betty Woodworth. My wife and I provide $1000 annually to the recipient of the award.]

Recipients of the C.W. Woodworth Award

Yea r	Winner	Affiliation	#
1969	Dr. Maurice T. James	Washington State University	1st
1970	Dr. Walter Carter	Pineapple Research Institute, Honololu	2nd
1971	Dr. Ray F. Smith	University of California, Berkeley	3rd
1972	Dr. Hartford Keifer	Department of Food and Agriculture, CA	4th
1973	Dr. Carl Barton Huffaker	University of California, Berkeley	5th
1974	Dr. Walter Ebeling	University of California, Los Angeles	6th
1975	Dr. Melville H. Hatch	University of Washington	7th
1976	Dr. D. Elmo Hardy	University of California, Berkeley (University of Hawaii, Manoa)	8th
1977	Dr. Paul DeBach	University of California, Riverside	9th
1978	Dr. William Harry Lange Jr.	University of California, Davis	10th
1979	Dr. William G. Wellington	University of British Columbia	11th
1980	Dr. George P. Georghiou	University of California, Riverside	12th
1981	Dr. Harry Laidlaw	University of California, Davis	13th
1982	Dr. Paul W. Oman	Oregon State University	14th
1983	Dr. George Tamaki	USDA ARS, Yakima Agricultural Research	15th

		Laboratory	
1984	(the records of this PBESA meeting were lost)	-	16th
1985	Dr. Carl A. Johansen	Washington State University	17th
1986	Dr. Roy Fukoto	University of California, Riverside	18th
1987	Dr. Robert Washino	University of California, Davis	19th
1988	Dr. John R. Anderson	North Carolina State University	20th
1989	Dr. Stanley C. Hoyt	Washington State University	21st
1990	Dr. Philip F. Torchio	Utah State University	22nd
1991	Dr. Thomas F. Leigh	University of California, Davis	23rd
1992	Dr. Wallace C. Mitchell	University of Hawaii, Manoa	24th
1993	Dr. Brian Croft	Oregon State University	25th
1994	Dr. Michael K. Rust	University of California, Riverside	26th
1995	Dr. Nabil N. Youssef	Utah State University	27th
1996	Dr. Marshall W. Johnson	University of California, Riverside	28th
1997	Dr. Jacqueline L. Robertson	USDA ARS, Pacific Southwest Research Station	29th
1998	Dr. Harry Kaya	University of California, Davis	30th
1999	Dr. Wyatt W. Cone	Washington State University	31st
2000	Dr. Jay F. Brunner	Washington State University	32nd
2001	Dr. Robert S. Lane	University of California, Berkeley	33rd

2002	Dr. James Hagler	USDA ARS, Western Cotton Research Laboratory	34th
2003	Dr. Keith S. Pike	Washington State University	35th
2004	Dr. Victoria Y. Yokoyama	USDA ARS, San Joaquin Valley Agricultural Sciences Center	36th
2005	Dr. John D. Stark	Washington State University	37th
2006	Dr. Jocelyn Millar	University of California, Riverside	38th
2007	Dr. Nick Toscano	University of California, Riverside	39th
2008	Dr. Brian Federici	University of California, Riverside	40th
2009	Dr. Charles G. Summers	University of California, Davis	41st
2010	Dr. Walter Leal	University of California, Davis	42nd
2011	Dr. Frank Zalom	University of California, Davis	43rd
2012	Dr. Steven Naranjo	USDA Arid Land Ag. Research Center, Maricopa	44th
2013	Dr. Vincent P. Jones	Washington State University	45th
2014	Dr. James Carey	University of California, Davis	46th

Table 10 Recipients of the C.W. Woodworth Award

1st Winner (1969) – Dr. Maurice T. James

Figure 147 Maurice T. James[584]

Maurice T. James was born on September 16, 1905 in Elwood, Indiana. He received an AB in 1932, and MA in 1934, and a Ph.D. in 1938 in Zoology, all from the University of Colorado.

He was first the curator of a museum at Colorado State University and then at the U.S. National Museum in Washington D.C. during WWII. Control of insects was important to the war effort in the Pacific. He then worked at Washington State University from 1947 until his retirement in 1970.

He published 185 scientific articles in his specialty area of dipteran systematics. Particularly important was his 1947 article, "The flies that cause myiasis in man." He was the author and coauthor of three editions of the widely used textbook series, *Entomology in Human and Animal Health* and its predecessor volumes.

He was the editor of the Entomological Society of America's *Annals* from 1948 to 1958, and was elected an honorary member in 1973.

He was the first recipient of the C.W. Woodworth Award and was the WSU Invited Address Speaker for 1970.

Upon his retirement, WSU named their insect collection the M.T. James Entomological Collection. It holds over 1.25 million specimens of insects and other arthropods and is one of the top 15 university collections in the United States. Before his death, Maurice and his wife Helen endowed the collection with a gift of property.[585]

21st Winner (1989) – Dr. Stanley C. Hoyt

Figure 148 Dr. Stanley C. Hoyt and the author in 2012[586]

25th Winner (2000) – Dr. Brian Croft

Figure 149 Dr. Brian Croft and the author in 2012[587]

32nd Winner (2000) – Dr. Jay F. Brunner

Figure 150 Dr. Jay F. Brunner and the author in 2010[588]

36th Winner (2004) – Dr. Vicki Yokoyama

Figure 151 Dr. Vicki Yokoyama and the author[589]

37th Winner (2005) – Dr. John D. Stark

Figure 152 Dr. John D. Stark and the author[590]

38th Winner (2006) – Dr. Jocelyn Millar

Figure 153 The author, Dr. Jocelyn Millar and my wife Joann Wilfert[591]

39th Winner (2007) – Dr. Nick Toscano

Figure 154 Joann Wilfert, Celina Richeson, Gail Woodworth, Betty Woodworth, Mary Detrich, Dr. Nick Toscano, Jim Woodworth, Kathy Detrich, Brian Holden[592]

40th Winner (2008) – Dr. Brian Federici

Figure 155 2008 Winner Dr. Brian Federici – front: CWW's neice Mary Detrich, CWW's great-neice Kathy Detrich, back: Joann Wilfert, Dr. Federici, Brian Holden[593]

42nd Winner (2010) – Dr. Walter Leal

Figure 156 Dr. Walter Leal after receiving the C.W. Woodworth Award[594]

43rd Winner (2011) – Dr. Frank Zalom

Figure 157 Dr. Frank Zalom receiving the C.W. Woodworth Award[595]

44th Winner (2012) – Dr. Steven Naranjo

Figure 158 Dr. Steven Naranjo receiving the C.W. Woodworth Award[596]

45th Winner (2013) – Dr. Vincent P. Jones

Figure 159 Dr. Vincent P. Jones[597]

46th Winner (2014) – Dr. James Carey

Figure 160 Dr. James Carey receiving the C.W. Woodworth Award[598]

Chapter 18 - Conclusions

The breadth and comprehensive nature of C.W.'s mind is still amazing. The fact that he published in seven diverse academic fields shows that his mind was something rare. He was able to contribute to the solution of almost any question.

He was respected by his colleagues and lived a positive, forward-looking life. He was very happily married and raised four intelligent and accomplished children.

He suggested the use of Drosophila. He wrote the first draft of one of California's earliest environmental laws. He led the first successful city-wide mosquito abatement program. He directed the first mosquito abatement of Nanjing, China. He redesigned the curricula for Cal's College of Agriculture. He played a part in the building of the Ortho brand of insecticides. He was a significant early contributor to the development of Integrated Pest Management. He defined the requirements for the landmarked Wellman Hall. He architected his landmarked home. He developed a novel distillation technique. He discovered a fundamental optics formula. He designed an eyepiece for the Lick Observatory. He attempted to build the world's largest telescope in his retirement using a novel multi-element reflector.

With all of that, his impact to economic entomology was the greatest. Without his many achievements, California's great agriculture industry and thus California itself may not have reached the heights that it has.

[Author's note: I am honored to be C.W.'s great-grandson and happy to be able to bring the story of his life to you.]

Chapter 19 – Acknowledgements

This was actually a really hard project. The breadth of C.W.'s work meant that I really had to come up to speed in each of the seven fields to which he contributed. My mind has been permanently expanded. I've become something of an amateur entomologist and have been able to handle several recent infestations around our garden with knowledge and ease.

I want to especially thank the two most important reviewers of this book for their diligence in reviewing every page of this book: Diane Alston of Utah State University and my Aunt Betty Woodworth.

I want to thank the entomologists at the Pacific Branch of the Entomological Society of America for being so encouraging to me over the years. Each of the twelve winners that I have had the privilege of presenting the award to has been a treat. The first winner that I presented to (the 36th winner) Vicki Yokoyama has always encouraged me greatly along the way. Each of the other recent winners, Dr. John Stark, Dr. Jocelyn Millar, Dr. Nick Toscano, Dr. Brian Federici, Dr. Charles Summers, Dr. Walter Leal, of course Dr. Frank Zalom, Dr. Steven Naranjo, Dr. Vincent Jones, and Dr. James Carey have inspired me, each in their unique way. Dr. Doug Walsh and Brian Bret of the PBESA have also helped me along.

I want to thank the folks at the Bancroft Library at Cal for their help in working with the archives there and Tim Lundgren of the Berkeley Historical Society for buying my Great-Aunt's photo album and then giving it to me.

I want to thank my Brother Craig Woodworth Holden, my Uncle Jim Woodworth, and my Cousin Mary Detrich for their review of the family sections. Also, thank you to my friend Chee Hu for the translation of C.W.'s plaque.

I especially want to thank my wonderful wife Joann for her love and for her support through the five years that it has taken to write this, and also for her suggestions. I also want to say a big thank you to my daughters, Katie and Ali and my stepdaughters Harmony and Meghan for their encouragement and interest.

Lastly, I would also like to thank C.W. himself for being such an inspiration.

Appendix 1 – Reference Abbreviations

The following abbreviations are used in the appendices and the end notes:

[CalAgEx] *University of California, College of Agriculture, Agricultural Experiment Station*

[CalObit] Charles William Woodworth, website of *University of California in Memorium, 1940,* http://content.cdlib.org/ark:/13030/hb367nb1mt/

[ContOptics] C.W. Woodworth, Contribution to the optics of the microscope, *Proceedings of the California Academy of Sciences*, 4th Ser., Vol. 9, No 5, 7/12/1919, LOC Q11.C253

CWW Charles W. Woodworth

[CWW-Corr] *Correspondence of C.W. Woodworth, 1899-1937,* University of California, Berkeley, Bancroft Library, 308x.W912.cor

[CWW-Papers] Charles William Woodworth papers, 1888-1939, University of California, Berkeley, Bancroft Library, BANC MSS 67/124 c

[EntoNews] *Entomological News*

[JEcoEnto] *Journal of Economic Entomology*

LOC United States Library of Congress

[RepAgExXX] *Report of Work of the Agricultural Experiment Stations of the University of California*

Replace XX with the following:

- *90 , 1890*
- *94 for the year 1892-1893 and part of 1894*
- *95 for the year 1894-95*

- *97* *for the year 1895-1896:1896-1897*
- *98* *for the year 1897-1898*
- *01* *for the year 1899-1901*
- *03* *for the years 1901-1903*
- *04* *for the year 1903-1904*
- *13* *from July 1, 1912 to June 30, 1913*
- *14* *from July 1, 1913 to June 30, 1914*
- *15* *from July 1, 1914 to June 30, 1915*
- *16* *from July 1, 1915 to June 30, 1916*
- *17* *from July 1, 1916 to June 30, 1917*
- *18* *from July 1, 1917 to June 30, 1918*
- *19* *from July 1, 1918 to June 30, 1919*

[ScienceObit] Obituary Charles William Woodworth, *Science,* Vol. 92, No. 2399, pages 570-572

Appendix 2 – C.W.'s Entomology and Plant Pathology Publications and Writings

Author of the following is C.W. Woodworth:

1. Jassidae of Illinois: Part I, *Bulletin of the Illinois state Laboratory of Natural History, Article II*, 1887
2. On the genus Cicadula. Zett., *Psyche*, vol v, pp76-77, August 1888
3. The Grape-leaf Roller, The Annual Report, 1888, pp. 121-127
4. Entomological Notes: Life history, injuries, and remedies of the tarnished plant-bug, *Arkansas Agricultural Experiment Station Bulletin No. 10*, June 1889, 18 pages
5. North American Typhlocybini, *Psyche,* vol v, pp 211-214, July 1889
6. Entomologists Report: Treatments of the grape leaf-folder, life history, natural enemies, and remedies, *First Annual Report, Arkansas Agricultural Experiment Station*, 1889, pp. 121-127
7. Entomology, *Arkansas Industrial University, Agricultural Experiment Station*, Bulletin 13, 1889
8. Studies on the Embryological Development of Euvanessa Antiopa, *Extract from Scudder's The Butterflies of the Eastern United States and Canada,* 1889, by Samuel Hubbard Scudder, page 95, LOC QL549.S43
9. The Tarnished Plant Bug, *The Southern Cultivator and Dixie Farmer*, June 1890, pp 254-256
10. Spray and Band Treatment for Codling Moth, *Annual Report, California Agricultural Experiment Station*, pp. 308-312, (also mentioned in "*Insect Life*" p100) (also mentioned on page 196 of "*True Gardens of the Gods*")

11. Variation in Hessian-fly Injury, *Annual Report California Agricultural Experiment Station*, pp. 312-318, (mentioned in "*Insect Life*" p100)

12. Insects, *Unknown publication*, Mentioned in Annals of Horticulture 1890, Bailey, page 224

13. The effects of the arsenites upon plants, *Arkansas Industrial University, Agricultural Experiment Station, Bulletin No. 10*, September 1890, pp14)

14. Some New Insecticides, *Unknown publication,* Mentioned in Annals of Horticulture 1890, Bailey, page 224

15. Report of the entomologist: Treatments of tarnished plant-bug, chinch bug, cotton and boll worms, *Second Annual Report Arkansas Experiment Station*, 1890, pp. 141-196

16. On the relation between scientific and economic entomology, Annual address of the retiring president of the Cambridge Entomological Club, *Psyche*, Volume 6, pp 19-21, transcript of speech

17. The Laboratory method of experimentation, *Insect Life*, v. 3, March 1891, pp. 266-269

18. Effects of Arsenites, *Orange Judd Farmer*, May 2, 1891, p. 276

19. Staff entomologist's report: Treatments of cutworms, white grubs, grain plant-louse, grape leaf-folder, cotton worms, and experiments with arsenites, *Third Annual Report Arkansas Agricultural Experiment Station*, 1891, pp. 70-97

20. Root knots on fruit trees and vines, *[CalAgEx], Bulletin 99*, December, 1892, republished in the*R[RepAgEx94]*, pp 436-440)

21. A synopsis of the families of insects, *[RepAgEx93]*, pp 271-314, OCLC: 80176553

22. *Laboratory Manual for the course in elementary and economic entomology at the University of California*, Berkeley, Cal., Published by author, 1893, LOC QL464.W89

23. Synopsis of the Family of Insects, Prepared for the Unscientific Public, *[RepAgEx93]*, pp 271-314

24. A Laboratory of Plant Diseases, *Science,* Vol. 20, December 30, 1892, pp 368-369, reprinted in *[RepAgEx94]*, pp 435-436

25. Winter Spraying of Apples and Pears, *[RepAgEx94]*, pp 441-460

26. Remedies for Plant Diseases, *[RepAgEx94]*, pp 461-462

27. Miscellaneous entomological notes: Use of arsenites, notes on thrips, *Fourth Biennial Report State Board of Horticulture California for 1893-94*, 1894, pp. 139-140

28. *The Entomologist's Daily Postcard: A California Journal of Entomology - Official Organ of the U.C. Entomological Society*, 118 issues, Jan 2, 1895 - May 23, 1895, Berkeley, CA, University of California Entomological Society, no bylines

29. The Crater Blight of Pears, *Pacific Rural Press*, February 29, 1896, also mentioned in a follow-up article in the March 21, 1896 issue on page 1, column 1

30. The black scale, *California Cultivator*, August 1896, pp. 236-237

31. Remedies for insects and fungi, *[CalAgEx], Bulletin 115*, December 1896, pp. 15, republished in the Report of Work of the Agricultural Experiment Station of the University of California for the year 1895-1896, pp 213-233

32. The Black Scale, *[RepAgEx95]*, 1896, pp. 253-262

33. The California Vine Hopper, *[CalAgEx], Bulletin 116*, May, 1897, LOC SB608.V5W6

34. Orchard fumigation, *[CalAgEx], Bulletin 122*, January, 1899

35. Sprays and Washes, *[RepAgEx99]*, pp 181-183

36. Paris Green for the Codling-Moth, *[CalAgEx], Bulletin 126*, May, 1899

37. Substitutes for Paris Green as Insecticides, Essay presented to the December 9, 1899 convention of Fruit Growers'

Convention at Unitarian Hall, San Jose, *Unknown Publication*, reference found in online version of *Pacific Rural Press*, Volume 58, Number 24, link at http://cdnc.ucr.edu/cdnc/cgi-bin/cdnc?a=d&d=PRP18991209.2.14&cl=CL2.1899.12&srpos=0&dliv=none&st=1&e=-------en-logical-20--1-----all---

38. For Crater Blight of Pears, *Sixth Biennial Report, Board of Horticulture,* 1900, page 139

39. Butterflies, *Nature-study bulletins*, 1900, The University Press

40. Notes from California, *Proceedings of the Twelth Annual Meeting of the Association of Economic Entomologists,* Washington, 1900, Government Printing Office, pp 90-94

41. The White-Flies of California, *Official Report of the Twenty-Sixth Fruit-Growers Convention of the State of California*, 1901, pp 155-160

42. Orange and Lemon Rot, *Culture of Citrus in California, [CalAgEx], Bulletin 139*, February 1902, reprinted in *State Board of Horticulture*, pp. 249-252

43. Grasshoppers in California, *[CalAgEx], Bulletin 142*, August 1902, (in google books PDF, cover is present but body is missing) (also summary in *Experiment Station Record*, 1903, p471)

44. The California Peach-Tree Borer, *[CalAgEx], Bulletin 143*, September, 1902, (in google books PDF, body is included behind cover of Bulletin 142) (also summary in *Experiment Station Record*, 1903, page 408)

45. The Red Spider of Citrus Trees, *[CalAgEx], Bulletin 145*, November 1902, (also summary in *Experiment Station Record*, 1903, page 782)

46. Remedies for insects, *[CalAgEx], Circular 7*, June, 1903

47. *Key to the Coccidae of California,* Published by the Author, Berkeley, California, 1903)

48. Fumigation Dosage, *[CalAgEx], Bulletin 152*, June 1903

49. New Observations on the Codling Moth, *Official Report of the Twenty-Ninth Fruit Growers' Convention of the State of California*, December 1903, State Horticultural Commission

50. Text book for reading course in economic entomology, *[CalAgEx], Circular 10,* March, 1904 [said 1906 in likely typo in list in 1918 report, page 111]

51. Reference book for reading course in economic entomology, *[CalAgEx],* March, 1904

52. Fumigation practice, *[CalAgEx], Circular 11,* March, 1904

53. Directions for Spraying for the Codling-Moth, *[CalAgEx], Bulletin 155,* March, 1904

54. Silk culture, *[CalAgEx], Circular 12,* June, 1904)

55. The wing veins of insects, Contributions from the Zoological Laboratory of the Museum of Comparative Zoology at Harvard College under the direction of E.L. Mark, *University of California Publications. Technical bulletins No. 181.* College of Agriculture. Agricultural Experiment Station. Entomology, 1906, Sacramento, W.W. Shannon, Supt. State Printing, 152 pp, LOC, LOCOC, call number QL494.W8, also QL461.C17 vol. 1, no. 1, (this was his 1902 rejected doctoral thesis at Harvard)

56. Caterpillars on oaks, *[CalAgEx], Circular 18,* February, 1906

57. Mosquito Control, *Official Report of the Thirty-First Fruit-Growers Convention of the State of California,* 1906, pp 107-112

58. Recent Work in Entomology, *Second Biennial Report of the Commission of Horticulture of the State of California for 1905-1906 (incorporates the Official Report of the Thirty-Second Fruit-Growers Convention of the State of California),* Ellwood Cooper, Commissioner, pp 437-445

59. White fly in California, *[CalAgEx], Circular 30,* June, 1907

60. White fly eradication, *[CalAgEx], Circular 32,* July, 1907

61. Winged Aiphids, *[EntoNews]*, XIX, 3 and 4, 1908 (also mentioned in *Bulletin de la Société entomologique* de France, Volume 13)

62. California Horticultural Quarantine, *[JEcoEnto]*, Vol 2, October 1909, pp 359-360

63. Synopsis of the Family of Insects inhabiting California, *Syllabus series, University of California, Issue 13*, 1909, The University Press, 12 pages

64. The Argentine Ant in California, *[CalAgEx], Circular 38*, August 1908

65. The Theory of the Parasitic Control of Insect Pests, *Science*, 1908

66. The Leg Tendons of Insects, *American Naturalist*, 1908

67. *Synopsis of the Families of Insects Inhabiting California*, The University Press, 1909

68. The Thorax of Insects and the Articulation of the Wings, *Science*, Vol. 30, No. 764, August 20, 1909, pp. 243-244

69. The Thoracic Teragum of Insects (Review of 3 books by R. E. Snodgrass), *Science*, Vol. 30, No. 764, August 20, 1909, pp 243-244

70. A Comparative Study of the Thorax in Orthoptera, Euplexoptera and Coleoptera, *Science*, Vol. 30, August 20, 1909, page 243

71. The Green Bug and Its Natural Enemies, *Science,* Vol. 30, No 782, December 24, 1909, pp 927-929

72. California horticultural quarantine (1909) *[JEcoEnto]*, 1909, 2, pp 359-360)

73. The control of the Argentine Ant, *[CalAgEx], Bulletin 207,* October, 1910

74. Map of the sewer system of Piedmont, California showing the locations of the infestations of the Argentine Ant, circa 1910, part of the *[CWW-Papers]*

75. Fumigation scheduling, *[CalAgEx], Circular 50,* April 1910
76. The Leakage Problem in Fumigation, *2nd meeting of the Pacific Slope Branch of the American Association of Economic Entomologists,* March 1911, proceedings never published due to travel by the secretary
77. The Quantity of Spray Required, *2nd meeting of the Pacific Slope Branch of the American Association of Economic Entomologists,* March 1911, proceedings never published due to travel by the secretary
78. Pure insecticides, *[CalAgEx], Circular 73,* October, 1911
79. Dosage tables, *[CalAgEx], Bulletin 129,* 1911
80. A new leakage gauge, *[CalAgEx], Circular 75,* February, 1912)
81. List of Insecticide Dealers, *[CalAgEx],* Circular 79, July, 1912)
82. Apples, Codling Moth, and Climate, *Monthly Weather Review,* vol. 40, issue 10, 1912, page 1574, portion of an address entitled "The Battle of the Arsenicals" read at the Watsonville Apple Show, October 1910
83. *Guide to California insects,* 1913, Berkeley, The Law press, QL475.C3 W6
84. *Check list of California insects IV. Lepidoptera,* 4/11/1913, 388, i, pp 941-948
85. *Insecticide Co-efficients,* 4/11/1913, presented to Pacific Slope Association of Economic Entomologists
86. *Fumigation Injury to Oranges,* ~1913, presented to Pacific Slope Association of Economic Entomologists
87. Codling moth control in the Sacramento Valley, *[CalAgEx], Circular 101,* June, 1913
88. The Woolly Aphis, *[CalAgEx], Circular 102,* June, 1913
89. The Amended Insecticide Law, *[CalAgEx], Circular 104,* August, 1913
90. A new self-regulating paraffin bath, University of California publications in zoology, 1914, LOC QU231.W7

91. Silk worm Experiments, *[CalAgEx], Circular 116*, March, 1914

92. The Rate of Hatch of Scale Insect Eggs, A note with statistical statement on the subject ,*The Canadian Entomologist,* Dec 1914

93. Classification of Orders and Insects, A note on systematic work in entomology, *[EntoNews],* Vol. 26, p 120

94. *School of Fumigation: conducted by C.W. Woodworth, University of California, held at Pomona, Calif,* 1915, Los Angeles, Braun Corp.

95. New Dosage tables, Fumigation Studies No. 7, *[CalAgEx], Bulletin 257*, July 1915

96. Aphids on grain and cantaloupes, *[CalAgEx] , Circular 125,* January, 1915

97. House fumigation, *[CalAgEx] , Circular 127*, March, 1915

98. The Toxicity of Insecticides, *Science,* Vol. 41, March 5, 1915, pp 367-369

99. Insecticide formulas, *[CalAgEx],Circular 128*, April, 1915)

100. A New Spray Nozzle, *Journal of Agricultural Research,* vol. 5, no. 25, pp1177-82, LOC S21.A75 vol. V, no. 25, (mentioned in Monthly Catalogue, United States Public Documents, No. 247, July 1915, page 479)

101. Time of Fumigation, *Citrograph,* Vol. I, No. I, Oct. 1915, p8

102. The Efficiency of Spray Machinery, *California Cultivator,* Vol XLI, No. 19, Nov 1915, p. 451

103. Quantitative Entomology, *Annals of the Entomological Society of America,* Vol. 8, number 4, December 1915, pp. 373-383

104. Theory of Toxicity, *[JEcoEnto],* Vol. 8, No. 6, pp. 509-512, Dec., 1915

105. A New Descriptive Formula, *[EntoNews]*, Vol. XXVII, pp.57-58, Feb 1916

106. The calibration of the leakage meter, Fumigation studies, *[CalAgEx], Bulletin* 264, 1916, 4 pages

107. Observations on the Silk Industry in China, *[JEcoEnto]*, 1918, Entomological Society of America

108. The Domestication of the Llama, *Science*, 10, May 1918, Vol 47, no. 1219, page 461

109. *Fly Swatter (Jan 2, 1923),* U.S. Patent 1,440,809, USPTO

110. Wings of Bombyx mori, *[EntoNews] and proceedings of the Entomological Section of the Academy of Natural Sciences of Philadelphia*, Vol XXXIV, No. 2, Feb 1923,

111. Silk Culture in China and California, *Unknown Publication*, circa 1924, 2 pages, found in [CWW-Corr]

112. Arrangement of the Major Orders of Insects, *Psyche* Vol. **37**, 1930, pp 157-162

113. What is Control, *Science,* Vol. 71, 1930, page 388

114. There is No Control, *Science,* Vol. 72, August 1930, page 141-a

115. Trabajos Publicados Por V.V. Popov, L. Masi Y, C.W. Woodworth en El periodo 1906-1935, *Unknown publication*

116. Cooperative Work in Economic [Entomology], *The Vedalia*, May 4, 1937, found mention of in letter from E.P. Felt in C.W. Woodworth correspondence in UCB Bancroft collection, found a separate partial link to the article in a google search

117. *Charles William Woodworth papers, 1888-1939,* University of California, Berkeley, Bancroft Library, BANC MSS 67/124 c

118. *Correspondence of C.W. Woodworth, 1899-1937,* University of California, Berkeley, Bancroft Library, 308x.W912.cor

Appendix 3 – C.W.'s Entomology Department and Administrative Publications

These publications are collective publications of the Agricultural Experiment Station. C.W. was running the Division of Entomology during this entire period and it is assumed that he wrote the Entomology portion of the larger document, which is signed by the Director of the station at the time.

The following years do not have reports:

- 1895-1897 – the article is in the form of the paper "Remedies for insects and fungi"
- 1897-1898 – there is no summary, only short papers
- 1898-1901 - Carroll Fowler did the report for 1899-1901 while C.W. was at Harvard.
- 1904-1912 – the Agricultural Experiment Station did not issue a general report
- 1916-1917 - an article on the agricultural emergency caused by WWI filled the report.
- 1917-1918 - E.J. Wickson's history article filled the report.
- Post-1919 – C.W. had stepped down as head of the Division of Entomology

1. Work in Entomology and Plant Diseases, *[RepAgEx94], page* 21
2. Plant Diseases and Entomology, *[RepAgEx98], pp 174-184*
3. Entomology, *[RepAgEx03]*, pp 104-108
4. The Division of Entomology, *[RepAgEx04]*, pp 85-87
5. Entomology, *[RepAgEx13]*, pp lv-lviii
6. Entomology, *[RepAgEx14]*, pp 109-118
7. Fumigation Methods, The Citricola Scale, Mealy Bugs, *[RepAgEx15]*, page 30

8. Action of Insecticides - Microscope Improvement *[RepAgEx16]*, pp 56-58
9. Silk Cuture – The Beet Leafhopper *[RepAgEx19]*, pp 68-70

Appendix 4 – C.W.'s Public Policy Publications

Author of the following is C.W. Woodworth:

1. The Entomological Equipment of the Horticultural Commissioner *Rept. Com. Hort.*, 1903-1904, pp322-28, (see note 112, "True Garden of the Gods", page 284)
2. Proposed Insecticide Law, *[CalAgEx], Bulletin 182, 1906, pp 175-188*
3. The California insecticide law, *[CalAgEx], Bulletin, 1911*
4. Requisites of a County Commissioner, *Proceedings of the Fortieth Fruit Growers' Convention*, 1911, pp 119-124 (plus following discussions)
5. The Educator, *2nd meeting of the Pacific Slope Branch of the American Association of Economic Entomologists*, March 1911, proceedings never published due to travel by the secretary
6. The Insecticide Industries in California, *[JEcoEnto]*, Vol. 5, August 1912, pp 358-364
7. The amended insecticide law, *[CalAgEx], Bulletin*, 1913
8. China's Greatest Need, *The Far Eastern Republic*, April 1920, Chinese National Welfare Society in America, pp. 25-28

Appendix 5 – C.W.'s Optics Publications

Author of the following is C.W. Woodworth:

1. A New Idea in Microscope Construction, *Science*, Vol. 10, August 4, 1893, pp 59-60, later summarized in *Proceedings of the American Microscopial Society*
2. A New Fundamental Equation in Optics, *Science*, Vol. 43, No. 1119, 9 June 1916, pp. 824-825
3. The Astigmatism of Lenses, *Journal of the Optical Society of America*, Vol. 1, Issue 4, 1917, p. 108
4. Astigmatism and Coma, *Science*, Vol. 47, 10 May 1918, pp. 459-460)
5. Contribution to the optics of the microscope, *Proceedings of the California Academy of Sciences*, 4th Ser., Vol. 9, No 5, 7/12/1919, LOC Q11.C253
6. A Focal-Length Equation, *Journal of the Optical Society of America*, Vol. 4, Number 5, September 1920, pp 243-244, page 255 of pdf, accessed via Google Books
7. The Treatment of Certain Special Cases in Lens Calculation, *Journal of the Optical Society of America*, Vol. 4, Number 5, September 1920, pp 286-293, page 298 of pdf file found on Google Books, in an abstract published in Science Abstracts, Volume 24, Institution of Electrical Engineers it is incorrectly referenced as Special Cases in Lens Calculation: Distant Focus Determination
8. Note on T. Smith's method of tracing rays through an optical system, *Journal of the Optical Society of America*, Vol. 5, issue 4, page 334, July 1921
9. Unknown optics paper, *Transactions of the Chinese Association for the Advancement of Science*, Science Society of China,

Somewhere in Vol. 1-5, 1922, page 118, accessed on Google Books (only snippet view)

10. Methods for machine calculation of rays through a lens system, *Journal of the Optical Society of America*, Vol. 7, issue 8, page 673, August 1923
11. *Microscope theory* (Shanghai, Commercial Press, 1924)
12. Wave Train Theory of Light, Early 1925, probably unpublished, mentioned in letter from U.C. Physics Professor Ralph S. Minor to CW in: *[CWW-Corr]*, 80% through folder
13. The Wave Front in the Focus of a Corrected Lens, *Bulletin of the American Physical Society*, Vol. 2, Issue 1, 1927, page 8
14. Sine-arc and arc-sine tables for lens calculation, self-published, Advertisement for it in *the Journal of the Optical Society of America*, 1930)
15. Notes on Microscope Theory, *Transactions of the Chinese Association for the Advancement of Science*, Science Society of China, Vol VIII, No. 1, 1924, accessed on Google Books (only snippet view)

Appendix 6 – C.W.'s Other Writings

Author of the following is C.W. Woodworth:

1. *Oil Refining Process*, U.S. Patent #2,166,193, July 18, 1939, USPTO
2. *Genealogical Records of the Woodworth Family*, handwritten records in the possession of Brian Holden, accumulated through his life, ~250 pages

Appendix 7 – Selected references to C.W.

Listed in alphabetical order:

1. City of Berkeley, *City of Berkeley Landmarks*, 1993, http://www.ci.berkeley.ca.us/onlineservice/planning/landmarks.pdf, photo of the Woodworth family home in Berkeley which he designed http://www.berkeleyheritage.com/berkeley_landmarks/images/2237_Carleton.jpg

2. Davenport, C.B., *The Early History of Research with Drosophila*, http://www.sciencemag.org/cgi/content/citation/93/2413/305-a

3. Essig, Edward Oliver, *A History of Entomology*, The Macmillan company, 1931, Original from the University of Michigan, Digitized Nov 3, 2005, 1029 pages, 30 pages

4. Essig, Edward Oliver , Charles William Woodworth, *Science*, Vol. 92, 20 December 1940, pp 570-572 http://www.sciencemag.org/cgi/search?src=hw&site_area=sci&fulltext=%22Charles+William+Woodworth%22&search_submit.x=11&search_submit.y=6

5. Fryer, John, *John Fryer Papers, [ca 1861-1921]*, (University of California, Berkeley, OCLC: 26631753

6. Hasse, Adelaide Rosalia, *Index of Economic Material in Documents of the States of the United States*, California 1849-1904, index of articles

7. Herms, W.B., Fly Control at Sewage Treatment Plants, *Sewage Works Journal*, Vol. 2, No. 1, Jan 1930 http://www.jstor.org/pss/25037072

8. Holden, Brian, *Brian's Family and Friends*, contains the family tree of Charles W. Woodworth, this tree used his geneaology research as its starting point, http://worldconnect.rootsweb.com/cgi-bin/igm.cgi?op=PED&db=brian2003&id=I642

9. Klose, Nelson, California's Experimentation in Sericulture, *Pacific Historical Review*, Vol. 30., No. 3, Aug 1961 http://www.jstor.org/pss/3636919

10. Kohler, Robert E., *Lords of the Fly: Drosophila Genetics and the Experimental Life*, University Of Chicago Press, 1 edition, May 2, 1994, English, ISBN-10: 0226450635, ISBN-13: 978-0226450636, 344 pages, mention on page 23

11. Morgan, T.H., *T.H. Morgan's Nobel Prize biography,* mentions C. W. Woodworth, http://nobelprize.org/medicine/laureates/1933/morgan-bio.html

12. National Research Council (U.S.) Committee on the Future Role of Pesticides in US Agriculture , *The Future Role of Pesticides in US Agriculture,* National Academies Press, 2000, ISBN 0309065267, 9780309065269, 301 pages, mention on page 24 (about the 1901 law)

13. New York Times, article about the multi-element telescope that he was building, *NY Times*, 3/30/1930, http://select.nytimes.com/gst/abstract.html?res=F10612FA3E5E10728DDDA90B94DB405B808FF1D3

14. New York Times, Obituary, *NY Times*, 11/21/1940, http://select.nytimes.com/gst/abstract.html?res=F40D16F63C5C10728DDDA80A94D9415B8088F1D3

15. Parish, John Carl, *Pacific Historical Review*, American Historical Association Pacific Coast Branch, Published by University of California Press, 1961, pp 223, 224

16. *Psyche, A Journal of Entomology*, Vol 6, No. 178, pp 33-34 - Proceedings of the Societies, Cambridge Entomological Club, 10 February 1888, extensive mentions

17. *Report of the Illinois State Entomologist Concerning Operations Under the Horticultural Inspection Act*, By Illinois State Entomologist, Published by , 1899, Original from the University of California, Digitized Apr 10, 2007, Page 9

18. Roeding, George Christian, *The Smyrna fig: at home and abroad : a treatise on practical fig culture,* Cornell University Library, January 1, 1903, ISBN-10: 1429761385, ISBN-13: 978-1429761383, 94 pages, mention on page 43

19. Snustad, D. Peter and Simmons, Michael J., *Principles of Genetics,* 888 pages, Wiley; 4 edition, November 4, 2005, ISBN-10: 047169939X ISBN-13: 978-0471699392, mention on page 101

20. Solbert, Winton U., *The University of Illinois, 1894-1904: The Shaping of the University*, University of Illinois Press, (2000), 415 pages, note 15 on page 390 is of a letter from Stephen Forbes to C.W. Woodworth written on June 18, 1904

21. Stoll, Steven, *The Fruits of Natural Advantage: Making the Industrial Countryside in California*, University of California Press, 1998, ISBN 0520211723, 9780520211728, 273 pages, pp 112-5, mention on page 221

22. Tyrrell, Ian R., *True Gardens of the Gods: Californian-Australian Environmental Reform, 1860-1930,* University of California Press, 1999, ISBN 0520213467, 9780520213463, 313 pages, mention on page 196

23. University of Arkansas, *History of Entomology at the University of Arkansas* http://entomology.uark.edu/history/

24. *University of California Chronicle, The*, Vol. VI, 1903, Berkeley, The University Press, page 323 (also mention of Howard O. Woodworth on page 232)

25. *University of California Chronicle, The*, Volume XXI, 1919, pp 10, 71, 98, mentions his lectures and return from Nanking

26. University of California, *In Memoriam, 1940* http://dynaweb.oac.cdlib.org:8088/dynaweb/uchist/public/inmemoriam/inmemoriam1940/@Generic__BookTextView/430

27. University of California, Berkeley, *History of Entomology at UC Berkeley* http://sunsite.berkeley.edu/uchistory/general_history/campuses/ucb/departments_e.html

28. University of California, Davis, *History of Entomology at UC Davis* http://entomology.ucdavis.edu/dept/history.cfm

29. White Fly in California, *Riverside Enterprise*, 14, August 1907 (note 113, True Garden of the Gods, page 284)

30. Note on Professor Woodworth's Formula For Focal Length, *Journal of the Optical Society of America*, Vol IV, Number 5, September 1920, pp 245-248

31. *Journal of the Society of Glass Technology*, By Society of Glass Technology, Published by The Society, 1920, Item notes: v.4 (1920), Original from the University of California, Digitized Mar 19, 2008, (Summary of Journal of the Optical Society of America article)

Appendix 8 - References to his son, Charles E Woodworth

1. Wedding of College Faculty Members Held in Berkeley, *Modesto News-Herald*, June 23, 1926, page 6, column 1, accessed via www.newspaperarchives.com

2. 35 Ounce Baby In Modesto, *Modesto News-Herald*, June 14, 1927, page 6, column 1, accessed via www.newspaperarchives.com

3. The Proposed Biological Science club, title of a sub-section in an article entitled Blue and White, *Modesto News-Herald*, Mar 15, 1927, page 5, column 3 (www.newspaperarchives.com)

4. A Wireworm Double Monster *Limonius canus Lec, Psyche*, 39-037, circa 1932

5. To Arrive Home, *Walla Walla Union-Register*, October 19, 1945, page 5, column 2, accessed via www.newspaperarchive.com

6. Onion Plant Treatment Suggested, *Walla Walla Union-Register*, August 21, 1957, page 5, column 1, accessed via www.newspaperarchive.com

7. Collection of the Essig Museum of Entomology at the University of California, http://essig.berkeley.edu/

8. Chest Drive Is Discussed in CP, *Walla Walla Union-Register*, August 21, 1957, page 15, column 8, accessed via www.newspaperarchive.com

Appendix 9 – Research dead ends

[Author's note: Inevitably you chase down a few blind alleys in the course of a project of this magnitude. Here are four dead ends that I reached:]

Google searches for our C.W. also turn up a C.W. Woodworth in a property-related court case in Sebastopol, California. Sebastopol is a sixty mile drive from Berkeley. However, the 1920 U.S. census shows a different Charles W. Woodworth, born 1848 in Missouri, living in Analy, California, nearby. [This one took me a while to dismiss given the proximity of the location to Luther Burbank's house in Santa Rosa.]

There was a professor of Geology at Harvard named Jay Backus Woodworth while C.W. was there. Numerous fossils in the collection of the Museum of Comparative Zoology were collected by him. Genealogical research shows that they were 6th cousins, which is barely cousins at all. There is no evidence that they knew each other. Woodworthia arizonica is the "rarest of petrified woods from Arizona.

Similarly, Dr. William McMichael Woodworth (1864-1912) was an assistant to Dr. Agassiz of the Harvard Museum of Comparative Zoology. C.W. definitely knew him as there was a mention in a letter that C.W. received of calling him WMMW. His research was in flatworms. *Phagocata woodworthi, Fonticola gracilis woodworthi, Asthenoceros woodworthi* and *Humbertium woodworthi* are presumably named after him. It also seems likely that *Admete woodworthi.* A crab found in the Maldive Islands *Pilumnus woodworthi* was also presumably named after him as it was described in the museum's bulletin. The frog *Rana woodworthi* also named *Limnonectes woodworthi* is also presumably named after him. The reptile genus Woodworthia was also described in a museum bulletin. A number of animals in the collection of the Museum of Comparative Zoology were collected by him. I could find no definitive genealogy information about him. One possible match would put him at closest, a sixth cousin, again barely a cousin at all.

There was an agronomy professor named Clyde Melvin Woodworth who was born in 1888 and came to the University of Illinois in 1920 and worked on the genetics of soybeans. I found his family tree and he is not a close relative.

Appendix 10 - Genealogical references

Charles Averill Barlow:
http://wc.rootsweb.ancestry.com/cgi-bin/igm.cgi?op=GET&db=brian2003&id=I4665
http://en.wikipedia.org/wiki/Charles_Averill_Barlow
http://www.barlowgenealogy.com/GeorgeofSandwich/HonCABar.html

Julia Caldwell Barlow:
http://wc.rootsweb.ancestry.com/cgi-bin/igm.cgi?op=GET&db=brian2003&id=I4664

Elizabeth Louise Woodworth Holden
http://wc.rootsweb.ancestry.com/cgi-bin/igm.cgi?op=GET&db=brian2003&id=I9

Justus Henry Nelson
http://wc.rootsweb.ancestry.com/cgi-bin/igm.cgi?op=GET&db=brian2003&id=I72
http://en.wikipedia.org/wiki/Justus_Henry_Nelson

Jessica Nelson North
http://wc.rootsweb.ancestry.com/cgi-bin/igm.cgi?op=GET&db=brian2003&id=I4165
http://en.wikipedia.org/wiki/Jessica_Nelson_North

Thomas Sterling "Sterling" North
http://wc.rootsweb.ancestry.com/cgi-bin/igm.cgi?op=GET&db=brian2003&id=I4197
http://en.wikipedia.org/wiki/Sterling_North

Mary Elizabeth "Elizabeth" Woodworth Plass
http://wc.rootsweb.ancestry.com/cgi-bin/igm.cgi?op=GET&db=brian2003&id=I2833

Raymond Benedict Plass

http://wc.rootsweb.ancestry.com/cgi-bin/igm.cgi?op=GET&db=brian2003&id=I4143

Charles E. Woodworth
http://wc.rootsweb.ancestry.com/cgi-bin/igm.cgi?op=GET&db=brian2003&id=I8
http://en.wikipedia.org/wiki/Charles_E._Woodworth

Harold Evans Woodworth:
http://wc.rootsweb.ancestry.com/cgi-bin/igm.cgi?op=GET&db=brian2003&id=I2830

James Vickers Woodworth
http://wc.rootsweb.ancestry.com/cgi-bin/igm.cgi?op=GET&db=brian2003&id=I1

Lawrence Ariel Woodworth:
http://wc.rootsweb.ancestry.com/cgi-bin/igm.cgi?op=GET&db=brian2003&id=I2832

Mamie Isabel Barlow Woodworth:
http://wc.rootsweb.ancestry.com/cgi-bin/igm.cgi?op=GET&db=brian2003&id=I4144

Sarah Louise Nelson Woodworth
http://wc.rootsweb.ancestry.com/cgi-bin/igm.cgi?op=GET&db=brian2003&id=I7

Index

The page numbers in this index are for the print edition. The e-book page numbers can be estimated from the page numbers of the Chapters, which can be found indexed alphabetically within the index.

Titles are omitted to aid the readability and compactness of the index.

End Notes

[1] Photo owned by author.
[2] Told to Brian Holden by Mary Young Detrich in 2008.
[3] U.S. Census, 9/16/1950
[4] Photo used by permission of Mary Detrich
[5] Photo used by permission of Mary Detrich
[6] Told to Brian Holden by Mary Young Detrich in 2008.
[7] Told to Brian Holden by Mary Young Detrich in 2008.
[8] Photo used by permission of Mary Detrich
[9] *Report of the Illinois State Entomologist concerning operations under the Horticultural Control Act*, page 24, found on google books
[10] Inscription on back of photograph of her that is owned by the author.
[11] Photo used by permission of Mary Detrich
[12] Judith Wellman (2004), *The Road to Seneca Falls,* University of Illinois Press, page 6
[13] Ibid, page 223
[14] Photo used by permission of Mary Detrich
[15] Told to Brian Holden by Mary Young Detrich in 2010
[16] Photo used by permission of Mary Detrich
[17] Photo used by permission of Mary Detrich
[18] *[CWW-Corr],* Letter dated July 25, 1898 from Thomas J. Burrill to CW
[19] *[CWW-Corr],* Letter dated December 14, 1898 from R.W. Brancher to CW
[20] *Pamphlets on Biology: Kofoid Collection*, Volume 2887, page 25, page 359 of collection, accessed on Google Books
[21] *Report of the Illinois State Entomologist concerning operations under the Horticultural Control Act*, page 24, found on google books
[22] Woman Teacher, *Oakland Tribune*, July 25, 1904, page 8, column 4
[23] *Report of the Agricultural Experiment Station* 1918, page 6
[24] *Catalog of Officers and Students 1920-1921*, Feb. 1921, page 55, page 390 in pdf, accessed on Google Books
[25] Photo used by permission of Mary Detrich
[26] *May 1926 Santa Cruz city directory*, page 11/22, 33 Soquel Ave h33, Santa Cruz, CA, Locksmith, accessed via http://www.ancestry.com
[27] Died April 9, 1941 in San Mateo, CA, *California Death Index,* accessed via http://www.ancestry.com
[28] *North Star*, July 28, 1848 as quoted in Frederick Douglass On Women's Rights, Philip S. Foner, ed. New York: Da Capo Press, 1992, pp. 49-51

[29] *Website of the National Park Service Women's Rights National Historic Park*, http://www.nps.gov/wori/index.htm
[30] Photo owned by author
[31] Photo owned by author
[32] Judith Wellman (2004), *The Road to Seneca Falls,* University of Illinois Press
[33] Ibid, page 201
[34] Ibid, page 206
[35] *History of Seneca Co., 1786-1876,* Ensign, Everts, Ensign, Philadelphia, 1876; reprinted by W.E. Morrison & Co., 1976, pp. 124-127.
[36] Photo owned by author
[37] Photo owned by author
[38] Told by Edward Lawrence to the author
[39] Photo owned by author
[40] Logo used by Fair Use doctrine to refer to the company
[41] Public Domain image of Stephen Crane, *Wikimedia Commons*
[42] Public Domain image of Robert Treat Paine's signature, *Wikimedia Commons*
[43] CWW, *Family tree of Charles W. Woodworth*, single copy of manuscript exists, Brian Holden used this tree used C.W.'s research as an important reference for his tree that can be found http://wc.rootsweb.ancestry.com/cgi-bin/igm.cgi?op=PED&db=brian2003&id=I642
[44] Public Domain image of Thomas Edison, *Wikimedia Commons*
[45] Public Domain image from the *Archival Research Catalog of the United States National Archive*
[46] *1913 Alumni Record of the University of Illinois,* accessed via http://www.distantcousin.com (link from Rootsweb WorldConnect Database "uialumni".
[47] Edward Emerson, Jr., *The College Year-book and Athletic Record*, Stone & Kimball, New York, 1897, page 337
[48] *Report of the Board of Trustees of the University of Illinois*, page 99 (accessed via Google Books)
[49] Edward Emerson, Jr., *The College Year-book and Athletic Record*, Stone & Kimball, New York, 1897, page 337
[50] *Semi-Centennial Alumni Record of the University of Illinois*, entry 456 – Sigma Xi is listed after high school and before Arkansas, but Sigma Xi was founded at Cornell in the same year 1886 as he graduated.

[51] *Pamphlets on Biology: Kofoid collection*, Volume 2887, page 4, page 260 of the collection, accessed via Google Books
[52] Image of Stephen Alfred Forbes, public domain image (pre-1923), found at: http://www.inhs.illinois.edu/organization/images/forbes2.gif from the document http://www.inhs.illinois.edu/organization/history.html
[53] *Report of the Board of Trustees of the University of Illinois*, page 99 (accessed via Google Books)
[54] L.O. Howard, *Biographical Memoir of Stephen Alfred Forbes, 1844-1930,* National Academy of Sciences of the United States of America, Biographical Memoirs, Volume XV-First Memoir, 1931, Pages 16-17, http://books.nap.edu/html/biomems/sforbes.pdf
[55] Ibid, page 19
[56] Ill. Hort. Soc Trans,. Vol. 19, pp. 103-124, 1886 (see list in Howard biography above)
[57] Ill. Ent. Off. Bul., no. 1, pp. 1-24, with 11 diagrams, 1187 (see list in Howard biography above)
[58] [VWOI], page 3
[59] Image of Thomas J. Burrill, public domain image (pre-1923), *Wikimedia Commons,* http://commons.wikimedia.org/wiki/File:Thomas_Jonathan_Burrill.jpg
[60] Dean A. Glawe, Thomas J. Burrill, Pioneer in Plant Pathology, *Annual Review Phytopathology*, 1992, 30:17-24, http://www.annualreviews.org/doi/pdf/10.1146/annurev.py.30.090192.000313
[61] Told to Brian Holden by Mary Young Detrich in 2008.
[62] C.H. Dietrich, Keys to the Families of Cicadomorpha and Subfamilies and Tribes of Cicadellidae (Hemiptera: Auchenorrhyncha), *Florida Entomologist,* Vol. 88(4), December 200, pp 502-517, http://www.fcla.edu/FlaEnt/fe88p502.pdf
[63] About Us, *Website of the Illinois Natural History Survey,* http://www.inhs.uiuc.edu/organization/
[64] *Text of New England Mutual Life Insurance Co. v. Woodworth* http://supreme.justia.com/us/111/138/case.html
[65] Logo used through the Fair Use Doctrine to refer to the company
[66] Photo used by permission of Mary Detrich
[67] *Website of the History of the Cornell University Graduate School*, mention of dates mid-page http://www.gradschool.cornell.edu/index.php?p=36
[68] Photo of Hermann August Hagen, public domain image (pre-1923), *Wikimedia Commons*

[69] Obituary, Prof. Herman August Hagen, *New York Times*, Nov 10, 1893, page 4
[70] Ibid
[71] [WVOI], page 3
[72] History & Hatch Act of 1887, *Oklahoma Agricultural Experiment Station (at OSU) website*, http://www.oaes.okstate.edu/hatch-act-of-1887-1
[73] Station Entomologists – Agricultural Experment Stations, Virginia Tech Pesticide Programs, http://vtpp.ext.vt.edu/museum-of-pest-management/early-days-of-virginia-agricultural-experiment-station/station-entomologists-agricultural-experiment-stations-1880s
[74] Station Entomologists – Agricultural Experment Stations, Virginia Tech Pesticide Programs, http://vtpp.ext.vt.edu/museum-of-pest-management/early-days-of-virginia-agricultural-experiment-station/station-entomologists-agricultural-experiment-stations-1880s
[75] Land Grant & Sea Grant: Acts, History & Institutions, *Website of the University of Florida Institute of Food and Agricultural Sciences,* http://www.ifas.ufl.edu/land_grant_history/
[76] Text of the amended Hatch Act of 1887, *Website of the USDA*, http://www.csrees.usda.gov/about/offices/legis/pdfs/hatch.pdf
[77] CWW, On the Relation Between Scientific and Economic Entomology, *Psyche,* February 1891, pp19-20
[78] *[CWW-Corr],* Draft of an undated letter from CWW to E.L. Mark, likely early 1900
[79] *[CWW-Corr],* Letter from CWW to UC President Benjamin Wheeler, September 14, 1900
[80] Photo owned by author
[81] *[CWW-Corr],* March 5, 1901 letter from E.W. Hilgard to CWW
[82] The Harvard University Museum of Comparative Zoology, Entomology Department http://www.mcz.harvard.edu/Departments/Entomology/about.html
[83] John Henry Comstock, *The Wings of Insects*, 1918, The Comstock Publishing Company, page vii (preface)
[84] Ibid, page 2
[85] *[CWW-Corr]*, Letter from E.L. Mark to CWW, September 4, 1901
[86] *[CWW-Corr],* Letter from E.L. Mark to CWW, September 17, 1901
[87] *[CWW-Corr],* Letter from E.L. Mark to CWW, January 25, 1902
[88] Short biography of James G. Needham on Cornell Library website: http://rmc.library.cornell.edu/ead/htmldocs/RMA00479.html
[89] Image of Cornell Professor James G. Needham, circa 1920, public domain image (pre-1923), Cornell limnology professor James G. Needham

finds something interesting with his students, ca. 1920: From Mann's 2009 Spring lobby exhibit: "*100 Years of Limnology at Cornell.*", date is believable given his older look in the 1928 image found on embryo website, this image found on Picasa at: http://picasaweb.google.com/lh/photo/I_mk0twFMvi2BNGdHjTcSg

[90] A Note on the Fallaciousness of the Theory of Pretracheation in the Venation of Odonta, Lt. Colonel F. C. Fraser, *Proceedings of the Royal Entomological Society of London*. Series A, General Entomology, Volume 13, Issue 4-6, pages 60–70, June 1938

[91] Gordon Patterson, *The Mosquito Crusades: A History of the American Anti-Mosquito Movement*, 2009, Rutgers University Press, Chapter 2

[92] Image of painting of Edward L. Mark by Leopold Seyffert, *Harvard Alumni Bulletin*, Vol. XXIV, Number 33, March 25, 1922, page 822, Public Domain image (Pre-1923)

[93] Charles B. Davenport, *Harvard Alumni Bulletin*, Vol. XXIV, Number 33, March 25, 1922, pages 822-826

[94] Image of William Ernest Castle, public domain image (pre-1923 as he is clearly younger than 56 in this picture), found on UCSB website at: http://www.nceas.ucsb.edu/~alroy/lefa/Castle.html

[95] George D. Snell and Sheldon Reed, William Ernest Castle, Pioneer Mammalian Geneticist, *Genetics* 133: 751-753 (April 1993)

[96] Ibid

[97] Ibid

[98] John Hugh Reynolds, *History of the University of Arkansas*, pp 285-286

[99] *Twenty Fifth Annual Report of the Entomological Society of Ontario*, 1894, page 92

[100] Sunstrokes, *Cornell Daily Sun*, Volume VIII, Issue 90, 28 February 1888, page 3

[101] Edward Emerson, Jr., *The College Year-book and Athletic Record*, Stone & Kimball, New York, 1897, page 319

[102] 1908 Public Domain image of a postcard of the Experimental Research station at Arkansas. Found on http://entomology.uark.edu/history/

[103] Stephen F. Strausberg, *A century of research: Centennial history of the Arkansas Agricultural Experiment Station*, 1989, **ISBN-13:** 9780962285806, page 10

[104] Ibid, page 11

[105] Edward Emerson, Jr., *The College Year-book and Athletic Record*, Stone & Kimball, New York, 1897, page 319.

[106] Public Domain image (pre-1923), Birdseye Map of Berkeley, 1891, High resolution image available, Call number: G4364.B5A3 .Mga Case D, http://cluster3.lib.berkeley.edu/EART/tour/birdseye.html

[107] Ibid
[108] Public Domain (pre-1923) image of Edward Wickson, *website of the History of the University of California, Davis*
[109] E.W. Hilgard, *University of California, College of Agriculture Report of the Professor in Charge to the President*, 1889, reference on pages 5 and 6
[110] E.W. Hilgard, *University of California, College of Agriculture Report of the Professor in Charge to the President*, 1890, reference on pages 6
[111] Website: *A Brief History of the University of California*, **http://content.cdlib.org/view?docId=hb4v19n9zb;NAAN=13030&doc.view=frames&chunk.id=div00002&toc.depth=1&toc.id=div00002&brand=calisphere**
[112] Public Domain image, *Wikimedia Commons*, **http://commons.wikimedia.org/wiki/File:Eugene_Woldemar_Hilgard.jpg**
[113] *[RepAgEx90]*, page 307, Assistant in Entomology
[114] E.W. Hilgard, *University of California, College of Agriculture Report of the Professor in Charge to the President*, 1891, reference on pages 18
[115] *[CWW-Corr]*, May 28, 1891 telegram from Clinton D. Smith to CWW
[116] Ralph E. Smith and collaborators, Protecting the Plants from Their Enemies, *California Agriculture*, Edited by Claude B. Hutchison, University of California Press, 1946, pp 239-316, quote on page 259, accessed on Google Books
[117] *[CWW-Corr]*, June 5, 1891 telegram from Mrs. Woodworth to CWW
[118] *History of Burrton, Kansas*, **http://www.burrtonkansas.com/history.htm**
[119] AT&SF 1891 route map, **http://en.wikipedia.org/wiki/File:Santa_Fe_Route_Map_1891.jpg**
[120] Public Domain image (pre-1923), from the *[RepAgEx89]*, page 25
[121] Public Domain image (pre-1923), from the *[RepAgEx89]*, page 32
[122] Gordon Patterson, *The Mosquito Crusades: A History of the American Anti-Mosquito Movement*, 2009, Rutgers University Press, Chapter 2
[123] Photo owned by author
[124] *[CWW-Corr]*, June 16, 1891 invitation from the Kelloggs to CWW
[125] Public Domain image (pre-1923) from the *University of California History Digital Archives*, **http://sunsite.berkeley.edu/~ucalhist/general_history/overview/presidents/index.html**
[126] The Graduate Handbook, C. A. Duniway, Harvard, Federation of Graduate Clubs, The Macmillan Company, 1897, page 125
[127] *[RepAgEx97]*, page xii
[128] Wilmar N. Tognazzini, Compiler, *One Hundred Years Ago 1897*, website at **http://wntog.tripod.com/97.html**

[129] *[CWW-Corr],* Note from John Henry Comstock to CWW, February 7, 1900
[130] Public domain (pre-1923) image of Anna Comstock, *Wikimedia commons*, **http://commons.wikimedia.org/wiki/File:Anna-Botsford-Comstock-1854-1930.jpg**
[131] *[CWW-Corr],* Letter from Vernon Kellogg to CWW, February 3, 1900
[132] Public domain (pre-1923) image of Vernon Kellogg, *Wikimedia commons*, **http://commons.wikimedia.org/wiki/File:Vernon_Lyman_Kellogg_(1867-1937).jpg**
[133] *[CWW-Corr],* Letter from Benjamin Wheeler to CWW on April 27, 1900
[134] *[CWW-Corr],* Letters from Carroll Fowler to CWW on April 22, 1900 and May 12, 1900
[135] *[CWW-Corr],* Letter from H.E. Summers to CWW on May 3, 1900
[136] *[CWW-Corr],* Letter from Lawrence Bruner to CWW on May 12, 1900
[137] *[CWW-Corr],* Letter from Lawrence Gillette to CWW on May 12, 1900,
[138] *[CWW-Corr*], Letter from E.J. Wickson to CWW on May 28, 1900
[139] The Potato-Worm in California, Warren T. Clarke, *[CalAgEx], Bulletin No. 135,* Berkeley, October 1901, page 6
[140] *[CWW-Corr],* Letter from E.W. Hilgard to CWW on February 12, 1901
[141] *[CWW-Corr],* Letter from E.W. Hilgard to CWW on March 29, 1901
[142] *[CWW-Corr],* Letter from E.W. Hilgard to CWW on July 22, 1901
[143] [ObitScience]
[144] *[CWW-Corr],* June 7, 1905 letter from EJ Wickson to CWW
[145] Public Domain (pre-1923) image of E.W. Hilgard from the 1913 *Report of the Agriculture Experiment Station*, frontispiece
[146] Public Domain image (pre-1923) from the *U.C. Davis Historical Timeline* website, **http://centennial.ucdavis.edu/timeline/**
[147] History of the University of Wisconsin college of Agriculture **http://digicoll.library.wisc.edu/cgi-bin/UW/UW-idx?type=turn&entity=UW.Babcock10.p0004&id=UW.Babcock10&isize=text**
[148] *[CWW-Corr]*, May 25, 1906 letter from Dean Henry to CWW
[149] Told by Dr. Frank Zalom of U.C. Davis to Brian Holden at PBESA meeting 2005.
[150] Rancher's Week at University Farm, *The San Francisco Call*, October 13, 1909, Column 3, **http://chroniclingamerica.loc.gov/lccn/sn85066387/1909-10-13/ed-1/seq-8/**

[151] University of California Digital Archives, UC Davis portion, accessed at: **http://sunsite.berkeley.edu/uchistory/general_history/campuses/ucd/departments_e.html**
[152] Photo owned by author
[153] Photo owned by author
[154] Underwood 1 page, *Website of Antiquetypewriters.com,* **http://www.antiquetypewriters.com/collection/typewriter.asp?Underwood%201**
[155] Various letters from CWW, *The State Historical Society of Missouri, Edwin P. Meiners, Collections, 1825-1960 (C3722)*
[156] [ObitScience]
[157] CWW, *Guide To California Insects*, 1913, The Law Press Berkeley, scanned by the Cornell University Historical Monographs Collection
[158] Ibid page 4
[159] Ibid page 34
[160] CWW, Entomology, *Report of the Agricultural Experiment Station*, 1914, page 109
[161] Public Domain (pre-1923) image
[162] CWW, University of California (1868-1952), College of Agriculture, Free Correspondence Courses, July 8, 1919, accessed at **http://www.ebooksread.com/authors-eng/university-of-california-1868-1952-college-of-a/free-correspondence-courses-in-agriculture-hci/1-free-correspondence-courses-in-agriculture-hci.shtml**
[163] Gordon Patterson, *The Mosquito Crusades: A History of the American Anti-Mosquito Movement*, 2009, Rutgers University Press
[164] *University of California Register 1920-1921 with announcements for 1921-1922*, page 47, page 64 in the pdf, accessed on Google Books
[165] Photo owned by the author
[166] Mary A. Agnew, Workers in Subjects Pertaining to Agriculture in State Agricultural Colleges and Experiment Stations, *United States Department of Agriculture Miscellaneous Publications, 1928, Issues 37-62*, heading is on page 51, reference is on page 5 of that section, accessed via Google Books
[167] [ObitScience]
[168] *[CWW-Corr],* August 5, 1935 Letter from Robert G. Sproul to CWW
[169] *[CWW-Corr],* October 25, 1935 Letter from Robert G. Sproul to CWW
[170] Photo owned by author
[171] Public domain image from the *[RepAgEx14],* page 109
[172] *Biennial Report of the President of the University on behalf of the Regents to His Excellency the Governor of the State, 1910-1912*, about 30% of the way through the page, two places

[173] *[CWW-Corr],* October 25, 1935 Letter from Robert G. Sproul to CWW He is addressed as the "Director, The Temple Institute"
[174] *History of the Baptist Temple church,* http://www.baptempl.org/aboutus.html
[175] Station Entomologists – Agricultural Experment Stations, Virginia Tech Pesticide Programs, http://vtpp.ext.vt.edu/museum-of-pest-management/early-days-of-virginia-agricultural-experiment-station/station-entomologists-agricultural-experiment-stations-1880s
[176] *Annual report of the Minister of Agriculture and Food, Ontario Department of Agriculture and Food*, 1890, page 37, access via Google Books
[177] Insect Life, United States Department of Agriculture, 1895, Vol. XII, page 214
[178] *[JEcoEnto]*, Vol 2, page xi
[179] Notes From California, *Proceedings of the Twelfth Annual Meeting of the Association of Economic Entomologists*, United States Bureau of Entomology, Published by the Govt. Printing Office, 1900
[180] *[CWW-Papers],* Twentieth Annual Entomologists Dinner, December 28, 1939, Columbus, Ohio (program for)
[181] *Bulletin of the Entomological Society of America*, Volume 35, page 79, found on Google Books (but only in the snippet view)
[182] *Journal of Economic Entomology,* Vol. 2, No. 3, June 1909, page 264
[183] *[JEcoEnto]*, Volume 5, page 340, August 1912.
[184] Ibid
[185] *Classic Cordilleran Concepts: A View from California*, 1999, The Geological Society of America, page 25
[186] *Journal of Economic Entomology*, Volume 12, Number 4, pp 281-344
[187] *Facts about Sugar*, Vol XIII, July 30, 1921, Domestic Sugar Producers Inc., page 93
[188] *[CWW-Papers], The Entomologist's Daily Post Card*
[189] *[CWW-Corr],* December 27, 1894 letter from CH Fernald to CW
[190] *[CWW-Papers],* Public Domain image (pre-1923) of the title of *The Entomologist's Daily Post Card*
[191] *The University of California Chronicle*, 1916, page 281
[192] Semi-Centennial Alumni Record of the University of Illinois, entry 456
[193] Proceedings of the Entomological Society of America, California Summer Meeting, *Annals of the Entomological Society of America,* Vol. VIII, pp 384-387
[194] *[EntoNews]*, Jan 1941, page 30, found on archive.org at: http://www.archive.org/stream/entomologicalnew52amer/entomologicalnew52amer_djvu.txt

[195] U.S. Department of Agriculture, Office of Experiment Stations, Bulletin No. 65, 1899, page 63, found on Google Books
[196] *[CWW-Corr],* Letter from H. Garman to CWW September 7 and September 9, 1900
[197] Semi-Centennial Alumni Record of the University of Illinois, entry 456
[198] Photo owned by the author
[199] The State Historical Society of Missouri, *Edwin P. Meiners, Collections, 1825-1960 (C3722),* pages 3-4, November 11, 1887 Letter from C.W. to E.P. Van Duzee
[200] Image of the Title of *Psyche, A Journal of Entomology*, Vol. 6, 1891-1893, Public Domain image (pre-1923), accessed via Google books
[201] The State Historical Society of Missouri, *Edwin P. Meiners, Collections, 1825-1960 (C3722)*, pages 5-6, December 10, 1887 Letter from C.W. to E.P. Van Duzee
[202] History of the Cambridge Entomology Club, page 35
[203] [203] CWW, On the Relation Between Scientific and Economic Entomology, *Psyche,* February 1891, pp19-20
[204] *[CWW-Corr*], Mentioned in a letter from E.L. Mark to CWW, September 4, 1901
[205] *Entomologica Americana*, Volumes 4-6, page 201, accessed via Google Books
[206] *[CWW-Corr],* Letter from AAAS Permanent Secretary R.S. Woodward to CWW
[207] Thomas H. Morgan, *The Nobel Prize in Physiology or Medicine 1933 Biography*, http://nobelprize.org/nobel_prizes/medicine/laureates/1933/morgan-bio.html
[208] *A History of Genetics*, Alfred Henry Sturtevant, 2001, page 43
[209] Herbert C. Morse III, Building a Better Mouse: One Hundred Years of Genetics and Biology, *The Mouse in Biomedical Research: Diseases*, James G. Fox et al, 2007, Academic Press, pp 1-10, quote on page 5, accessed on Google Books
[210] Edward B. Lewis*, Thomas Hunt Morgan and His Legacy,* 20 April 1998, http://nobelprize.org/nobel_prizes/medicine/articles/lewis/index.html
[211]Michael Ashburner and Casey M. Bergman, *Drosophila melanogaster: A case study of a model genomic sequence and its consequences*, Genome Research 2005 15: 1661-1667
[212] Public Domain (pre-1923) image, *Wikimedia Commons*
[213] CWW, Synopsis of the Families of Insects, prepared for the use of the unscientific public, *[RepAgEx94]*, pp 271-314
[214] CWW, Work in Entomology and Plant Diseases, *[RepAgEx94]*, page 21

[215] CWW, Remedies for Plant Diseases, *[RepAgEx94]*, pages 461-462
[216] CWW, A Laboratory of Plant Diseases, *[RepAgEx94]*, pages 435-436
[217] CWW, Experiments in Winter Spraying of Apples and Pears, *[RepAgEx94]*, pages 441-460
[218] CWW, Root Knots on Fruit Trees and Vines, *[RepAgEx94]*, pages 436-440
[219] *[CWW-Corr]*, Letters from US Patent Office dated January 10, 1896 and February 16, 1897
[220] *[RepAgEx97]*, pages 213-233
[221] Ralph E. Smith and collaborators, Protecting the Plants from Their Enemies, *California Agriculture*, Edited by Claude B. Hutchison, University of California Press, 1946, pp 239-316, quote on page 259, accessed on Google Books
[222] *[RepAgEx98]*, pages 181-2
[223] CWW, Recent Work in Entomology, *Second Biennial Report of the Commission of Horticulture of the State of California*, 1905, pp 437-
[224] UC Publications in Entomology, *website of the University of California Press*, http://escholarship.org/uc/ucpress_ucpe
[225] UC Publications in Entomology, *website of the University of California Press*, http://www.ucpress.edu/series.php?ser=ucent&s=sv&o=desc&r=10&page=2#
[226] *University of California Publications in Entomology, Vol. 1,* 1906-1922, University of California Press, Berkeley, California
[227] Spray Systems Washjet nozzles using C.W.'s design http://www.spray.com/cat70/cat70pdf/ssco_cat70_c41.pdf
[228] Flat spray nozzle from Wintrax, model 23990, website at: http://www.windtrax.com/search_results.asp?txtsearchParamTxt=23990&txtsearchParamType=ALL&txtsearchParamCat=ALL&txtsearchParamMan=ALL&txtsearchParamVen=ALL&txtDateAddedStart=&txtDateAddedEnd=&txtPriceStart=&txtPriceEnd=&txtFromSearch=fromSearch&iLevel=1&btnSearch.x=75&btnSearch.y=15
[229] CWW, New Dosage Tables Fumigation Studies No. 7, *[CalAgEx], Bulletin No. 257*, July 1915
[230] Quantitative Entomology, *Annals of the Entomology Society of America,* Vol. VIII, pp 373-383
[231] Public domain (pre-1923) image taken from Quantitative Entomology, *Annals of the Entomology Society of America,* Vol. VIII, pp 373-383
[232] Quantitative Entomology, *Annals of the Entomology Society of America,* Vol. VIII, page 383
[233] *Science*, Vol. LXIII, No. 1637, page 493, Barro Colorado Island Biological Station, Vernon Kellogg

[234] List of U.S. Citizens, in the Passenger List of the S.S. Parismina, arrived in New Orleans from Havana on August 10, 1925, found on ancestry.com, New Orleans Passenger Lists, 1813-1945, scanned image 705 of 890
[235] Photos owned by author
[236] History of the STRI, *Website of the Smithsonian Tropical Research Institute,* http://www.stri.si.edu/english/about_stri/history.php
[237] *Website of the Smithsonian Tropical Research Institute* http://www.stri.si.edu/english/about_stri/index.php
[238] Ibid [history]
[239] Public domain (pre-1923) photo from the STRI website
[240] *[CWW-Corr],* September 9, 1937 Letter from Zetek to C.W. Woodworth
[241] *Proceedings of the California Academy of Sciences: 4th Series, Volume 11,* page 606
[242] CWW, The Arrangement of the Major Orders of Insects, *Psyche*, 32, June 1930, pp 157-162
[243] Sabater-Munoz et al, *Genome Biology*, 2006, 7:R21, Figure 1
[244] Public domain image from the Wikimedia Commons, http://commons.wikimedia.org/wiki/File:RJTillyard1881-1937.jpg
[245] CWW, The Arrangement of the Major Orders of Insects, *Psyche*, 32, June 1930, pp 157-162
[246] Photo taken by author on 2/3/2012
[247] The Eastern Occurrences of the San José Scale, *Insect Life*, 1895, page 163.
[248] CWW, Notes From California, *Proceedings of the Twelfth Annual Meeting of the Association of Economic Entomologists*, United States Bureau of Entomology, Published by the Govt. Printing Office, 1900
[249] Public domain (pre-1923) image
[250] CWW, *Key to the Coccidae of California*, Published by the Author, Berkeley, California
[251] CWW, For Crater Blight of Pears, *Sixth Biennial Report of Horticulture,* 1900, page 139
[252] Public domain image from the Wikimedia Commons, http://commons.wikimedia.org/wiki/File:Hessian_Fly.jpg
[253] Public domain image from Wikipedia, http://en.wikipedia.org/wiki/File:Tpb7.jpg
[254] CWW, White-Flies of California, *Proceedings of Twenty-Sixth Fruit-Growers' Convention, 1901*, p155
[255] Ibid
[256] Ibid

[257] Grape Whitefly, *Website of the UC Davis Integrated Viticulture,* http://iv.ucdavis.edu/Viticultural_Information/?uid=101&ds=351
[258] CWW, Orange and Lemon Rot, *[CalAgEx],* Bulletin No. 139, Berkeley, February 1902, 12 pages
[259] CWW, California State Bulletin 142, Grasshoppers in California, summarized in the *Experiment Station Record, 1903*, page 471. U.S. Department of Agriculture
[260] CWW, California State Bulletin 143, The California Peach-Tree Borer, summarized in the *Experiment Station Record, 1903*, page 468. U.S. Department of Agriculture
[261] Image from *Wikimedia Commons* with a Creative Commons Attribution 3.0 license, *{{Information |Description={{en|1=Synanthedon exitiosa}} |Source=http://www.forestryimages.org/browse/detail.cfm?imgnum=1435199 |Author=Clemson University - USDA Cooperative Extension Slide Series, , United States |Date=August 12, 2002 |Permission= |other)*
[262] *Saratoga's First Hundred Years*, 1967, Florence R. Cunningham, Valley Publishers, page 233-4
[263] Public Domain (pre-1923) image
[264] *UC ANR Publication 3433,* http://www.ipm.ucdavis.edu/PMG/r5301011.html
[265] Ibid
[266] Ibid
[267] The Week, *Pacific Rural Press*, May 10, 1902, page 310, column 1, mention at bottom of column 2
[268] Public domain (pre-1923) image
[269] CWW, The Red Spider of Citrus Trees, *[CalAgEx],* Bulletin No. 145, November, 1902
[270] Public domain (pre-1923) image
[271] Public domain (pre-1923) image
[272] *[CWW-Papers]*

[273] *[CalAgEx]* Bulletin 207, page 94
[274] Agricultural Club, *Blue and gold [1904]: being a record of the college year, published by the Junior Class,* page 191
[275] *Bulletin, Issue 118*, United States, Division of Entomology, United States Bureau of Entomology, page 44
[276] Public Domain image (pre-1923, *Blue and Gold [1904]: being a record of the college year published by the Junior class*, unnumbered pages after page 64 in alphabetical order, accessed on google books, aliasing in the Google Books original image for all similar images, the photos in the yearbook are probably half-tone images that alias with the scanner.

277 Caliothrips fasciatus, website of *Thrips of California*, **http://keys.lucidcentral.org/keys/v3/thrips_of_california/data/key/thysanoptera/Media/Html/browse_species/Caliothrips_fasciatus.htm**
278 Photo of female Caliothrips fasciatus from the *Thrips of California*, used by permission of UCR Professor Mark Hoddle per 2/6/12 email to author
279 E.P. Van Duzee, Nomenclatural and Critical Notes on Hemiptera, *The Canadian Entomologist*, 1914, pp 377-389, **http://biostor.org/reference/58769.text**
280 A.P. Liang, L.B. O'Brien, External morphology of the wax glands of Epiptera woodworthi, *Southwestern entomologist*, June 2002, v 27 (2) , reference to this article at: **http://openagricola.nal.usda.gov/Record/IND23295414**
281 Public Domain image of Edward P. Van Duzee, from Wikimedia Commons
282 Edward Van Duzee, Notes on some hermiptera taken near lake tahoe, *University of California publications in entomology, Volume 1, 1906-1922*, California Agricultural Experiment Station, University of California, Berkeley (1868-1952), pages 229-249, description on pages 245-6
283 G.O. Shinji, New Aphids from California, *[EntoNews]*, Vol. XXVIII, pp 61-64, **http://www.archive.org/stream/entomologicalnew28acad/entomologicalnew28acad_djvu.txt**
284 Albert F. Swain, A Synopsis of the Aphididae of California, *Miscellaneous Studies in Biology and Agriculture*, 1919, University of California Press, **http://cluster.biodiversitylibrary.org/m/miscellaneousstu00univ/miscellaneousstu00univ_djvu.txt**
285 Obituary of Ray F. Smith, *website of U.C. Berkeley*, http://berkeley.edu/news/berkeleyan/1999/0908/obit.html
286 C.B. Huffaker, Some Ecological Roots of Pest Control, acceptance speech to the Pacific Branch of the Entomological Society of America containing a quote from Ray F. Smith's speech, published in *BioControl*, Vol 19, Number 4, December 1974
287 Ray F. Smith, History and Complexity of Integrated Pest Management, *Pest Control Strategies*, Edited By Edward H. Smith and David Pimentel, 1978, Academic Press, pp 41-52, quote on pp 44-45
288 Carl B. Huffaker, Overall Approach to Insect Problems in Agriculture, *Biometrology in Integrated Pest Management*, 1982, Academic Press, edited by Jerry Hatfield and Ivan Thomason, pp 171-192, accessed via Google Books preview

[289] R.E. Frisbie and P.L. Adkisson, IPM: Definitions and Current Status in U.S. Agriculture, *Biological Control in Agricultural IPM Systems*, edited by Marjorie Hoy and Donald C. Herzog, 1985, Academic Press, pp 41-49

[290] G.H. Walter, Insect Pest Management and Ecological Research, 2003, Cambridge University Press, quote is on page 61

[291] Gordon Patterson, *The Mosquito Crusades: A History of the American Anti-Mosquito Movement*, 2009, Rutgers University Press

[292] Mosquito Control, *Official Report of the Thirty-First Fruit-Growers Convention of the State of California – 1906,* pp 107-112

[293] Ibid

[294] Ibid

[295] Ibid

[296] Ibid

[297] *[RepAgEx13],* page lviii

[298] Fruitmen to Hear Address, *The San Francisco Call*, December 6, 1905, column 2, accessed at UCR website at: **http://chroniclingamerica.loc.gov/lccn/sn85066387/1905-12-06/ed-1/seq-6/**

[299] Ibid

[300] Gordon Patterson, *The Mosquito Crusades: A History of the American Anti-Mosquito Movement*, 2009, Rutgers University Press

[301] District History, *Website of the Alameda Country Mosquito Control District*, **http://www.mosquitoes.org/history.htm**

[302] Public domain (pre-1923) image of the life stages of *Bombyx mori*, from the Wikimedia commons, from the 1885-1890 *Myers Konversations-Lexikon*

[303] *[CWW-Corr],* Letter from L.O. Howard to CWW, Feb 14, 1900

[304] CWW, Division of Entomology, *[RepAgEx04]*, pp 85-87

[305] Silk Worm Experiments, *[CalAgEx]*, Circular No. 116, March, 1914

[306] Public Domain (pre-1923) image

[307] *The Far Eastern Republic*, by Chinese National Welfare Society in America, April 1920, page 1

[308] *Millard's Review of the Far East*, Saturday March 2, 1918, found through google books (snippet view)

[309] Photo owned by author

[310] Translation by Chee Hu and Jialin Song

[311] Quacquarelli Symonds, Ltd., *Asian University Rankings 2010 – Top 200* **http://www.topuniversities.com/university-rankings/asian-university-rankings/2010**

[312] Professor Woodworth Home From China, *Berkeley Gazette*, December 23, 1918, (clipping so page number is unknown)

[313] *The University of California Chronicle*, 1919, page 98
[314] *The University of California Chronicle*, 1919, page 193
[315] *The Far Eastern Republic*, December 1919, page 27 "California Professor Honored in China
[316] *University of California Record, Volume 2, Number 1*, January 1922, University of California Press, Berkeley California, item 6, accessed via archive.org
[317] Ibid
[318] *The Rockefeller Foundation Annual Report, 1922*, page 256 in section on the China Medical Board
[319] William J. Haas, *China Voyager: Gist Gee's Life in Science*, 1996, M.E. Sharpe, Inc., page 151, accessed via Google Books
[320] *Entomological News, and the proceedings of the Academy of Natural Sciences of Philadelphia*, Vol. XXXIV, January, 1923, No. 1, accessed via archive.org
[321] Biography of Edwin C. Van Dyke **http://essigdb.berkeley.edu/cgi/eme_people_query?name_full=Edwin+C.+Van+Dyke&one=T**
[322] CWW, U.S. Patent #1,440,809, Fly Swatter, U.S. Patent and Trademark Office, 3 pages
[323] Told by Mary Detrich to author, 2008 and 2011
[324] CWW, The Wings of Bombyx mori, *Entomological News and the proceedings of the Academy of Natural Sciences of Philadelphia*, Vol. XXXIV, February, 1923, No. 2, accessed via archive.org
[325] ibid
[326] List of U.S. Citizens, from the passenger list of the S.S. President Roosevelt, April 5, 1923, found on ancestry.com file New York, Passenger Lists 1820-1957, Number 6, 116 stamped, scanned page 213 of 1206
[327] *Journal of the New York Entomological Society*, March 1924, page 75, Proceedings of the New York Entomological Society, Meeting of April 19
[328] List of U.S. Citizens, from the passengers of the S.S. President Wilson, document 23472-104, June 27, 1924, found on ancestry.com file "California, Passenger and Crew Lists 1882-1957, scan of a microfilm, scanned page 348
[329] Scan of letter from CWW to his sister Celina, November 10, 1939, page 1, original of letter is in the possession of Mary Detrich, used by verbal permission
[330] Told by Elizabeth Holden to the author, 1970's
[331] Photo owned by author
[332] Photo owned by author
[333] Photo owned by author
[334] Photo owned by author

[335] Berkeley Architectural Heritage Association, *Historic Resources Inventory*, September 29, 1977, in file for house at the BAHA office, listed in text on reverse side, his daughter Elizabeth is listed as one of two sources for the text

[336] Regina Ochoa, History of the Berkeley Public Library, http://ochoaberkeley.blogspot.com/

[337] S.D. Waterman, *History of the Berkeley Schools*, 1905, Robert Ernest Cowan, pages 125-126, accessed on archive.org at: http://www.archive.org/stream/historyofberkele00wate/historyofberkele00wate_djvu.txt

[338] *[CWW-Corr]*, Letter from CWW to Benjamin Wheeler, September 14, 1900

[339] California State Bulletin 142, Grasshoppers in California, summarized in the *Experiment Station Record*, 1903, page 471. U.S. Department of Agriculture

[340] http://sciencegeist.net/http:/sciencegeist.net/chemistry-in-the-age-of-impressionism/

[341] George E. Colby, Arsenical Insecticides. Paris Green; Commercial Substitutes; Home-Made Arsenicals, *[CalAgEx], Bulletin No. 151*, Berkeley, May 1903, 38 pages

[342] Law Notes, January 1902, *Indecent Exposure as Contributory Negligence*, page 200

[343] Allen B. Lemmon, *State Pesticide Laws*, http://science-in-farming.library4farming.org/Insects_2/Warnings-as-to-Insecticides/Pesticide-Laws.html

[344] Reproduced in Colby, *[CalAgEx], Bulletin 151*, pages 37-38

[345] E.O. Essig, Charles W. Woodworth, *Science*

[346] Presidents Address, *Proceedings of the Thirty-Fourth Annual Convention of the Association of Official Agricultural Chemists, 1917*, page 15, published in the *Journal of the Association of Official Agricultural Chemists*, Vol. IV, No. 1, August 15, 1920

[347] Christopher J. Bosso, *Pesticides and Politics*, June 1987, University of Pittsburg Press, page xi, referenced on the website Living History Farm: http://www.livinghistoryfarm.org/farminginthe40s/pests_07.html

[348] *[JEcoEnto]*, Volume 5, page 358, August 1912

[349] California Codes, Food and Agricultural Code, Section 12811-12837, http://www.leginfo.ca.gov/cgi-bin/waisgate?WAISdocID=8746751593+0+0+0&WAISaction=retrieve

[350] Burbank Finds Golden Promise in the Cactus, *San Francisco Call*, December 21, 1911

[351] CWW, California Horticultural Quarantine, *[JEcoEnto]*, Vol 2, October 1909, pages 359-360
[352] Berkeley Architectural Heritage Association, *Historic Resources Inventory*, September 29, 1977, in file for house at the BAHA office, listed in text on reverse side, his daughter Elizabeth is listed as one of two sources for the text
[353] Clipping of *Berkeley Gazette* article, "City's Heritage", written by Fillmore Eisenmayer, likely in the 1970's given that Fillmore Eisenmayer was the author of the 1977 Historic Resources Inventory on the house. The clipping is found in BAHA's file on the house.
[354] "Minority Children Aided by MAC", *Berkeley Daily Gazette article* from June 15, 1974 in the People section written by Pauline Metz. This article is about the Minority Adoption Committee is included in the Berkeley Architectural Heritage Association file about the house nearby the September 29, 1977 Historic Resources Inventory. It seems likely that this article was provided to the person doing the survey by C.W.'s daughter Elizabeth who is listed as a source on the survey
[355] The Chung Mei Home for Boys, http://www.windrush.org/about/history/chung-mei
[356] Charles Shepard, *Chung Mei, Where Drifting Chinese Boys Find Anchorage*, 1945, 14 pages, in UC Berkeley Bancroft Library, F870 C5P18, accessed con Calisphere at http://content.cdlib.org/ark:/13030/hb5t1nb0z2/?order=2&brand=calisphere
[357] Public domain image from Wikimedia Commons http://commons.wikimedia.org/wiki/File:Cydia_pomonella_(Falter).jpg
[358] Public domain image from Wikimedia Commons http://commons.wikimedia.org/wiki/File:Borer_(PSF).jpg
[359] CWW, "Spray and Band Treatment for Codlin Moth", *[RepAgEx90]*, State printing office, pages 308-312
[360] CWW, Substitutes for Paris Green as Insecticides, Essay presented to the December 9, 1899 convention of Fruit Growers' Convention at Unitarian Hall, San Jose, reference found in online version of *Pacific Rural Press*, Volume 58, Number 24, link at http://cdnc.ucr.edu/cdnc/cgi-bin/cdnc?a=d&d=PRP18991209.2.14&cl=CL2.1899.12&srpos=0&dliv=none&st=1&e=-------en-logical-20--1----all---
[361] Steven Stoll, *The fruits of natural advantage: making the industrial countryside in California*, 1998, University of California Press, 273 pages, quote from page 114

[362] Description of the Ortho Brand, website of *America's Greatest Brands*, http://www.americasgreatestbrands.com/volume5/pdf/ortho.pdf
[363] Logo used by Fair Use Doctrine to refer to the company
[364] CWW, Apples, "Codling Moth, and Climate", *Monthly Weather Review*, October 1912, pages 1574-5
[365] Ibid
[366] *[JEcoEnto]*, Volume 5, page 358, August 1912
[367] List of U.S. Citizens, from the list of passengers of the S.S. Eastern Prince, Number 1, stamped 140, found on ancestry.com New York, Passenger Lists, 1820-1957, scanned image 266 of 871
[368] EPA administrative Order of site on Omaha, *website of the EPA* http://www.epa.gov/region7/businesses/consent_agree_final_order/2004/california_spray-chemical_co_omaha_ne121404.pdf
[369] Michael Seville, "Toxic legacy lingers on", *Register-Pajaronian*, February 7, 2003
[370] *Remedial Action Certification Form*, http://envirostordev.ecointeractive.com/regulators/deliverable_documents/6045301139/Calspray.CertPkg.pdf
[371] Michael Seville, "Toxic legacy lingers on", *Register-Pajaronian*, February 7, 2003
[372] *Environmental, Chemical & Nanotechology Update*, Issue 184, March 20, 2007, Page 3, Shook Hardy & Bacon LLP
[373] Told by Doug Simons to the author after his lecture to the PBESA in March 2011, the day before the PBESA conference
[374] A New Idea in Microscope Construction, *Science*, Vol. 22, Number 548, August 4, 1893, page 59
[375] Photo owned by author
[376] Info about the fair at http://www.sfcityguides.org/public_guidelines.html?article=349&submitted=TRUE&srch_text=&submitted2=&topic=Events
[377] Public domain (pre-1923) image found at http://content.cdlib.org/ark:/13030/tf167nb3sr/, cropped by author
[378] *Report of Work of the Agricultural Experiment Station of the University of California for the Year 1892-93 and Part of 1894*, The Experiment Station Exhibit at the World's Fair and Midwinter Fair in San Francisco, R.H. Loughridge, page 465
[379] Ibid, page 473
[380] Public domain (pre-1923) image from [ContOptics], page 177
[381] Public domain (pre-1923) image from [ContOptics], page 182
[382] Public domain (pre-1923) image from [ContOptics], page 186
[383] Public domain (pre-1923) image from [ContOptics], page 195

384 *Microscope Theory*, 1924, Commercial Press, Shanghai, LOC QH211.W6, 240 pages
385 "*Microscope Theory*", 1924, Commerical Press, 1924, Shanghai, page 23
386 Public Domain image (pre-1923) from the 1917 "The Astigmatism of Lenses" by CWW
387 *[CWW-Corr],* May 19, 1925 letter from Ralph S. Minor to C.W.
388 Advertisement, Five-place Arcs Sines and Cosines, *Science*, Vol 88, No. 2287, page 7
389 *[CWW-Corr],* Letter from Harlan Shapley to CWW, Dec 3, 1928, 80% through book
390 *The Amateur Astronomer*, Albert G. Ingalls, May 1930
391 Letter from CWW to his niece Celina, December 24, 1937, on the stationary of the Milner Hotel in Jacksonville, FL, page 2, original in the possession of Mary Detrich
392 Renaud Foy and Francoise-Claude Foy, *Optic in astrophysics,* 2005, Springer, page 64, page view of mention of Guido Horn d'Arturo: http://books.google.com/books?id=qE_sFOr6gLMC&pg=PA64&lpg=PA64&dq=%22segmented+mirror+telescope%22+history&source=bl&ots=aLex8Y99_T&sig=6O-ipr1PuIKz64Z3XOzf22emwzE&hl=en&ei=QTrnTMK7Doa4sAOlt72xCw&sa=X&oi=book_result&ct=result&resnum=6&ved=0CEEQ6AEwBQ#v=onepage&q=%22segmented%20mirror%20telescope%22%20history&f=false
393 *[CWW-Corr], Ja*nuary 29, 1936 letter from F.A. Eaton to C.W.
394 Website of *History of Bausch & Lomb*, rangefinder discussion starts on page 8, http://www.bausch.co.nz/en_US/corporate/corpcomm/general/150_FinalCopyEnglish.pdf
395 *U.S. Navy manual*, describes the use of two Bausch & Lomb rangefinder models. http://www.hnsa.org/doc/rangefinder/index.htm
396 Letter from CWW to his niece Celina, December 24, 1937, on the stationary of the Milner Hotel in Jacksonville, FL, page 3, original in the possession of Mary Detrich
397 *The Information: A History, a Theory, a Flood* (2011), James Gleick, Pantheon (ebook), ebook page 342/1042
398 Public Domain image (work of the U.S. Federal Government) of Vannevar Bush from the Wikimedia Commons, http://commons.wikimedia.org/wiki/File:Vannevar_Bush_portrait.jpg

[399] This is coarsely calculated via several online sources. 16 candle power is around 200 lumens which is in the ballpark of what is put off of a 20W incandescent bulb.
[400] Photo taken by author of a hard copy he owns.
[401] Public domain image (product of U.S government office)
[402] Told by Elizabeth Holden to the author, 1970's
[403] *Website of InCon Processing, LLC*, description of their thin-film evaporators, **http://www.incontech.com/equip_syst.htm**
[404] Told by Mary Detrich to Brian Holden, 3/2008
[405] *Elizabeth Woodworth's photo album*, given by Tim Lundgren to author in 2011, photo taken by author
[406] Recorded by Harold Woodworth on Leonora Stern Woodworth's September 7, 1924 certificate of death
[407] *1881 Gazetter and Business Directory Cities and Towns, Missouri*, page 7
[408] Told by Mary Young Detrich to Brian Holden in 2011
[409] Marriage License, C.W. Woodworth and Lenora Stern, September 4, 1889, Rolla, Phelps County, Missouri
[410] 1886 Arkansas and 1895 Missouri historic rail maps found on the website - **http://menotomymaps.com/rail_maps.asp**
[411] Train station listing and picture for Monett, Missouri, *website of the library of Springfield, Missouri,* **http://thelibrary.springfield.missouri.org/lochist/frisco/depots/barry.cfm**
[412] Picture of a locomotive of the Meteor, *website of the Dallas Railway Museum* **http://www.dallasrailwaymuseum.com/frisco.html**
[413] Picture almost certainly public domain (pre-1923). Found on the website: **http://thelibrary.springfield.missouri.org/lochist/frisco/depots/barry.cfm**
[414] From Elizabeth Woodworth's photo album, given by Tim Lundgren to author in 2011, photo taken by author
[415] *The Blue and Gold Handbook, 1924*, Ancestry.com U.S. School Yearbooks index (search for Leonora Woodworth)
[416] *The website of the Pryanean Society,* **http://www.ocf.berkeley.edu/~prytnean/index.htm**
[417] WWI Draft Record, accessed on Ancestry.com **http://search.ancestry.com/iexec?htx=View&r=an&dbid=6482&iid=WA-1991533-3238&fn=Joseph+Arnold&ln=Stern&st=r&ssrc=&pid=26972817**

[418] WWI Draft Record, accessed on Ancestry.com
http://search.ancestry.com/iexec?htx=View&r=an&dbid=6482&iid=WA-1991533-3238&fn=Joseph+Arnold&ln=Stern&st=r&ssrc=&pid=26972817
[419] *Great Register, Primary Election, Alameda County*, accessed on ancestry.com
http://search.ancestry.com/browse/view.aspx?dbid=1249&iid=alamedacounty_14-00499&rc=317,623,396,642;247,1883,308,1903;248,1914,308,1934;324,1914,403,1934&pid=286003451&ssrc=&fn=joseph&ln=stern&st=g
[420] Photo owned by author
[421] Photo owned by author
[422] Photo owned by author
[423] Refuse to Pose as Models in Pantomime, *Oakland Tribune*, December 3, 1909, Page 14, column 6, near bottom
[424] *Mining and Metallurgy*, The American Institute of Mining and Metallurgical Engineers, March 1920 issue, page 60-1 has a short biography of Lawrence Woodworth as he is applying for membership. The first article of this issue is a record of the inaugural address of Herbert Hoover, who has just been elected president of the A.I.M.M.E.
[425] Photo owned by author
[426] *1920 U.S. Census*, CA, Alameda, Berkeley, District 293, mis-recorded as Woodward
[427] U.C. Professor Leaves $26.458, *Oakland Tribune*, Jan 23, 1941, Section C, page 3, column 1, top
[428] Letter from CWW to his sister Minnie, November 10, 1939, page 1, original of the letter is in the possession of Mary Detrich
[429] 12/27/10 email from Betty Woodworth to Brian Holden
[430] Photo owned by author
[431] *University of California Register 1916-17 with Announcements for 1917-1918*, 1917, University of California Press, Berkeley, page 10
[432] *The Mosquito Crusades: A History of the American Anti-Mosquito Movement from the Reed Commission to the First Earth Day* (Kindle Edition), Gordon Patterson, Rutgers University Press, 2009, location 1280 of 3619
[433] Ibid, location 1282 of 3619
[434] Ibid, location 1290 of 3619
[435] Ibid, location 1346 of 3619
[436] *1920 Blue and Gold*, 1919, H.S. Crocker Co., Inc., page 400
[437] *The Philippine Agriculturalist*: Volume 43, 1959, page 103, (found via snippet view of Google Books)

[438] *The University of the Philippines General Catalog 1921-1922*, page 292, (found via Google Books)
[439] *Biography of Charles Averill Barlow*: http://www.barlowgenealogy.com/GeorgeofSandwich/HonCABar.html
[440] Wallace M. Morgan, *History of Kern County,* Historic Record Company, Los Angeles, CA – 1914 (http://www.barlowgenealogy.com/GeorgeofSandwich/HonCABar.html)
[441] U.C. Professor Leaves $26.458, *Oakland Tribune*, Jan 23, 1941, Section C, page 3, column 1, top
[442] *Bakersfield City Council Minutes*, Jan-June 1953, page 4 http://www.bakersfieldcity.us/WEBLINK7/DocView.aspx?id=711&page=5&dbid=0
[443] *California Death Index* (ancestry.com)
[444] 12/27/10 email from Betty Holden to Brian Holden
[445] http://www.ecasebriefs.com/blog/law/wills-trusts-estates/wills-trusts-estates-keyed-to-dukeminier/construction-of-trusts-future-interests/estate-of-woodworth/2/
[446] Photo owned by author
[447] Charles Edward Woodworth, *The Sawflies of California*, May 1923, 86 pages, Main (Gardner) Stacks Locked Case UCB, Call No. 308t.W912
[448] *1920 Blue and Gold*, 1919, H.S. Crocker Co., Inc., pages 400-1
[449] http://www.visitmodesto.com/areainfo/history.asp
[450] Used by permission of Modesto Junior College per 1/24/12 email to author. Thank you to Sue Adler and Barbara Page of MJC for arranging and providing the permission. http://www.mjc.edu/community/resources/foundation-alumni/alumni/history.html
[451] *Science*, Vol. LXIII, No. 1637, page 493, Barro Colorado Island Biological Station, Vernon Kellogg
[452] Photo used by permission of Mary Detrich
[453] Photo owned by author
[454] Wedding of College Faculty Members Held in Berkeley, *Modesto News-Herald*, June 23, 1926, page 6, column 1
[455] 35 Ounce Baby In Modesto, *Modesto News-Herald*, May 14, 1927, page 5, column 2
[456] Photo owned by author
[457] Woodworth, C. E. (1930). *The effect of reduced pressure on the respiration of the honey bee*. Thesis (Ph.D.) University of Wisconsin--Madison, 1930., 122 pages, UW Madision Shelving Faciltiy, Catalog number AW W8788 (M38-L-5)

[458] Photo owned by author
[459] More to Return Home, *Walla Walla Union Bulletin*, Feb 3, 1946, column 3 at end of article
[460] Photo owned by author
[461] Told by Elizabeth L. Woodworth Holden to the author in the 1970s.
[462] Dr. C.E. Woodworth Is Home from Eastern Trip, *Walla Walla Union Bulletin*, April 30, 1947, page 6, Column 4
[463] *Website of the Essig Museum*, Search the museum's database with a query of "Woodworth" at http://essigdb.berkeley.edu/query_specimens.html
[464] *Directory of Organization and Field Activities of the Department of Agriculture: 1941*, Miscellaneous Publication No. 431, page 77
[465] Dr. C.E. Woodworth Is Home from Eastern Trip, *Walla Walla Union Bulletin*, April 30, 1947, page 6, Column 4
[466] Woodworth is Badly Burned, *Walla Walla Union Bulletin*, December 14, 1948, page 1, column 7, toward bottom
[467] *Washington State University Bulletin*, 1961, page xxxi
[468] I was the principal contributor to the Wikipedia article on Charles E. Woodworth. I reused some of the text that I wrote here.
[469] Annual Meet of Church Held, *Walla Walla Union Bulletin*, Jan 24, 1947, page 2, column 2
[470] Scout and Cub Roundup Event Draws Throng to Wa-Hi Gym, *Walla Walla Union Bulletin*, December 12, 1946, page 3, column 1
[471] Photo owned by author
[472] 12/27/10 email from Betty Woodworth to Brian Holden
[473] From Elizabeth Woodworth's photo album, given by Tim Lundgren to author in 2011, photo taken by author
[474] U.C. Professor Leaves $26.458, *Oakland Tribune*, Jan 23, 1941, Section C, page 3, column 1, top
[475] 12/27/10 email from Betty Woodworth to Brian Holden
[476] 12/27/10 email from Betty Woodworth to Brian Holden
[477] http://www.berkeleyhistoricalsociety.org/
[478] Photo taken by author
[479] Photo owned by author
[480] Foresters Enjoy Evening, *Oakland Tribune*, July 20, 1904, page 8, column 5
[481] *Foresters website*, http://www.foresters.com/
[482] Letter from CWW to his niece Celina, May 18, 1940, the original is in the possession of Mary Detrich
[483] *Website of the City Commons Club of Berkeley, California* http://www.citycommonsclub.org/

[484] *Website of the Streit Council,* http://streitcouncil.org/
[485] *Oakland Tribune*, September 8, 1924, page 16, column 7, 3/4ths down, accessed on ancestry.com
[486] Letter from CWW to his niece Celina, December 24, 1937, on the stationary of the Milner Hotel in Jacksonville, FL, pages 1 and 2, original in the possession of Mary Detrich
[487] *Ancestry.com,* public member tree christfc
[488] *1930 U.S. Census*, record in Berkeley, Alameda County, CA, District 293, mis-captured as Woodward
[489] *1930 U.S. Census*, record in Berkeley, Alameda County, CA, District 293, mis-captured as Woodward
[490] *County of Alameda Standard Certificate of Death*, California, filed May 7, 1930
[491] Letter from CWW to his niece Celina, December 24, 1937, on the stationary of the Milner Hotel in Jacksonville, FL, page 2, original in the possession of Mary Detrich
[492] Photo used by permission of Mary Detrich
[493] Photo used by permission of Mary Detrich
[494] Photo owned by author
[495] Photo owned by author
[496] 12/27/10 email from Betty Woodworth to Brian Holden
[497] Photo owned by author
[498] Photo owned by author
[499] Letter from CWW to his sister Minnie, November 10, 1939, page 2, original letter in the possession of Mary Detrich
[500] *Hastings Law Library database of California Ballot Propositions*, http://holmes.uchastings.edu/cgi-bin/starfinder/1484/calprop.txt
[501] Photo of book owned by author
[502] Photo of book owned by author
[503] [ObitScience]
[504] American Chess Magazine, Vol 1, No. 5, p. 290
[505] Letter from CWW to
[506] [ObitScience]
[507] *[CWW-Corr]*, July 29, 1892 letter from James Hays letter to CW
[508] *[CWW-Corr],* Credentials, 55% through book
[509] 12/27/10 email from Betty Woodworth to Brian Holden
[510] [ObitScience]
[511] *[CWW-Corr]*, October 16, 1893 letter from President Kellogg to CW
[512] Requisites of a County Commissioner, *Proceedings of the Fortieh California Fruit Growers' Convention of California*, 1911, p119

[513] *Far Eastern Republic*, by Chinese National Welfare Society in America, April 1920, pages 25-28
[514] Ibid, page 26
[515] Ibid, page 28
[516] What is Control?, *Science*, Vol. 71, No. 1841, page 388
[517] Letter from CWW to his niece Celina, December 24, 1937, on the stationary of the Milner Hotel in Jacksonville, FL, original in the possession of Mary Detrich
[518] Marriage License, C.W. Woodworth and Lenora Stern, September 4, 1889, Rolla, Phelps County, Missouri
[519] *History of the First Baptist Church of Fayetteville* http://storage.cloversites.com/firstbaptistchurchfayettevillearkansas/documents/History.pdf
[520] Letter from CWW to his niece, Celina Young, November 1939, in the possession of Mary Detrich
[521] *2009 Report of the First Baptist Church of Berkeley*. Page 36 says that it was established in 1889, although the congregation first met 15 years earlier. http://www.fccb.org/pdfs/FCCBAnnual%20Report2009web.pdf
[522] *Website of the First Baptist Church of Berkeley*, http://www.fbc-berkeley.org/index.html
[523] *Psyche*, Volume 6, Jan 1891, pages 19-21, On the Relation Between Scientific and Economic Entomology
[524] Told by Elizabeth Woodworth Holden to the author, 1970's
[525] *Pacific Unitarian*, March 1895, Vol. 3, No. 5, San Francisco, page 133
[526] Wedding of College Faculty Members Held in Berkeley, *Modesto Bee*, June 23, 1923, page 6, Column 1, top, page titled "Modesto Clubs"
[527] Church Study Group Has Monday Meet, *Walla Walla Union Bulletin*, April 22, 1952, page 6, column 8, top
[528] Regents make Appointments, February 12, 1930, *Oakland Tribune*, page 16, column 1
[529] [CalObit] http://content.cdlib.org/view?docId=hb367nb1mt&query=&brand=calisphere
[530] Photo owned by author
[531] Letter from CWW to his niece Celina, December 24, 1937, on the stationary of the Milner Hotel in Jacksonville, FL, page 3, original in the possession of Mary Detrich
[532] Photo owned by author
[533] Photo owned by author
[534] [CalObit]

[535] UCB library listing of campus buildings, http://www.lib.berkeley.edu/ENVI/buildings.html#wellman photo http://seismo.berkeley.edu/seismo/photos/wellman_2.jpg
Nice kite photos of Wellman Hall at http://arch.ced.berkeley.edu/kap/gallery/gal156.html
[536] Public Domain image (pre-1923) of John Galen Howard in 1886 from Wikimedia Commons
[537] Order Plans For College Building, *Oakland Tribune*, July 25, 1904, page 8, column 2
[538] Public Domain (pre-1923) image of Agriculture Hall, *[RepAgEx13]*, page lxxii
[539] Photo owned by author
[540] *Catalog of Officers and Students 1920-1921*, Feb. 1921, page 55, page 390 in pdf, accessed on Google Books
[541] Photo owned by author
[542] The State Historical Society of Missouri, Edwin P. Meiners, Collections, 1825-1960 (C3722), pp 1-2, address found at end of a letter from C.W. to Dr. E.P. Van Duzee,
[543] Per email from Joyce Kennedy to Brian Holden dated 6/9/10
[544] *The Harvard Index*, Harvard University, Collins Press Corporation, page 404, listed as "3G", in New York City Public Library, accessed via Google Books
[545] About our Building, *Website of the University Lutheran Church*, http://www.unilu.org/building/index.htm
[546] Address listed on the Town of Berkeley Application For Building Permit #512, June 30, 1905, accessed in *the files of the Berkeley Architectural Heritage Association*
[546] Berkeley Landmark #180,
[547] Told to author by John Stone
[548] Town of Berkeley Application For Building Permit #512, June 30, 1905, accessed in *the files of the Berkeley Architectural Heritage Association*
[549] 1905 Berkeley plat maps, accessed at the BAHA office
[550] Berkeley Landmark #180, http://www.berkeleyheritage.com/berkeley_landmarks/landmarks101-200.html
[551] Photo used by permission of Mary Detrich
[552] Photo owned by author, taken 2008
[553] Photo owned by author, taken 2008
[554] Berkeley Architectural Heritage Association, *Historic Resources Inventory*, September 29, 1977, in file for house at the BAHA office

[555] Floor plan of CWW house from brochure, used by permission of Tarpoff and Talbert Residential Real Estate, per email 10/11
[556] Photo taken by author
[557] Photo taken by author
[558] Photo taken by author
[559] Photo taken by author
[560] Photo taken by author
[561] Photo taken by author
[562] Article about clinker bricks: http://www.oldhousejournal.com/exteriors_savvy_clinker_bricks/magazine/1495
[563] Photo owned by author, taken of public monument, taken 2008
[564] Lola Blankenship's name and address per Andrew at BAHA
[565] Public domain photo (pre-1923) owned by BAHA
[566] Wedding of College Faculty Members Held in Berkeley, *Modesto Bee*, June 23, 1923, page 6, Column 1, top, page titled "Modesto Clubs"
[567] Told by Bill Jackson to the realtor Pat Talbert during an open house of the CWW house in November 2011.
[568] Letter from CWW to Celina Young, May 18, 1940, in the possession of Mary Detrich
[569] From a scan of "*A Climber's Guide to the High Sierra*" (1954), Edited by Hervey Voge, found at: http://www.yosemite.ca.us/library/climbers_guide/
[570] Told by the 1992-2012 John Stone to the Author in 2008
[571] Ibid
[572] Told by Anthony of the Berkeley Architectural Heritage Association to Brian Holden in 2/2010.
[573] Patents accessed via Google Patents
[574] *The Pocket Guide to Digital Prepress*, by Frank J. Romano, Delmar Cengage Learning, June 29, 1995, page 179
[575] *Infoworld*, Vol. 12, No. 51, December 17, 1990, page 38
[576] Electronic file "*2237.pdf*" collected by the Berkeley Architectural Heritage Association.
[577] Date and price per *Zillow.com*
[578] Mortgages, *Oakland Tribune*, Feb 20, 1906, page 3, Column 3 near top
[579] Agreements, *Oakland Tribune*, June 16, 1906, page 19, column 3 near bottom
[580] *History of Berkeley, From the Gound Up*, website, created by Allen Cohen, Chapter 9, accessed at http://historyofberkeley.org/chapter09.html
[581] Per Google Maps

[582] Logo of ESA used by Fair Use Doctrine to refer to the organization
[583] Bulletin of the Entomology Society of America, Volumes 14-15, 1968, page 277, accessed via Google Books
[584] Photo of Maurice T. James used by permission of the Maurice T. James Entomological Library
[585] facts from the *Bulletin of the Entomological Society of America*, Sept 1982, volume 28, number 3, pp 342-343
[586] Photo owned by author
[587] Photo owned by author
[588] Photo owned by author
[589] Photo owned by author
[590] Photo owned by author
[591] Photo owned by author
[592] Photo owned by author
[593] Photo owned by author
[594] Photo owned by author
[595] Photo owned by author
[596] Photo owned by author
[597] Used by permission of Vincent Jones
[598] Photo owned by author

79580013R00250

Made in the USA
Columbia, SC
26 October 2017